The Excellent Way

Also by R. T. Kendall

The Excellent Way

365 Readings
to Transform Your Life

From the Writings of
R.T. KENDALL

Edited by
David Moloney

HODDER &
STOUGHTON

Unless indicated otherwise, Scripture quotations are taken from the
Holy Bible, New International Version.
Copyright © 1973, 1978, 1984 by International Bible Society.
Used by permission. All rights reserved.
Scripture quotations marked AV are taken from the Authorised Version.
Scripture quotations marked JB are taken from the Jerusalem Bible.

This anthology first published in Great Britain in 2009 by Hodder & Stoughton
An Hachette UK company

1

Selected and edited by David Moloney

Typeset in Monotype Sabon by Palimpsest Book Production Ltd, Grangemouth, Stirlingshire

Printed and bound by Clays Ltd, St Ives plc

Hodder & Stoughton policy is to use papers that are natural, renewable
and recyclable products and made from wood grown in sustainable
forests. The logging and manufacturing processes are expected to conform to
the environmental regulations of the country of origin.

Hodder & Stoughton Ltd
338 Euston Road
London NW1 3BH

www.hodderfaith.com

Contents

Introduction

One of the most humbling experiences I have had in a long time was to be presented with the manuscript of the present book, *The Excellent Way*. David Moloney, my former editor at Hodder & Stoughton, came up with the idea, chose the title and also selected the 366 readings that follow (one for every day of the year and one for leap year!), taken from some of my books. The 'excellent way' (1 Corinthians 12:31) is the way Paul introduced 1 Corinthians 13, the famous love chapter of the Bible. I have to tell you that my ministry is certainly not worthy of that title. I just wish I could live a life of consistently keeping 'no record of wrongs' (1 Corinthians 13:5).

I was honoured by Hodder's request to publish this book, and have been very touched indeed by David's kind words as well as his choice of readings for this volume. He has obviously worked very hard to come up with these particular excerpts, and, knowing him as I do, has prayed earnestly to be led by the Holy Spirit in the preparation of this book.

I have been asked by Hodder to write this Introduction, but it is rather embarrassing to do so.

If you happened to read my book *Did You Think to Pray?*, you may recall that in the Preface I mentioned a rather amazing occurrence – or coincidence – that came the first day or so of writing it. Doing a book on prayer was not on either Hodder's agenda or mine, but one morning I felt compelled to start writing that book. I felt a bit uneasy, saying to myself, 'There must be a thousand books on prayer, what publisher will want another book on this subject?' But I kept writing and did so with a considerable sense of guidance. The same day – or the very next – David phoned to say, 'Have you thought of writing a book on prayer? I am wondering if this is something you should think about' (or words to that effect). What an encouragement that was!

If, then, you have had a look at my book *Did You Think to Pray?*, you will know I emphasise the amount of time one should spend in prayer – and reading your Bible. For this reason, therefore, although the present book *The Excellent Way* is designed to form part of your daily devotional life, please do not let it substitute for reading your Bible or compete with your time in prayer. It would be a huge mistake if you let these brief readings become the sum total of your quiet time. David has chosen paragraphs from my books that he trusts would appropriately fit in with your own devotional life.

Some forty years ago I read a collection of 365 readings from Dr Martyn Lloyd-Jones's sermons. I read and reread them. I never dreamed that one day I would be in his pulpit or that I would be asked to do a similar book. God has been so good to me. I doubt you have any idea what it is like for a man from the hills of Kentucky to move across the Atlantic with his wife and two children, first to read for a research degree at Oxford University, then be asked to be the minister of Westminster Chapel. I have never got over it – to this day. So I am amazed at the thought that my publisher would come up with this book.

My relationship with Hodder & Stoughton goes back a long way – beginning with my early weeks as minister of Westminster Chapel. Edward England, my first editor at Hodder, called on me at the vestry one day in 1977. We had not met, but he wanted me to do a book with them. Since I was preaching on the book of Jonah at that time, he said, 'Let's do Jonah.'

'Are you sure?' I asked. 'How do you know you are not making a mistake?'

'We don't make mistakes at Hodder,' he actually replied, and stuck to his guns; my writing career began. That same day I told Lady Elizabeth Catherwood, one of Dr Lloyd-Jones's daughters, that a publisher had asked to do my sermons on Jonah. 'Which publisher?' she asked. I said it was with Hodder & Stoughton. She replied, 'If you are with Hodder, *you're there*.' That made me feel good. I have since realised what a privilege it has been to be associated with Hodder & Stoughton over these years.

My wife Louise and I continually have to pinch ourselves that we were ever at Westminster Chapel – or even in London. We love England, we love London, we love Westminster, we love Pimlico, we love those streets and shops near our flat in Ashley Gardens and think all the time of those memorable years when we walked by Big Ben nearly every day. Some of our best and dearest friends are in London. Our best memories are in London. Our worst memories are in London. Although our twenty-five years at Westminster Chapel were not always easy, we'd go back in a second if given the chance.

Hard years? Oh yes. Following the greatest Bible expositor in the world was without question the most intimidating experience of my life. Rightly or wrongly, I always felt it was Dr Lloyd-Jones's pulpit, not mine. I even felt I was trespassing each time I mounted that awesome pulpit. But I kept telling myself that it was God who put me there – even if he used Dr Lloyd-Jones to make it happen.

I am frequently asked, 'Of the books you have written, which is your favourite?' I always say (if you're a parent), 'That's like asking you to choose which of your children you like best!' I honestly do not know if I have a favourite. My most popular book seems to be *Total Forgiveness*. It was born in the darkest hour of our lives when my old friend Josif Tson lovingly cautioned me: 'R.T., you must totally forgive them; release them and you will be released.' I could not have known these words would change my life and lead to a book that I would be best known for. *Total Forgiveness* has reached a lot of people, has been translated into several languages, and most of my unsolicited letters come from people who have read that book to tell me how it helped them.

But the most important book I have written is (to me) *The Sensitivity of the Spirit,* which actually preceded *Total Forgiveness* by one year. I originally wanted to call the book 'The hyper-sensitivity of the Spirit' (but they talked me out of it). I regard my deepest insight during my twenty-five years in London to be how sensitive the Holy Spirit is and how easy it is to grieve him. We grieve him chiefly by bitterness and holding a grudge (Ephesians 4:30–32). The easiest thing in the world to do is to grieve the Holy Spirit. The greatest challenge in the world is never to grieve the Spirit. A young pastor asked me, 'What has a veteran like you got to say to a young preacher like me?' I replied: *find out what grieves the Holy Spirit – and don't do that.* There is no way to convey to you how the concept of living by the un-grieved Spirit has shaped my thinking. The Bible teacher Joyce Meyer wanted a copy of each of my books, some of which she had read. I was honoured. But the only book she asked me to sign was *The Sensitivity of the*

Spirit. This impressed me about her, that she would discern how important this insight is. It is the key to all I believe.

And yet I would have to say that the one verse, above all others, I have sought to be *governed* by (but not always succeeding) is John 5:44 – which reveals why the Jews missed their Messiah: 'How can you believe if you accept praise from one another, yet make no effort to obtain the praise that comes from the only God.' I was brought up on the Authorised Version that translates, 'the honour that comes from *God only*'. I am *so glad* it reads that way; it almost certainly taught me more acutely to want the honour that comes *only from God* and not to be so influenced by the praise of people. This is why I called the book describing my twenty-five years at the Chapel *In Pursuit of His Glory*.

Since retiring from Westminster Chapel and returning to America, I was given an opportunity to meet some interesting people in the Middle East, among them the late Yasser Arafat and Rabbi David Rosen. This came through Canon Andrew White, who was the Archbishop of Canterbury's envoy to the Middle East. My friendship with Arafat caused many to say, 'R.T., you will never reach a Jew for Christ now, since you are seen as siding with their enemy.' My reply: I did not open this door, I only walked through it. I knew it was what Jesus would do. But on the last day I saw Arafat I breakfasted with David Rosen in Jerusalem. David is Israel's most distinguished Orthodox rabbi. Our book *The Christian and the Pharisee* was born that same day – the exchange of our unedited letters (I try to lead him to Christ; David replies why he does not believe Jesus is Israel's Messiah). It demonstrates that if you keep your eyes on Jesus, instead of looking over your shoulder, God will open doors no one can shut. *The Christian and the Pharisee* (David Rosen's choice for a title) was launched at Westminster Abbey, and quite a number of Jews were present. Jews, evangelical Christians and Messianic Jews have praised the book, but I have to admit, sadly, that, as far as I know, no Jew has come to Christ as a result of this book (which is what I wanted).

One of my most successful writing ventures came as a result of my begging Hodder to publish a book on tithing. They were not very interested, but came back with a question: would I buy 1,000 copies if they printed it? Yes, I said. That very book (now called *The Gift of Giving*) did exceedingly well, being reprinted several times in the UK and has had over thirty printings in America. It has been endorsed by John Stott, Sir Fred Catherwood, Billy Graham and Lord Carey. One British businessman used his tithe to buy copies of *Tithing* and gave copies to every member of his parish. Their giving doubled the first month! It has been a much needed book. However, since it does not lend itself well to daily devotional readings, David did not quote from it in the present volume.

I thank God he put me in Westminster Chapel, I thank God for Hodder & Stoughton. Thank you, David, for your hard work. Thank you, Katherine Venn, for the final editing. Thank you, Louise, T.R. and Melissa, for your love and support during those unforgettable years in London. Thank you, all my readers, for your blessing me as you have done. May this book bless all of you and bring great honour and glory to God.

R. T. Kendall
Hendersonville, Tennessee
March 2009

Editor's Note

I was R. T. Kendall's editor at Hodder & Stoughton for ten happy years and have always known him to be a skilled and wise writer – as well as an honest and gracious friend. The process of compiling this book has further increased my admiration for R.T.'s talent for unearthing the complex theologies of the Bible, digging them up, untangling them and presenting them in deceptively simple, relevant, motivational language for those of us who are not gifted with such brilliant insight. I thought I knew his books inside out but this task has required me to look at the structure of his writing from a new perspective and – even though I edited most of them – I don't think I ever truly appreciated just how much wisdom is packed between the covers of every single book he has written. R.T. has so much to say – nuggets of biblical insight and exposition, lessons for life, personal anecdotes and an acute understanding of human nature – and wastes not a single word. I was required to choose 366 extracts from 18 books, each one a self-contained, mini sermon of approximately 300 words, based on a passage of the Bible. No small challenge, but I honestly think I could have found 732!

If you are not familiar with all of his books, I hope *The Excellent Way* will encourage you to read more of them. R.T. says that it is no shame to be blessed with the gift of 'helps' (1 Corinthians 12:28), and I believe he has this gift in spades. God uses R. T. Kendall to help us understand his excellent way, and we should be ever thankful for that.

This book is arranged to introduce you to as much as possible of R.T.'s teaching over the course of a year, with no requirement to start on 1 January or any other date. Every day's reading stands in its own right, although some have also been arranged in sequence to allow you to explore certain themes in greater depth. For example, the Lord's Prayer is unpacked line by line between 1 March and 10 March, and the fortnight between 24 April and 7 May comprises R.T.'s most important theological principles as revealed in his memoir, *In Pursuit of His Glory*.

The readings are selected from the following books, the vast majority of which are still in print: *The Anointing* (1998), *The Christian and the Pharisee* (with David Rosen, 2006), *The Day the World Changed* (2001), *Did You Think to Pray?* (2008), *Does Jesus Care?* (2006), *He Saves* (1988), *In Pursuit of His Glory* (2002), *Out of the Comfort Zone* (2005), *Pure Joy* (2004), *Second Chance* (2008), *The Sensitivity of the Spirit* (2000), *Stand Up and Be Counted* (1984), *Thanking God* (2003), *The Thorn in the Flesh* (1999), *Total Forgiveness* (2001), *Totally Forgiving Ourselves* (2007), *Worshipping God* (1989) and *Your Words Have Power* (2006).

David Moloney

January

And find out what pleases the Lord.

Ephesians 5:10

We learn what pleases those closest to us primarily by spending time with them. By trial and error we also discover things they like and dislike, and when we want such a relationship to develop it becomes fun to make the other happy.

The Lord has his own ways too, and he wants us to know them and adjust to them. We may think they are odd at first; but the benefits of accepting him as he is and adjusting to what pleases him will result in great blessing and peace.

That Paul would urge the Ephesians to 'find out' what pleases the Lord can only mean that this was an achievable goal – without the whole of the New Testament. Presumably they had only that one letter of Paul's to them (it was hundreds of years before all the Church had all of the New Testament as a source), which means they had to find out what pleases the Lord largely by experience – by trial and error. They had to spend time with the Lord and take seriously the warning not to grieve the Holy Spirit (Ephesians 4:30).

We have the wonderful advantage over the early Church of having the whole Bible at our fingertips. This surely leaves us without excuse. And yet if we let the Bible replace the immediate witness, guidance and voice of the Spirit we quench him in one stroke. For we too must learn – by experience – what pleases the Lord. This means spending time with the Lord and developing a sensitivity to his ways.

The Sensitivity of the Spirit

'I make known the end from the beginning, from ancient times, what is still to come. I say: "My purpose will stand, and I will do all that I please."'

Isaiah 46:10

Who would want to pray to a God who was not in total control? And yet some church leaders on both sides of the Atlantic have flirted with an idea which I can only call sub-Christian that maintains God does not know the future, that he waits for us to know what to do next and has no absolute assurance that he will win out. Indeed, one of the leading theologians from Canada who upholds this view of God was asked, 'How do you know for certain that Jesus Christ will win in the end? Does not your very theology leave open the possibility that God might not win in the end?' To give him full marks for being consistent, he agreed. And yet there were church leaders who applauded the notion.

The God of the Bible is sovereign, has a mind of his own, knows what is going to happen because he has declared the end from the beginning! This pronouncement from Isaiah reminds me of a friend of mine whose six-year-old son knelt at his bedside and prayed, 'God bless Daddy and Mummy and me and, oh yes, please take care of yourself because if anything happens to you we are going to be in an awful mess.' If God is not sovereign, there is no hope that our Lord Jesus will triumph in the end as he did when God raised him from the dead.

Out of the Comfort Zone

And the LORD said, 'I will cause all my goodness to pass in front of you, and I will proclaim my name, the LORD, in your presence. I will have mercy on whom I will have mercy, and I will have compassion on whom I will have compassion.'

Exodus 33:19

I will now define what I mean by sovereignty of God: it is God's *authority* to do what he pleases with whomever he wills whenever he chooses. He does not need to explain himself, he is answerable to nobody. God blesses whom he chooses, withholding judgment (which is what mercy is) from those who deserve it and bestowing grace (undeserved favour) on those who don't deserve it.

This is not easy for some to accept, because of the implication that not all are chosen. Why aren't all chosen? You tell me. I wish they were. I would have no objection if that were true; and I will be thrilled beyond words to find out one day that I have got it wrong. For if all were chosen, then all would be saved. This is known as 'universalism' – the belief of some that God is too kind to let anybody go to hell; therefore he will ensure that all will be saved in the end. I wish it were true – oh, how I wish this. But the God of the Bible does not reveal himself in such a manner that we can make a sound doctrine out of it. I wish he were that nice.

Out of the Comfort Zone

I thank Christ Jesus our Lord, who has given me strength, that he considered me faithful, appointing me to his service. Even though I was once a blasphemer and a persecutor and a violent man, I was shown mercy because I acted in ignorance and unbelief. The grace of our Lord was poured out on me abundantly, along with the faith and love that are in Christ Jesus.

1 Timothy 1:12–14

Saul of Tarsus never really got over God saving him. He loved to relate the account of his conversion again and again. He was *so* thankful. Likewise I will never get over the fact that God has saved me, forgiven me of so much and kept me from falling a thousand times. Moreover, he has been pleased to use me, for which I am eternally grateful.

He has given me a wonderful wife and beautiful family, he has given me the best friends anyone ever had, not to mention health and other blessings upon blessings. The list is endless.

I am conscious that you may say, 'I haven't been blessed like you, R.T. It is easy for you to be thankful. You have no idea what I've been through and am still going through.' I assure you that I too could tell a long (very long) tale of woes. But the truth is, I am literally thankful for the *worst* things that have happened as well. Here is why: my trials have 'made' me. A trial, or any measure of suffering, can 'make or break' a person. How do we respond? Our difficulties might have led us to bitterness or despair; they could have broken us, but in a good sense. 'The sacrifices of God are a broken spirit; a broken and contrite heart, O God, you will not despise' (Psalm 51:17).

Thanking God

Do not be anxious about anything, but in everything, by prayer and petition, with thanksgiving, present your requests to God.

Philippians 4:6

The first step I took to indicate a change in my life was to begin every day by thanking the Lord for all I could recall over the previous twenty-four hours. For many years I have kept a journal, which goes into considerable detail. For example, I could tell you where I was at three in the afternoon on 3 April 1983 – and what was on my heart as I awakened that morning.

But beginning on 7 November, the day after I preached for the first time on Philippians 4:6, as well as writing in my journal I began thanking the Lord for *every single item* I could think of over the previous twenty-four hours. Ever since that day, every morning as soon as I have commenced by praying for the renewal of the sprinkling of Christ's blood on me, I get out my journal and begin reading it. I thank the Lord for every single thing I can think of over the previous twenty-four hours. I wanted to make up for lost time. I have never been sorry for this decision, and I have not been the same since.

Writing a daily journal may not be what you can do – although many have found this to be a great blessing. What I am saying is that the habit of thankfulness needs to be part of our daily life, something from our hearts but a discipline we try to keep to.

Thanking God

First, I thank my God through Jesus Christ for all of you, because your faith is being reported all over the world.

Romans 1:8

Perhaps you have heard (and believed) that religion is a very personal matter – that you should keep it to yourself. That may be true with religion. But not salvation. God calls men to confess his Son before everybody. If salvation by Jesus Christ were merely a 'personal matter', Christianity would have died in the first generation. Bur Paul could say to the people that were saved in Thessalonica, 'The Lord's message rang out from you not only in Macedonia and Achaia – your faith in God has become known everywhere' (1 Thessalonians 1:8). Paul could say to Christians in Rome – right under the shadow of the Caesar, 'Everyone has heard about your obedience, so I am full of joy over you' (Romans 16:19).

If you really believe in your heart that Jesus Christ is the Son of God, how can you keep quiet about it? You cannot. This is why confession ratifies what is in the heart – thus proving that it *is* in the heart indeed. You sign your name to a letter because you are not ashamed of what you have written. You confess Jesus Christ with your mouth because you are not ashamed of what you have believed. Confession without the belief in the heart will not save, however. This is why coming forward does not save anybody. Something must happen in the heart. But if it does happen in the heart, you are required to prove that by your confession. Your refusal to confess Christ openly casts serious doubt on whether you really believe in the Lord Jesus Christ in your heart.

Stand Up and Be Counted

By faith Moses, when he had grown up, refused to be known as the son of Pharaoh's daughter. He chose to be ill-treated along with the people of God rather than to enjoy the pleasures of sin for a short time. He regarded disgrace for the sake of Christ as of greater value than the treasures of Egypt, because he was looking ahead to his reward.

Hebrews 11:24–26

The most painful decision that a man ever made was when Moses, aged forty, chose to suffer affliction with the people of God. He actually esteemed the 'reproach of Christ' as having greater value than the treasures of Egypt. That is the way this man declared himself. There was nothing secret about it. Forty years later he instructed the children of Israel to sprinkle blood over and on the sides of the doors of their homes. The night of the Passover was a visible demonstration of their obedience – it was a public pledge. It was their pledge to God and God's pledge to them and it was their witness before the world. And God said, 'When I see the blood, I will pass over you' (Exodus 12:13). The One in whom this Passover ordinance would be fulfilled was later to say 'Whosoever therefore shall confess me before men, him will I confess also before my Father which is in heaven' (Matthew 10:32).

After the children of Israel crossed the Red Sea and were wandering in the wilderness, there was a fresh need for commitment. There was a time when Moses addressed the children of Israel with these words, 'Who is on the Lord's side? Let him come unto me. And all the sons of Levi gathered themselves together unto him' (Exodus 32:26).

After Moses died, his successor Joshua addressed the children of Israel in yet another time of spiritual crisis. 'Choose you this day whom ye will serve.' The people responded, 'We will serve the Lord.' Joshua then asked for a public demonstration of their commitment (Joshua 24:15–27). An open demonstration of one's heart – a public pledge – is a consistent strain in the Bible.

Stand Up and Be Counted

'For God so loved the world that he gave his one and only Son, that whoever believes in him shall not perish but have eternal life.'

John 3:16

It is strange how Jesus is admired by so many. They claim he was a good man and a good teacher. But Jesus had more to say about the wrath of God than any writer in the New Testament! What is more, Jesus went into detail to *describe the pains* one will experience from God's coming wrath. Hell has been called a place of 'darkness, where there will be weeping and gnashing of teeth' (Matthew 8:12); 'the fiery furnace, where there will be weeping and gnashing of teeth' (Matthew 13:42). 'It is better for you to enter life maimed or crippled than to have two hands or two feet and be thrown into eternal fire' (Matthew 18:8). 'Depart from me, you who are cursed, into the eternal fire prepared for the devil and his angels' (Matthew 25:41).

Martin Luther called John 3:16 'The Bible in a nutshell'. John 3:16 demonstrates why Jesus died and what will *not* happen to those who believe: 'For God so loved the world that he gave his one and only Son, that whoever believes in him *shall not perish* but have eternal life.'

Eternal punishment for those who do not believe in the Son was an assumption underlying all Jesus taught. His coming into the world did not create hell. Those who take the gospel to the heathen do not create hell for them. All men are condemned anyway. 'Whoever does not believe stands condemned already.' I do not understand it. But this is his teaching.

It is not for you or me to criticise this teaching. We may not like it. I, for one, do not like it. I did not originate it, I would never have thought of it. Let us lower our voices and adopt the spirit and word of Abraham when he saw Sodom's impending doom: 'Will not the Judge of all the earth do right?' (Genesis 18:25).

He Saves

But when the chief priests and the teachers of the law saw the wonderful things he did and the children shouting in the temple area, 'Hosanna to the Son of David', they were indignant. 'Do you hear what these children are saying?' they asked him. 'Yes,' replied Jesus, 'have you never read, "From the lips of children and infants you have ordained praise"?'

Matthew 21:15–16

Running right through the Bible is the theme that God cares about each individual as though there were no one else to care for. Whether you are five years old, or fifty, or ninety years old, God cares about your worship. He is not interested in your status in life, he looks at *you*.

There are not many people alive now who were present at the Welsh Revival. But a little while ago I was speaking to a lady who was there when she was a child of six. She lived in London, but when her father heard that revival had broken out in Wales he took her out of school and sent her there. He argued that she could always go to school but she might never see revival again.

She told me that at the peak of the revival, her older brother, who was eight, stood up in the service and began to pray. She said his face shone like an angel, and he prayed on and on until finally heir grandfather went up to him and said, 'All right, you can sit down now.' Such was the worship of a child.

You see, not only do so-called unimportant people matter, but God does not care whether or not you are in a strategic position from which to help spread his name. You may sometimes think, 'I'm not going to be able to do anything for God where I am. Why should he show me anything or give me any insights?' But God wants our worship irrespective of our 'usefulness'.

Worshipping God

Then John gave this testimony: 'I saw the Spirit come down from heaven as a dove and remain on him. I would not have known him, except that the one who sent me to baptise with water told me, "The man on whom you see the Spirit come down and remain is he who will baptise with the Holy Spirit."'

John 1:32–33

When Paul cautioned, 'And do not *grieve* the Holy Spirit of God, with whom you were sealed for the day of redemption' (emphasis mine, Ephesians 4:30), he used a Greek word (Greek: *lupeite*, grieve) that means getting your feelings hurt. We hurt the feelings of the Holy Spirit, for example, when we refuse to forgive those who have hurt us.

Have you ever seen a person in grief? Have you ever been in a state of grief? It is not a pleasant feeling. And yet when I think that I am capable of bringing *grief* to the Holy Spirit, it makes me want to be careful not to do this. I do not want to cause the Holy Spirit to have any grief over my actions or attitudes.

All Christians have the Holy Spirit (Romans 8:9), but not all Christians enjoy the presence of the ungrieved Holy Spirit. When he is *ungrieved* – a wonderful condition to enjoy – it is like the Holy Spirit coming down on Jesus as a dove and *remaining* on him (John 1:32–33). I know what it is for the Dove to come down on me. It is absolutely wonderful. The peace, the joy, the feeling that all is under control. There is nothing quite like it. But my problem is that the Dove doesn't stay down long! Hours later I sense that something went wrong – I grieved him and he fluttered away. It may have been by a wrong attitude, speaking curtly to someone on the phone, getting angry in traffic. I'm sorry, but it doesn't take a lot to grieve him. He gets hurt easily.

I know of no greater challenge on earth than this: to find out what grieves the Spirit and also to *stop yourself* from grieving him when you are about to do it.

Did You Think to Pray?

'The Son of Man must be lifted up, that everyone who believes in him may have eternal life.'

John 3:14–15

I am a great believer in a soul-winning programme called Evangelism Explosion. It was designed by Dr D. James Kennedy, the minister of the Coral Ridge Presbyterian Church in Fort Lauderdale, Florida. There are two 'diagnostic questions' one asks someone – regardless of whether they are non-Christians or professing Christians (it does not matter): (1) 'Do you know for sure that if you were to die today you would go to heaven?' (2) 'If you stood before God and he were to ask you, "Why should I let you into my heaven?", what would you say?' In most cases, people we meet will say they think they would get into heaven – if there is such a place – by their good works. At this stage one presents the gospel. Should these people accept the gospel and pray the 'sinner's prayer', we then say to that person: 'Who have you just trusted for your salvation?' If they reply, 'Jesus who died for me on the cross,' we then say, 'That being true and if you died today, where would you go?' They would reply 'To heaven'. Many times the people will be tearful or emotional, sometimes not. In either case, the question is put in such a manner that they *reflect* on what they have just done (trusting Christ for their salvation). They are thus assured of being converted, born again. I am certainly not saying that all who pray the prayer or who give the right answers are absolutely saved. I am only pointing out that this is a way many of us have come to realise that we have the hope of heaven; it is because we know we have trusted Christ. It is the reflective act – the indirect act of faith. God uses this and it has considerable comfort and assurance to many.

Pure Joy

'For God so loved the world that he gave his one and only Son, that whoever believes in him shall not perish but have eternal life.'

John 3:16

Too often the heart of the Christian message becomes clouded with what in fact are but secondary benefits of the gospel. For example, 'We are so much better off here below.' Or, 'Our lives have changed. We are much happier than before. Even society is all the better when the gospel has made an impact.' True. I know what people mean by that.

But the main reason Jesus died on the cross was to make it possible for us to go to heaven when we die. Believe it or not, Christianity is essentially about our death. The wages of sin is death (Romans 6:23). Jesus came to reverse what Adam lost in the Garden of Eden. The gospel is essentially about this Great Reversal. Some say, 'If there were no heaven or hell I'd still be a Christian.' I know what people mean by this, too, but it is contrary to the thinking of Paul. 'If only for this life we have hope in Christ, we are to be pitied more than all men' (1 Corinthians 15:19). Paul is saying, 'If there is no heaven to come, it's not worth it as far as I am concerned.' This seems to surprise some people. But the wonderful thing is, we are going to heaven! Sometimes I can hardly wait.

Thanking God

Look, he is coming with the clouds, and every eye will see him,
even those who pierced him; and all the peoples of the earth will
mourn because of him. So shall it be! Amen.

Revelation 1:7

There will be no faith in heaven. Faith is described in Hebrews 11:1: 'Now faith is being sure of what we hope for and certain of what we do not see.'

In order for faith to be *faith* it follows that one must trust God without complete evidence. Faith is best defined, simply, as believing God – a definition Dr Martyn Lloyd-Jones gave me years ago. It is not merely believing that there is a God. After all, the devil believes in God. 'You believe that there is one God. Good! Even the demons believe that – and shudder' (James 2:19). Faith is believing God – relying on him – alone. It is believing his word to be true. It is proving this by trusting that word.

In heaven all the evidences of God and his word will be before our eyes. Faith will become sight!

'Seeing is believing,' says the world. But to God it is the other way around: to believe is to see. But in heaven everybody will see everything clearly and there will be no faith.

Thanking God

14 January

Christ Jesus, who died – more than that, who was raised to life – is at the right hand of God and is also interceding for us.

Romans 8:34

One Monday morning, 31 October 1955, driving from near Palmer, Tennessee, back to where I was a student at Trevecca Nazarene College of Nashville, the glory of the Lord filled my car. All of a sudden there was Jesus himself interceding before the Father on my behalf. I had never witnessed anything like it. I wept with joy as I drove. When I get to heaven I want to see a video replay of the whole thing – if only to know how I was able to drive the next sixty miles. All I now remember was an hour later, coming past Smyrna, Tennessee, when I heard Jesus say to the Father, 'He wants it.' The Father answered back, 'He can have it.' In that moment the most incredible warmth and peace surged into my heart as if a liquid flame had entered. It was tangible. I beheld the face of Jesus for several seconds, less than a minute. The experience ended. Ten minutes later I got out of my car, went to my room and shaved, then went to my first class at Trevecca.

The experience changed my theology. I thought I had discovered something new, that I must have been the first since the Apostle Paul to have experienced and believed what I felt. In hours I was not only transformed but also reformed in my theology, but I didn't realise that then.

The Anointing

I am not ashamed of the gospel, because it is the power of God for the salvation of everyone who believes: first for the Jew, then for the Gentile.

Romans 1:16

Two things are urgently needed today: that there should be a people who are unashamed of the gospel and that great care be taken in clarifying to people what that gospel is. The devil hates the gospel, and he will do anything to divert us from it, even ever so slightly; and the way he does it sometimes seems so innocent.

The devil knows just how to bring in things, even good things, that camouflage the gospel. One of the greatest enemies of the gospel is the subtle but superficially plausible attempt to *destigmatise* the gospel. The gospel inherently contains a stigma. There's nothing more offensive than the blood which Jesus shed when he died upon the cross. There is no greater offence than the premise that a person is actually saved from the wrath of God by simple trust in the blood of Jesus, and the devil will do anything to get us away from that. The offence shows itself by our being ashamed, embarrassed and afraid: afraid that in putting *all* our eggs into one basket, namely the gospel, we will be left 'high and dry'; that mere faith in the gospel is not enough.

Perhaps the best way we know what we really believe is by asking: what do we trust when the time comes to die? It is possible to be saved five minutes before we die but only a fool would wait until then. For first of all we don't know that our mind will be clear by then; and in any case we may not get a five-minute warning.

However, if you knew that you were going to die in five minutes, is it possible to be saved? Yes. But how? Well, obviously it's too late then to do anything more than to lean on the mere mercy of God. *What is true for five minutes before you die is true now*, even if you have thirty years left to live. Paul believed this, and thus said, 'I am not ashamed of the gospel.'

He Saves

'Whoever acknowledges me before men, I will also acknowledge him before my Father in heaven. But whoever disowns me before men, I will disown him before my Father in heaven.'

Matthew 10:32–33

This is a very strong statement. It is sobering. If I had only one verse in the Bible to support the call for people to pledge themselves publicly to Christ, it would be this one. Not that one must walk forward in a public service in order to honour that scripture (for it equally refers to the whole of the Christian life). But pledging publicly one's commitment to Jesus Christ most certainly *does* honour it. It is a way of coming out of hiding.

All men and women will come out of hiding sooner or later. For Jesus also said, 'There is nothing concealed that will not be disclosed, or hidden that will not be made known' (Matthew 10:26). 'For there is nothing hidden that will not be disclosed, and nothing concealed that will not be known or brought out into the open' (Luke 8:17). In other words, it is only a matter of time before everybody will learn the truth of our secrets. When the Lord comes, he 'will bring light to what is hidden in darkness and will expose the motives of men's hearts' (1 Corinthians 4:5). But to the one who confesses that Jesus Christ is Lord, provided that he believes in his heart that God has raised Jesus from the dead, there is the promise of salvation (Romans 10:9). Salvation assures us that our sins will not be held against us. 'I will forgive their wickedness and will remember their sins no more' (Hebrews 8:12). In a word: to come out of hiding now provides assurance that we will not be condemned at the final judgment.

Stand Up and Be Counted

My message and my preaching were not with wise and persuasive words, but with a demonstration of the Spirit's power, so that your faith might not rest on men's wisdom, but on God's power.

1 Corinthians 2:4–5

Here is a very simple definition of preaching: 'preaching is God's word reaching man through human personality.' The chief thing about preaching is that it must bring a real sense of God, not just of the word of God, but of God himself. And we will never worship unless that happens.

God uses ordinary men, and the preacher's personality actually becomes the very instrument of God. But for this to happen, the preacher must be called, prepared, uncontrived and unafraid. If he does not have these characteristics, there will be bad preaching.

It is possible to have good speaking, but bad preaching. Notice that in the verse I have just quoted, Paul refers to 'my speech and my preaching'. He distinguished between the two. It is possible to be only speaking and not actually preaching, even though it may be called preaching.

And it is possible for there to be bad speaking but good preaching. In 2 Corinthians 10:10, Paul refers to the way some of the people at Corinth talked about him. We read, 'For his letters, say they, are weighty and powerful; but his bodily presence is weak, and his speech contemptible.' They thought his speaking amounted to nothing. Imagine anyone saying that about the great Apostle Paul!

Worshipping God

*Several days later Felix came with his wife Drusilla, who was a
Jewess. He sent for Paul and listened to him as he spoke about faith
in Christ Jesus. As Paul discoursed on righteousness, self-control and
the judgment to come, Felix was afraid and said, 'That's enough for
now! You may leave. When I find it convenient, I will send for you.'*

Acts 24:24–25

Preaching which is gripping may still be ineffectual.

Where Felix was concerned, Paul's preaching was not effectual. And
this can be the case not only when the preaching is to non-Christians
but when it is to Christians in the Sunday services. I am quite sure
that many people are often gripped by the Sunday sermon, but they
just think, 'I'm not ready to do that yet.' Like Felix, they say, 'When
I find it convenient, I will send for you.'

When preaching is effectual, worship takes place, for then the
preaching is not with the words of man's wisdom, but by the demonstration of the Spirit and of power, so that the listener is caught up
into the heavenlies and loses sight of everything but God's voice. Some
people may even start to laugh or to cry while the preacher is speaking,
but the intercourse between God and man goes on unbroken. And this
is what every preacher longs for.

Effectual preaching leads to repentance, which means 'a change of
mind leading to a change of life'. For one person this may mean a one
hundred and eighty degree turn, whereas for another, who is already
walking in the light, it may lead to only a slight shift in direction.

Worshipping God

I came to you in weakness and fear, and with much trembling.

1 Corinthians 2:3

Sometimes only one person in a congregation responds to preaching with repentance, or maybe hundreds will: and this is a time of great rejoicing indeed. Then the preacher and the listener are in the Spirit, and a surge of heaven – a wave of glory – sweeps over the congregation, so that everyone knows that everyone else feels the same way. This is what we mean when we speak of unction.

The preacher may be aware of three things while he is preaching. Sometimes he may feel nothing at all – yet the congregation feels the presence of God's Spirit. The preacher may be like Moses, who did not know 'the glory of his countenance' (2 Corinthians 3:7). I think there are few things more encouraging (it has happened to me more than once) than to leave the pulpit feeling an utter failure, only to find that after all someone was spoken to or converted.

But sometimes when I am preaching I enjoy myself considerably – only to come down from the pulpit and find I was the only one!

Thirdly, and joy of joys, is when the preacher and congregation together are filled with a sense of the presence of God: where there is the unction I have just referred to. This is a weighty responsibility for the minister because up to a point he can control this surge of the Spirit. It is a great mystery, but it is absolutely true. This is one of the reasons why Paul told the Corinthians, 'I was with you in weakness, and in fear, and in much trembling.'

Worshipping God

The Spirit of the LORD *will rest on him—*
   the Spirit of wisdom and of understanding,
   the Spirit of counsel and of power,
   the Spirit of knowledge and of the fear of the LORD
and he will delight in the fear of the LORD.

Isaiah 11:2–3

One of the most frightening comments I have heard since I entered the ministry was uttered by an Episcopalian priest in America: 'If the Holy Spirit were taken completely from the Church, 90 per cent of the work of the Church would go right on as if nothing had happened!'

What a travesty of what the Church was meant to be! And can it be true also of our personal lives – that many of us are churning out 'Christian' activity that has no touch of God upon it?

There is only one antidote to such a situation: it is breathtaking in its possibility, it is awesome in its power, it is liberating in its effect. It is quite simply – the anointing.

The anointing is the power of the Holy Spirit. At the end of the day there is no better definition. But there is a more refined definition which I would like to offer at this stage.

Several years ago someone came into my vestry and asked me, 'What do you mean by the anointing?' I remember replying something like this: 'It's a gift that functions easily when it's working.' I had never said it like that before but I must have thought it. The person who is filled with the Holy Spirit is able to do extraordinary things but to them it seems quite natural. It is easy. That is, when it's working.

The Anointing

The wind blows wherever it pleases. You hear its sound, but you cannot tell where it comes from or where it is going.

John 3:8

You can't turn the anointing on and you can't turn the anointing off. A Spirit-filled nurse may be walking down a hospital corridor to give a patient an injection when she suddenly feels a sense of God's presence. She continues with her work but does so with the knowledge that God is with her in a special way. There is no greater feeling. Whether one is a secretary, professional person, homemaker, lorry driver or minister, the possibility of the anointing is there all the time; one never knows when God will manifest himself in an unusual way. Therefore, in my own work – whether in public speaking or in the solitude of intense preparation – I never know when that sense of God will come on me.

Why? There are probably *two* explanations. First, me. My mood, how much sleep I had, who I have just been talking with, how clear my mind feels, whether I am rushed or having to meet a deadline. It could be largely physical or emotional. It has much to do with whether I am under pressure. Or even if I have something to look forward to, like spending time with a trusted friend. It may therefore have little to do with the Holy Spirit. The second explanation is the sovereignty of the person of the Holy Spirit. The anointing *is* the Holy Spirit and the Holy Spirit is a person. God the Father is a person with a personality. God the Son – Jesus Christ – is a person with a personality. The Holy Spirit likewise has his own personality. He therefore moves in at will when we least expect it, and sometimes when we are least deserving of it. A lot of prayer no doubt has something to do with it, but there are times when the Spirit operates sovereignly when I haven't prayed as much as I should. The anointing is unmerited favour – it is sheer grace.

The Anointing

Then she called, 'Samson, the Philistines are upon you!' He awoke from his sleep and thought, 'I'll go out as before and shake myself free.' But he did not know that the LORD had left him.

Judges 16:20

After the Feast was over, while his parents were returning home, the boy Jesus stayed behind in Jerusalem, but they were unaware of it. Thinking he was in their company, they travelled on for a day. Then they began looking for him among their relatives and friends.

Luke 2:43–44

These two passages show that the special presence of God can be withdrawn and yet the people who have been experiencing that same presence feel nothing when it happens. This shows the painless way I can lose the anointing. I can displease the Lord and feel nothing. It even demonstrates the very real possibility that I could spend years doing what I presumed was God's will – preaching, teaching, witnessing and being involved in church work – when God was hardly in it at all. I may also have the applause and respect of people the whole time and they not have a clue I have moved ahead of Jesus.

One of the mysteries of the anointing is that one can be unaware of it when it is working most powerfully and, on the other hand, not be conscious should it be lifted. When Moses came down from Mount Sinai, he was 'not aware that his face was radiant' (Exodus 34:29). But Samson, who could tear a lion apart with his bare hands 'as he might have torn a young goat' (Judges 14:6), was as weak as a kitten when the anointing left him, but was unconscious of this until he tried to do what had seemed so natural the day before. For the supernatural often seems natural to the anointed man or woman.

The Sensitivity of the Spirit

'You may ask me for anything in my name, and I will do it.'

John 14:14

Is John 14:14 true or not? The phrase people overlook are these words: 'in my name'. The name of God is not to be used as a magic wand that you wave over a request. Some think that the mere mention of 'Jesus' ensures you can ask for anything from a Rolls-Royce, to healing, to win the election, to have tea with the Queen or win the Lottery – since God must honour Jesus' name.

What we forget is that God's name is 'Jealous': 'Do not worship any other god, for the LORD, whose name is Jealous, is a jealous God' (Exodus 34:14).

Truly to pray in Jesus' name is to *submit* to the name of God. It is not a name to be used for our manipulative, selfish purposes as if it were a good-luck charm. To pray in the name of Jesus is to embrace him as he is – and submit to all he wants.

James said, 'When you ask, you do not receive, because you ask with wrong motives, that you may spend what you get on your pleasures' (James 4:3). What many have done in this 'me generation' is to lift passages from God's infallible Word and apply them to situations absolutely alien to the purpose of those passages.

Take for example these words of Jesus: 'Ask and it will be given to you; seek and you will find; knock and the door will be opened to you. For everyone who asks receives; he who seeks finds; and to him who knocks, the door will be opened' (Matthew 7:7–8). These words are from Jesus' sermon on the mount, and the context is the kingdom of heaven. This is to be desired above all else. When Jesus said these words, 'Ask and it will be given to you,' he assumed that those who listened (or read) what came before, actually *wanted* the kingdom to come. The trouble is that people sometimes come from a worldly perspective, then seize certain words and apply them to a situation that is devoid of wanting to honour God's Word.

Did You Think to Pray?

'Why have we fasted,' they say, 'and you have not seen it? Why have we humbled ourselves, and you have not noticed?'

Isaiah 58:3

It is possible to spend hours every day talking to God like this. But the problem is that it is *we* who are doing all the talking, all the thinking, all the groaning and we shut God out. We think we are open to him when in fact we are only talking to him. And all the time he may be wanting to communicate with us at the level that we need, not at the level at which we are addressing him. We want to talk about one thing and God is saying, 'That's not your problem; your problem is over here.' We are looking in one direction and he's trying to get us to look in another.

Now when anyone develops a hearing problem, it usually doesn't happen overnight. It is a gradual and almost unnoticed event. And the same thing is true at the spiritual level: we hardly know it is happening. In the end we have to be jolted and made to realise what has been going on. It is like not realising we have been asleep until we wake up.

Worshipping God

'Here I am! I stand at the door and knock. If anyone hears my voice and opens the door, I will come in and eat with him, and he with me.'

Revelation 3:20

There are two reasons why God has difficulty in getting us to listen to him. The first is our inability to absorb or take in his counsel. Jesus said it like this: 'I have yet many things to say unto you, but ye cannot bear them now' (John 16:12). His disciples wouldn't have admitted to that. They would have said, 'Try me. See if I can't take it. Speak plainly.' But Jesus said, 'You couldn't take it.' We all overestimate our capacity to grasp and take in things, not realising that if God were to tell us all there is to know, our minds would snap. God has to deal with us where we are.

The second reason why God has difficulty in getting us to listen to him is that there is uncleansed sin within us as a result of not walking in the light.

A lady once came to Arthur Blessitt and asked him, 'Why doesn't God speak to me like he seems to speak to you?'

And Arthur said to her, 'Did you ever feel the impulse to speak to a stranger about the Lord but then were ashamed and didn't do it?'

When the lady replied, 'Yes, I have,' Arthur said, 'Well that's your problem. When you start to obey the impulse of the Spirit, God's voice gets clearer and clearer.'

God is trying to reach us and we hear him to the degree that we are walking in the light. Is it possible that God is trying to speak to you along a certain line but you are saying, 'I know God wouldn't say that to me'?

Worshipping God

After they prayed, the place where they were meeting was shaken.
And they were all filled with the Holy Spirit and spoke the word of
God boldly.

Acts 4:31

A vital ingredient of worship is expectancy: believing that something
good is going to happen. Nothing is sadder than going to church when
you aren't expecting anything to happen, and even know that nothing
is going to happen. When you feel that way – what a surprise – nothing
does happen! Yet so many people throughout the world go to church
feeling like that. It is not surprising that churches are closing down.
You would be shocked if you knew how many evangelical churches in
Britain have not had a conversion in five years – and are not even
expecting to see any conversions.

Of course, we have just as great a need for expectancy in our private
devotional life. When you come to read your Bible and pray, do you
expect something to happen? The peak moment of my day is when I
can be alone with God. I get out my Bible and expect God to speak
to me. Every time I open my Bible, I think, 'Lord, what are you going
to say to me today?'

And when I feel this way, and look for God to speak, then he often
does. This is how it should be with everyone. No one should come to
pray thinking, 'Oh, I suppose I've got to pray.' How dare we claim to
love God if coming to him is a duty!

Worshipping God

Therefore, my brothers, be all the more eager to make your calling and election sure. For if you do these things, you will never fall, and you will receive a rich welcome into the eternal kingdom of our Lord and Saviour Jesus Christ.

2 Peter 1:10–11

I have watched how evangelists, even pastors, play into the emotions of people to get them to 'walk the aisle' and make a public decision for Christ. The most reprehensible thing of all is to give the impression that these people who walk the aisle, join a church, sign a card or get baptised are actually converted. This would make God nice indeed. Nice God would not require people to be convicted of their sins by the Holy Spirit and make their calling and election sure by holy living.

Only the Holy Spirit can convert a man or woman; getting people to make a public decision without the inward persuasion of the Spirit is manipulation and abuse. It is nice preachers making God look nice by promising them a home in heaven – whether their hearts have been changed or not. 'Just come forward, let us baptise you', so your name can be added to the list of our many church members and can make statistics look good. This abuse of God's holy Name grieves the Spirit. The Dove flutters away and nobody feels a thing.

When we are governed by the sovereignty of God we will find it makes all the difference in what we try to get people to do. You cannot save the non-elect and you will not dislodge God's chosen. The preaching of the gospel will save some and condemn others, but it will accomplish God's purpose. New Testament evangelism stands in stark contrast to the Nice God who would not offend anyone.

Out of the Comfort Zone

The LORD was with Joseph and he prospered, and he lived in the house of his Egyptian master.

Genesis 39:2

Louise and I went to Russia in 1985, when it was the Soviet Union. We learned that there was a growing feeling among many, from the top down, that Christianity wasn't so bad after all. They found in every case, that if the worker was a Christian, they would get a good day's work out of them. If the employee was a Christian, then he or she didn't steal; that they could be trusted. Christians were soon getting promotions because they did such good jobs. What one can do is to be such a good employee, that you speak blessings to people. Don't be like so many Christians (forgive me) who are 'strange'. At work some people say, 'We know about her, she's a Christian and she sulks and sits in the corner.'

Arthur Blessitt, the man who has carried the cross around the world, had a profound influence on us at Westminster Chapel. He motivated us to talk to people about Jesus. I love the story he told about the lady who said, 'I don't ever tell people at work I am a Christian because I want my life to show.' One day somebody came to her after watching her for some time and said, 'You know, I have been watching you, you're different!' She began to think, 'It's paid off – thank you, Lord, I knew it would pay off one day.' She said, 'Yes, I am different.' 'Yes, I have been noticing you. I am going to ask you. Tell me, are you a vegetarian?'

If you are a Christian, then be nice. Speak blessings. Don't be unpleasant, bossy, always pointing the finger, especially if others know you are a Christian, which they should. There is a right way and a wrong way to witness. Don't witness on the job like we do on Saturdays on the streets. You don't go up to people and slap a Jesus sticker on them. But there is an intelligent way for people to know. You have what they don't have. God is with you.

The Thorn in the Flesh

*'It is mine to avenge; I will repay. In due time their foot will slip;
their day of disaster is near and their doom rushes upon them.'*

Deuteronomy 32:35

In 1741, taking his text from Deuteronomy 32:35, 'Their foot shall
slide in due time' (AV), Jonathan Edwards began to read his lengthy
sermon, word for word. He held the manuscript up to his eyes, hardly
the way most ministers today would preach a sermon! But as he spoke
the congregation began to moan and groan with emotion. Edwards
depicted his congregation as being held over the flames of hell by a
mere thread, and warned them that God could sever that thread at
any moment, allowing people to slide into hell. Jonathan Edwards
stressed that it was by the very mercy of God that they were not in
hell already. The noise of people under conviction as he spoke became
more intense. At one stage he asked them to be quiet before he
continued. But so powerful was the Holy Spirit's seal on the sermon
that people began to grab on to their pews to stop them from sliding
into hell. Strong men were seen outside the church building, trying to
hold on to tree trunks to stop themselves sliding into hell. One esti-
mate is that five hundred were eventually converted from that sermon.
When it went to press, the printer gave it the title *Sinners in the Hands
of an Angry God.*

I'm sorry, but many of today's generation appear to have lost real
respect for God. There is no real fear of God in the land, or even
among many of God's people. The irony is, the more that theology
is presented from man's perspective the less people will fear God or
even care about him. Only a robust view of the sovereignty of God,
which puts him back on the throne, will bring people to their senses.

Thanking God

Then Moses said, 'Now show me your glory.' And the LORD said, 'I will cause all my goodness to pass in front of you, and I will proclaim my name, the LORD, in your presence. I will have mercy on whom I will have mercy, and I will have compassion on whom I will have compassion.'

Exodus 33:18–19

The God of the Bible is the only true God. To grasp the truth about the God of glory we need to understand the sovereignty of God.

Two meanings are implied in God's right to do whatever he pleases. First, his privilege, or prerogative. The English aristocracy are said to be 'born to privilege'. Whether all these are just rights given to them is another matter, for so much in life seems to be unfair and quite wrong.

But God was not 'born'; he always was, is and shall ever be. What are the privileges, then, of being God? Does he have a 'right' to do this or that because he is God?

The second meaning implied in God's right is his rightness – indeed, righteousness – in what he does. God makes the rules; what he does is right. But does this mean he can break the rules – even break his own rules? Does he teach us one thing but live another way himself? No. Within the right or privilege that is God's are also his unchanging characteristics, among them being that he is holy, he cannot lie, and 'Will not the Judge of the earth do right?' (Genesis 18:25): Yes!

Thanking God

Our God is in heaven;
he does whatever pleases him.

Psalm 115:3

When the phrase 'sovereignty of God' emerges it is difficult to know which, if either, has priority: God's will or his power. But probably his will. 'In him we were also chosen, having been predestined according to the plan of him who works out everything in conformity with the purpose of his will' (Ephesians 1:11). This is a declaration of God's sovereignty if there ever was one. What surfaces at once is God's will. Hence Psalm 115:3: 'Our God is in heaven; he does whatsoever pleases him.' This too arises out of the assumption that whatever God does is absolutely just. Thus the idea of his will, or prerogative, is probably the main ingredient when it comes to the subject of God's grace and sovereignty.

But behind the assumption that God can exercise any right, which he is pleased to do, lies the equal assumption that he *can* do anything; that is, he has the power to do what he chooses to do. Some who sit on a throne may exercise their will, but do they have the power to pull it off? It is said of the Queen that she does not rule, she reigns. But God not only reigns but rules; he controls and carries out what he pleases to do.

The word 'power' basically has two meanings: force and authority. Indeed, two Greek words are often translated 'power' into English. First, *dunamis*, 'power', from which we get the word 'dynamite'. It refers to force or energy. It is used in Luke 24:49 and Acts 1:8. Second, *exousia*, 'authority', which means 'having the right', or 'privilege'. It is used in Matthew 28:18, John 1:12 and John 17:2.

The sovereignty of God encompasses both these words. God has the power to do anything because he can make it happen! He has power over his creation. He has power over all who appear to be in control. He has power over Satan.

It is by his mercy that we are not consumed (Lamentations 3:22). As Jonathan Edwards put it, it is by the sheer mercy of God we are not in hell. In a word: God can do anything, and whatever he does is right.

Thanking God

February

'He that is faithful in that which is least is faithful also in much: and he that is unjust in the least is unjust also in much.'

Luke 16:10 (AV)

What we are individually, twenty-four hours a day, is more important than what happens in church once a week. The secret of acceptable worship lies in how we are at home, or at work, and when we are alone and nobody knows what we are doing. It lies in our total lifestyle. If we don't get our act together before we come to church, we can't expect to worship at church. We can't expect something magical to happen once we're inside the church doors. We mustn't think 'All I need to do is get to church,' because it doesn't work that way. If we are hypocrites, if our profession of faith lacks reality, when we come to church to sing and worship we will be out of tune, and will not be making music pleasing to God.

Worshipping God

From him the whole body, joined and held together by every
supporting ligament, grows and builds itself up in love, as each part
does its work.

Ephesians 4:16

It is said that the great conductor Arturo Toscanini had such a perfect ear that he could detect if the fifth violinist on the fourth row back was slightly out of tune. Well, I don't know if it is possible for any minister to have that kind of sensitivity about his congregation. But God knows when there is perfect harmony and a lifestyle that is in accord with the Spirit – and he is not to be fooled or played around with.

The way we guard against being a hypocrite six days a week and acting piously on Sundays is by applying the word of God to our lives. Revival in a church may be quite extraordinary, but it is only a question of whether each member is following the conductor's score in his private life. In an orchestra, the sound is no greater than the sum of the different parts. So our worship ought to be a glorious symphony to God – no one out of tune, no one playing too loudly, each person following his or her own score.

Though our worship is not a performance designed to attract other people, or to pander to our own love of display, there is a sense in which it is a performance – a performance for God.

Worshipping God

Now the body is not made up of one part but of many. If the foot should say, 'Because I am not a hand, I do not belong to the body,' it would not for that reason cease to be part of the body. And if the ear should say, 'Because I am not an eye, I do not belong to the body,' it would not for that reason cease to be part of the body.

1 Corinthians 12:14–16

Everybody has an anointing. The Apostle Paul called it 'gifts' in 1 Corinthians 12:4–11. The Greek word *charismata* really means 'grace-gift'. It is God's gift, which he graciously bestows on those who don't deserve it. The difficulty is, ambition gets into the picture and some don't like it if their own anointing does not result in a high profile. Paul compared these grace-gifts, which I am calling anointings, to the parts of the human body.

Some anointings, then, have a high profile – like the eye or the head. Some anointings have a lower profile – like the hand or the feet. 'The eye cannot say to the hand, "I don't need you!" And the head cannot say to the feet, "I don't need you!" On the contrary, those parts of the body that seem to be weaker are indispensable' (1 Corinthians 12:21–2). Some people have an anointing with no apparent profile at all – like the kidneys or intestines which are indispensable (1 Corinthians 12:23ff.). God's design is that there should be 'no division in the body, but that its parts should have equal concern for each other' (1 Corinthians 12:25). Paul draws a conclusion: 'Now you are the body of Christ, and each one of you is a part of it' (1 Corinthians 12:27). There are those with the high profile, as apostles, prophets and teachers; some have an anointing (not listed in 1 Corinthians 12:8–10) which the Authorised Version merely calls 'helps' – 'those able to help others' (1 Corinthians 12:28).

The question is, will we accept our own anointing?

The Anointing

A man can do nothing better than to eat and drink and find satisfaction in his work. This too, I see, is from the hand of God, for without him, who can eat or find enjoyment?

Ecclesiastes 2:24–25

The anointing God gives will always be a legitimate anointing – what is just or fair; what is right. Whatever God does is just, even though we don't deserve it. Examine your own anointing. Is it not fair? He has not asked you to do what you cannot do. Your anointing will be an anointing you can use without fatigue. It comes easily. Because you can do it and you know you can do it.

God's anointing and promotion will mean that all you have been given by creation and refined by education and culture will cohere so that you will not be stunned and scared by where he puts you. The job will be right. Your ability to function will flow. It will be because you have come to terms with your anointing. It is legitimate because God set the standard. You can achieve your goal because the standard God set is never beyond the level of your competence. There is also a legitimate basis for feeling good about yourself because you are doing what he has equipped you to do. When, therefore, you come to terms with your own anointing you can stop looking over your shoulder at another's anointing. You find a gratification in the works of your own hands – which God made possible.

The Anointing

Now the Lord is the Spirit, and where the Spirit of the Lord is, there is freedom.

2 Corinthians 3:17

When we live within the limitations of our anointing there is freedom. The more I am myself the greater my liberty. This is because I am affirming God, who made me as I am. When I move outside my anointing I am trespassing. When I try to mimic somebody else I am stealing another's anointing and it always backfires on me.

A well-known Texas preacher of a previous generation had an eccentric habit of cupping his left hand over his ear when he began to soar in his preaching. Nobody knew why he did it. Young ministers all over Texas and Oklahoma would do the same thing; when they thought they were ringing the bell the left hand would come up over the ear. They thought they had the anointing! As it happened they made that same man Professor of Preaching at Southwestern Baptist Theological Seminary in Fort Worth, Texas. You could always tell one of his students!

Now I told the above story *at* Southwestern Baptist Theological Seminary a few years ago. I did it to see if I could find out why the old preacher did that. It worked. One of the older professors came up to me afterwards. 'I know exactly who you are talking about,' he said.

'But why on earth did he do that with his left hand over his ear?' I asked.

'Because he was hard of hearing,' came the answer. 'He could hear his own voice better.'

Hardly the anointing. But when anybody begins to imitate another who happens to have a great anointing, that person will not get the true anointing but will ape his eccentricity.

The Anointing

And the LORD *said, 'I will cause all my goodness to pass in front of you, and I will proclaim my name, the* LORD, *in your presence. I will have mercy on whom I will have mercy, and I will have compassion on whom I will have compassion.'*

Exodus 33:19

One of the mysteries regarding prayer is how some prayers are answered immediately, some take weeks or months, some years and years – while others remain (apparently) unanswered. I know what it is to put a brand-new prayer request to the Lord, write it down – expecting to repeat it daily indefinitely – only to have that request answered the same day! I can also tell you of many more requests that I have been bringing back to the Lord over and over again for the last twenty years – with no answer at all (that I can discern).

This is a mystery to me.

Exodus 33:19 is foundational to understanding the sovereignty of God. The sovereignty of God refers to God's prerogative to do what he pleases with whom he chooses. This covers every subject under the sun – salvation, healing, finances, relationships, gifts, callings, pay rises, jobs, guidance, and when he shows or hides his face. In a word: answered prayer begins with the sovereign will of God.

Yes, God may appear to change his mind, as in the illness and healing of Hezekiah (2 Kings 20:1–6); or in his declaration concerning destroying Nineveh (Jonah 3:9–10). And if I were Hezekiah or the king of Nineveh, I too would do what they did – plead with God with all my heart and soul! But I know at the same time that God will end up doing what he deems right in his own eyes, and we must trust his judgment, unwavering love and faithfulness when he does not come through for us in the way we wish he would.

Did You Think to Pray?

Then Jesus told his disciples a parable to show them that they should always pray and not give up.

Luke 18:1

The prayer of Isaiah, 'Oh, that you would rend the heavens and come down' (Isaiah 64:1) was the heart-cry in every synagogue in ancient Israel for hundreds of years as they prayed for their Messiah to come. He came, but they did not recognise him. Jesus wept over the city of Jerusalem which had rejected him and lamented, 'If you, even you, had only known on this day what would bring you peace – but now it is hidden from your eyes . . . you did not recognise the time of God's coming to you' (Luke 19:42, 44).

Israel's prayer was answered, but it was shaped by their readiness at the time. They weren't ready – that is why they missed their Messiah.

We must say what we mean and mean what we say when we pray – and stay at it. Do not ever forget that Jesus gave that parable to show that we should 'always pray and not give up'.

Ask yourself: what is it you once asked for – but stopped asking for? Praying for a loved one? A different job? A husband or wife? To have children? Healing? Revival? A new home? You may say: 'There is no way God could answer any of these requests and it will be under a cloud if it is answered.' I reply: don't be so sure; the shape that answered prayer takes is determined by our readiness at the time. God wants you to be found believing when he steps in.

Did You Think to Pray?

The things that mark an apostle – signs, wonders and miracles –
were done among you with great perseverance.

2 Corinthians 12:12

Unanswered prayer is God's deliberate *answer* to prayer as much as
any answered prayer is. Deliberate? Yes. He gives as much attention
to his denial of our request as he does approval of it.

Although it was not the response Paul was hoping for, God answered
Paul's request that the thorn in the flesh be removed: 'My grace is
sufficient for you, for my power is made perfect in weakness' (2
Corinthians 12:9). Nothing passes by the throne of grace without God's
careful attention. He acts upon every request that comes to him in the
name of his Son.

You don't have to be the Apostle Paul to get God's attention. God
loves every person as if there were no one else to love and answers
every prayer that comes to him in Jesus' name. It is only that you may
not like his answer – at first.

I know that I have lived long enough to thank God for unanswered
prayer. In fact, the longer I live, the more I thank him for the prayers
he did not answer with 'yes'. As Alec Motyer put it, if God was
compelled to answer all my prayers with 'yes', I would never have the
courage to pray for anything else again. It took me a while, however,
to come to this place.

Did You Think to Pray?

For it is we who are the circumcision, we who worship by the Spirit of God, who glory in Christ Jesus, and who put no confidence in the flesh.

Philippians 3:3

The Jews in Paul's day said that the people of God were those who had been circumcised. To this day, one is a Jew if one has had a Jewish mother. Being a Jew is either inherited or initiated by circumcision. Many think it is the same with Christianity. They think that to be a Christian you must be born into a Christian home, or be baptised or attend a Christian church.

Not so, says Paul. God's elect are a people of the Spirit. In Romans 9:6–7 Paul says, 'For they are not all Israel, which are of Israel. Neither, because they are the seed of Abraham, are they all children: but, in Isaac shall thy seed be called.' Ishmael, though a son of Abraham, was regarded as strictly of the flesh, whereas Isaac was the child of promise, and he was of the Spirit.

When Paul says, 'we are the circumcision', he means that God's people are circumcised in the heart: 'Circumcision is that of the heart' (Romans 2:29). And this is a sovereign work of the Holy Spirit. Jesus said, 'It is the Spirit that quickeneth; the flesh profiteth nothing' (John 6:63). And Paul said in Romans 8:2: 'For the law of the Spirit of life in Christ Jesus hath made me free from the law of sin and death.' The only people who truly worship God are the people of the Spirit, who have had this operation of the Holy Spirit upon the foreskins of their hearts. Only the elect can worship God with spiritual worship. All others may say that they worship, but they are worshipping idols.

Our churches should not be places where the unregenerate come on Sundays because they 'like the worship'. Our churches ought to be places where the unregenerate feel uncomfortable because it is the Spirit who is important and who comes first. Our controlling principle must be obedience to the Spirit – no matter where he leads us.

Worshipping God

'A priest happened to be going down the same road, and when he saw the man, he passed by on the other side.'

Luke 10:31

It seems to me that a missing note among Christians – nowadays more than ever – is a solid conviction in the justice and sovereignty of God. For far too long the 'me generation' has crept into our thinking. It is one of the main reasons why so many in the Church are weak and anaemic. And ungrateful.

Our gratitude to God will almost certainly be in proportion to our sense of feeling unworthily blessed, because the same God who could have passed us by didn't. I am tempted to use the word 'lucky' – a biblical word, in fact. The word 'happiness' (when something good 'happens' to you) actually comes from the word that means lucky. It is used in the parable of the Good Samaritan; a priest 'happened' to be going down the same road (Luke 10:31). (So the world has stolen a perfectly good word from us, so that now we are afraid to use it.) But the feeling of being 'lucky' – when in fact it was not 'chance' at all but God's sovereign blessing – can give the Christian a keen sense of gratitude, because God blessed us when we didn't deserve it. Our gratitude, then, is going to be in proportion to our sense of awe that God did what he did so graciously – but didn't have to.

Thanking God

*Then King David went in and sat before the LORD, and he said:
'Who am I, O Sovereign LORD, and what is my family, that you
have brought me this far? And as if this were not enough in your
sight, O Sovereign LORD, you have also spoken about the future of
the house of your servant. Is this your usual way of dealing with
man, O Sovereign LORD?'*

2 Samuel 7:18–19

David was struck with awe when he said, 'The boundary lines have
fallen for me in pleasant places' (Psalm 16:6). He knew God had been
singularly good to him. This is the way he felt when he reflected on
the news that he would not be allowed to build the temple. God saved
this for Solomon. David was disappointed, but even then sat before
the Lord and said, 'Who am I, O Sovereign LORD, and what is my
family, that you have brought me this far? . . . Is this your usual way
of dealing with man, O Sovereign LORD?'.

When God grants us sovereign mercy it ought to make us exceedingly grateful. This is why the Apostle Paul never got over being saved.
Knowing as he did that he was dedicated to the destruction of the
Christian faith, being 'a blasphemer and a persecutor and a violent
man', he could only say, 'I was shown mercy' (1 Timothy 1:13; 'I
obtained mercy', AV).

'Have pity on me!' cried the lepers of Luke 17. 'Pity' is the NIV
translation of the Greek word that is almost always translated 'mercy'
everywhere else, as in Hebrews 4:16. It is a word that proud people
loathe using in connection with God. Such people prefer to feel that
God owes *us* something, that *he* has a lot to answer for.

But the truth is, we are as unworthy and helpless as those lepers.
If only we knew our place as they did! Perhaps then we too would
not care who is eavesdropping and will cry out for mercy!

Thanking God

On the contrary, they saw that I had been entrusted with the task of preaching the gospel to the Gentiles, just as Peter had been to the Jews.

Galatians 2:7

I wonder how many people are afraid of becoming a Christian because they fear that the moment they become a Christian God is going to send them to Africa or South America or some other far-flung place. Well, as soon as Paul was converted he had something worse than that – he was sent to the Gentiles. Every Jew in those days thanked God daily that he wasn't a Gentile; that he wasn't a woman; and that he wasn't a dog.

To us it just doesn't add up. All his life Paul was looking over his shoulder, trying to reach Jews at every opportunity. He said, 'The gospel is to the Jew first' (Romans 1:16), and I can tell you, every chance he got, he was talking to a Jew. I am quite convinced this is what eventually got him into trouble. There is little doubt in my mind that when those people came to him and said, 'Don't go to Jerusalem', they were led of the Spirit (Acts 21:4–11). Luke says, 'By the Spirit they said, "Don't go."' Paul said, 'I'm going!' He kept thinking that one day, somehow, he was going to convert the Jews. When he went to Jerusalem, it was a big disaster. It didn't happen.

Maybe that's you. You are still hoping somehow to do something else. You say, 'I am not going to do this all my life!' You try to do what God won't let you do, and it just doesn't come off. Paul's lasting success was with the very people he had grown up to think very little of. It was an unwanted calling.

The Thorn in the Flesh

Likewise the tongue is a small part of the body, but it makes great boasts. Consider what a great forest is set on fire by a small spark. The tongue also is a fire, a world of evil among the parts of the body. It corrupts the whole person, sets the whole course of his life on fire, and is itself set on fire by hell.

James 3:5–6

There is a difference between temptation and sin. It is not a sin to be tempted; it is not a sin to have the thought. The sin is in our words – when we say what is tempting us. The temptation could be to lust or self-exaltation, name dropping or speaking ungraciously. The temptation to say such things is not sin; it is sin when we cave in to the temptation to cause another to lust, to say what makes us look good or to say what will make another look bad. Tongue control indicates whether the temptation was aborted and sin did not come forth.

The tongue therefore proves whether you are in control of your whole being. That is the fruit of the Spirit – self-control. The perfect man or woman therefore is not the one who doesn't have evil thoughts or wrong feelings; perfection is buttoning your lip so you do not say what you feel like saying. When we say what we feel in such circumstances it makes things worse.

Your Words Have Power

'Whoever acknowledges me before men, I will also acknowledge him before my Father in heaven.'

Matthew 10:32

Does Jesus care if we acknowledge his deity? Is this something that Jesus himself wants? Would he be embarrassed by it? What does it mean to him? Does he *want* us to do it? How important is it that we acknowledge his deity?

The proof that you have been truly converted to Christ by the Holy Spirit is not only that you believe in your heart but that you will confess *with your mouth* that Jesus is God in the flesh. Why with the mouth? So that others will know that you believe it. Are you ashamed of it? 'If anyone is ashamed of me and my words in this adulterous and sinful generation, the Son of Man will be ashamed of him when he comes in his Father's glory with the holy angels' (Mark 8:38).

Perhaps you have wondered whether or not God *has* ever been at work in you. Perhaps you have worried whether or not you are a Christian. Could it be that the devil himself has almost convinced you that you are not the Lord's. Are you wondering if you are one of God's own? I can answer that question for you. It is no guesswork. It is absolutely right. If you are not ashamed to confess that Jesus Christ is God in the flesh, you are a Christian. Worry no more, my dear friend. May God defeat Satan as you read these very lines. May the 'accuser of the brethren' (Revelation 12:10) be cast down!

This is an infallible test. If you from your heart – without trying to convince yourself by having to look for more evidence of 'proofs' – confess that Jesus is God in the flesh, you may know that the blessed Holy Spirit enabled you to do that.

Does Jesus Care?

'A wicked and adulterous generation looks for a miraculous sign, but none will be given it except the sign of Jonah.'

Matthew 16:4

And what was the sign of Jonah? Preaching.

Jonah marched into Nineveh with a simple but direct message, 'Forty more days and Nineveh will be destroyed' (Jonah 3:4). Paul said, 'For since in the wisdom of God the world through its wisdom did not know him, God was pleased through the foolishness of what was preached to save those who believe' (1 Corinthians 1:21).

In other words, God convinces men of himself by preaching Jesus Christ. When Paul came to Corinth, the seat of learning and sensuality of the day – where there was no 'God framework', he said 'for I resolved to know nothing while I was with you except Jesus Christ and him crucified' (1 Corinthians 2:2). Paul, knowing that he was going to the famous Corinth, might have said to himself, 'I'd better bone up on my Aristotle and Plato if I am going to a place like Corinth. I must show myself to be the erudite man they will listen to.' But no. He knew that there was only one way by which men would be convinced of the true God, and that was by preaching Jesus Christ. As Peter put it, 'Through him you believed in God' (1 Peter 1:21).

Does Jesus Care?

Because the patriarchs were jealous of Joseph, they sold him as a slave into Egypt. But God was with him and rescued him from all his troubles. He gave Joseph wisdom and enabled him to gain the goodwill of Pharaoh king of Egypt; so he made him ruler over Egypt and all his palace.

Acts 7:9–10

The challenge of unhappy employment is a test from God. All the angels are watching. What will you do? Joseph was treated unjustly by his brothers, became a slave in a foreign country, had to do tasks for which he was not trained and, on top of it, was falsely accused. So what's the challenge? Make the best of a bad situation. Don't always run away to look for another job. Don't promote yourself to the level of your incompetence. Don't jump out of the frying pan into the fire. Remember that God put you there for a purpose. God could change everything overnight. Remember that this life is not all there is. Many around you don't have heaven to look forward to, and God doesn't want any of us to be *too* happy here below.

Unhappy employment may also help one to appreciate all the more the good things in one's life. It may be helpful and self-edifying to thank God for things that are positive. Do you have good health? Do you have a home? Do you have loved ones? Do you have friends you can share with? Do you also have a good relationship with God?

Your relationship with God is more important than your job. Get your joy from the inward anointing. There are some Christians who are happy with their jobs – so happy that they are not very spiritual. They don't pray, they don't have intimacy with God. With unhappy employment you may be enjoying a relationship with God that you might not otherwise have. God loves you and wants your company, and knows what you would be like if you were too comfortable.

The Thorn in the Flesh

Even from birth the wicked go astray; from the womb they are wayward and speak lies.

Psalm 58:3

St Augustine (AD 354–430) put forward four stages of humankind which set the pace for the Christian Church's doctrine of sin for hundreds of years:

1 *Posse pecare* (able to sin) – that is, Adam and Eve before the Fall in Genesis 3.
2 *Non posse non pecare* (not able not to sin) – that is, the state into which all people are born after the Fall.
3 *Posse non pecare* (able not to sin) – that is, those who have faith in Christ.
4 *Non posse pecare* (not able to sin) – that is, once we are in heaven.

It is the second stage above – 'not able not to sin' – our fallen state – into which we are all born. This is the way we all are by nature; there are no exceptions. You and I were born into a state whereby we cannot help sinning and this condition begins at our birth and is why we came from our mother's womb speaking 'lies' (Psalm 58:3). You don't need to teach a child how to lie – we come by it naturally. It is not until we are glorified that we will be unable to sin (Romans 8:30). The point is, God knows our frame and remembers we are dust – even before the Fall.

Furthermore, God is so gracious – he knows and sympathises with our struggles (Hebrews 4:15). He commands us to do the Father's will but also tenderly leads us, inch by inch, day by day, to bring us to full obedience to him. But at the same time we need to know that forgiving ourselves is a serious matter and it is something we must do.

Totally Forgiving Ourselves

If our hope in Christ has been for this life only, we are the most unfortunate of all people.

1 Corinthians 5:19 (JB)

It is fashionable nowadays to say, 'If there were no heaven or no hell, I would still be a Christian.' Although I know what people mean by this, I must tell you as lovingly as I know how that the Apostle Paul would be horrified at this thought! He said the very opposite. And yet the Christian faith is too often presented as being something that exists mainly for us in the here and now. People seem not to want to face the fact that the Christian faith has been designed for us because we are a dying people and the wages of sin is death (Romans 6:23). If there really is a heaven and there really is a hell, and when you consider that eternity lasts a long time, nothing is more important than eternal values.

To put it another way, there is an inherent stigma in the Christian faith. Caution: never, never, never try to outgrow the stigma (offence of the cross). It offends the sophisticated person to hear that the main thing about the gospel is that it fits us for heaven. I don't mean to be unfair, but I sometimes fear that there is a subtle, perhaps unconscious, attempt by some to de-stigmatise the gospel. This is a big mistake. It is like trying to get a car to run without fuel, or expect a bird to fly without wings, or fish to swim out of water. Paul knew he was on safe ground with the Galatians because of the *stigma* of the gospel he was upholding. What helps to prove that the gospel one preaches is the true gospel is that it *offends* (Galatians 5:11; 6:12–13); and de-stigmatising the gospel seeks to remove the offence of the cross.

Did You Think to Pray?

Although they claimed to be wise, they became fools and exchanged the glory of the immortal God for images made to look like mortal man and birds and animals and reptiles.

Romans 1:22–23

Ludwig Feuerbach opined that God was nothing more than man's projection upon the backdrop of the universe; that people want to believe in something, especially a God who will take care of them in time of trouble and then give them a home in heaven when they die. Such people mentally project such a God and claim he really does exist. Such a God does not exist of course, says Feuerbach, but he exists in their minds and gives comfort.

It is my view that many Christians do this. They know full well there are things in the Bible they don't want to believe but they are not prepared to throw out everything in the Bible so they fancy a God who approves of their own comfort zone. This God is happy with Christians who reject Bible-denying liberal theology while at the same time approving of their unease with the total revelation of God as revealed in the Old and New Testament.

What does God himself think of this? Is he so neglected by the masses that he is simply thrilled to have anybody – anywhere – whatever their level of conviction, to give him any attention at all? Is he so hard up or starved for recognition that he will make any measure of concession to any person who makes any effort at all to acknowledge him? Will he therefore show his approval toward any kind of profession of faith because some tipping of the hat toward him is better than nothing?

The nice God of today's religious people might do just that. But not the God of the Bible.

Out of the Comfort Zone

'What good is it for a man to gain the whole world, yet forfeit his soul?'

Mark 8:36

It is amazing what some people will do for money. The very soldiers who were guarding the tomb of Joseph of Arimathea on Easter morning – the nearest to examples of eye-witnesses to Jesus' resurrection that we are likely to discover – actually took money rather than tell what they knew was true! 'You are to say, "His disciples came during the night and stole him away while we were asleep"', the chief priests commanded them. '"If this report gets to the governor, we will satisfy him and keep you out of trouble." So the soldiers took the money and did as they were instructed' (Matt. 28:12–15).

I will repeat my advice for anybody reading these lines: handle every penny and every pound as though a television camera were monitoring your every move for the world to see. After all, an equivalent of a video replay or DVD will be played for all to see at the Judgment Seat of Christ. Count on that.

There are some, however, who excuse themselves for handling money in a questionable manner because they are so generous with others. It is like saying, 'I may not want everybody to know how I spend, how I arrange the bookkeeping and how I may not be totally careful with every penny, *but I do give away a lot of money* – this should make it all right.' Really?

If you have had a fall that came about through the handling of finances, but you want to be restored, I must lovingly ask: 'Do you still have the same old love of money and material things?' Remember: 'For everything in the world – the cravings of sinful man, the lust of his eyes and the boasting of what he has and does – comes not from the Father but from the world' (1 John 2:16).

Second Chance

If you ever forget the LORD your God and follow other gods and worship and bow down to them, I testify against you today that you will surely be destroyed. Like the nations the LORD destroyed before you, so you will be destroyed for not obeying the LORD your God.

Deuteronomy 8:19–20

God hates ingratitude but loves our being thankful. In Romans 1 Paul demonstrates the justice of God's wrath on men. They suppress the truth by their wickedness. 'The wrath of God is being revealed from heaven against all the godlessness and wickedness of men who suppress the truth by their wickedness' (Romans 1:18). What is known about God is made plain to them so that they are without excuse (Romans 1:19–20). Such people 'neither glorified him as God *nor gave thanks to him*' (Romans 1:21).

Paul lists conditions of wickedness in the last days. 'People will be lovers of themselves, lovers of money, boastful, proud, abusive, disobedient to their parents, *ungrateful*, unholy' (2 Timothy 3:2). In a generation that did as they 'saw fit' (Judges 21:25), their backsliding was rooted in ingratitude.

How do we show our gratitude? By telling him. But that is not all. We also show gratitude by a holy life. Never forget that we are not saved by being holy; we are holy because we have been saved. But because we are still sinners, we easily forget and become careless.

Thanking God

After consulting the people, Jehoshaphat appointed men to sing to the LORD *and to praise him for the splendour of his holiness as they went out at the head of the army, saying: 'Give thanks to the* LORD, *for his love endures for ever.'*

2 Chronicles 20:21

For what are you grateful? If you cannot think of things to show how thankful you are, take the time to make a prayer list – or 'praise' list! Here are some suggestions to begin with:

- salvation: God sending his Son to die on a cross;
- that he gave you faith;
- your church – that person who had a hand in leading you to Christ;
- your minister, whose preaching and pastoring feeds your soul;
- your job – your income;
- your health;
- the Bible;
- what God is doing for you today and what he did for you yesterday.

When you begin to count your blessings you will see that the list is endless! For there is no end to the list by which we can demonstrate our gratitude to God.

Thanking God

For it is time for judgment to begin with the family of God; and if it begins with us, what will the outcome be for those who do not obey the gospel of God?

1 Peter 4:17

Why does God step in and judge some, but leave others to continue in their sin? The answer is that it has mostly to do with God's sovereign and inscrutable purposes, but also his infinite patience. And yet it may also have something to do with how angry God is, in which case he may prefer to wait and deal with some disobedient servants at the Final Judgment. However, all sin will be judged sooner or later – whether in this life or at the Judgment Seat of Christ.

The Apostle Peter stated that judgment 'must begin at the house of God' (1 Peter 4:17, AV; the word 'family' is used instead of 'house' in the NIV). This is because God has chosen to delay judging the world generally until he has first called his own people to give an account regarding their covenant responsibility. He therefore starts the process of judgment with his elect people first.

When Peter said that judgment must begin with the house, or family, of God I don't think he was referring to an order of events at the Final Judgment, although it could imply that. If so, it could therefore suggest that the *saved* will be dealt with before the lost are held accountable at the Final Judgment. However, I think Peter's statement that judgment must begin with the family of God refers to the way that God has chosen to deal with his own people in the here and now – in advance of the Final Judgment.

Second Chance

But if we judged ourselves, we would not come under judgment.

1 Corinthians 11:31

We must never forget this incontrovertible fact: we are *all* going to face God's Final Judgment. We should live our lives accordingly. That is one of the reasons that the Bible tells us there is a coming Judgment – to change our lives *now* and to prepare us for that frightening Event.

But it is equally true that God can give us a taste of the Final Judgment – in advance of that Day. As a matter of fact, good preaching on the subject of the Final Judgment should do this. When the reality of eternity is brought home so that it invades the present, the people will sense the fear of God and even feel something of what it will be like on that Day.

And yet a foretaste of the Final Judgment is what is actually taking place when you read of certain people who have been 'caught'. People like this who are being exposed is no accident; it is what *God* does. It is judgment in advance of the Judgment. When Paul says that if we judge ourselves, we will not be judged (1 Corinthians 11:31), referring to the Lord's Supper, he is telling us that you and I can be spared this judgment below – and the full effects of the Final Judgment – if we deal with sin in the here and now. Dealing with our sin in the here and now means (1) acknowledging it, not denying it; and (2) repenting of it.

It could be more painful to be found out *then* – at the Judgment Seat of Christ – than to be exposed *now* in advance of the Judgment. There is an observable pattern in the history of God's dealings with his people: the angrier God is, the longer he sometimes waits before showing his ire. However painful it must be to be caught and judged here below, it will be worse at the Judgment Seat.

Second Chance

When Mary reached the place where Jesus was and saw him, she fell at his feet and said, 'Lord, if you had been here, my brother would not have died.' When Jesus saw her weeping, and the Jews who had come along with her also weeping, he was deeply moved in spirit and troubled. 'Where have you laid him?' he asked. 'Come and see, Lord,' they replied. Jesus wept.

John 11:32–35

Jesus was affected by Mary and Martha's hurt. He let himself get involved. Why? He loved them.

Jesus felt what they were feeling and entered into their sorrow, even though he knew that in moments the whole situation would be changed. But he knew that they did not know that. He lived with them fully in the present.

That is the way Jesus loves. He is not like an annoyed parent who will say, 'Stop crying. You'll feel better tomorrow.' Rather, our Lord lives in the exact present as though there were no tomorrow.

This to me is one of the most astonishing things about God. Why would he waste time in comforting me with his presence and any number of verses from his word when he already knows that I may well soon feel better anyway? I say, this is most extraordinary. The God who knows the happy outcome lives with me in the very present moment to comfort me as though he had nothing on his mind but my feelings at the time. I call that love.

Does Jesus Care?

Oh, the depth of the riches of the wisdom and knowledge of God!
How unsearchable his judgments, and his paths beyond tracing out!
Who has known the mind of the Lord? Or who has been his coun-
sellor?

Romans 11:33–34

Sometimes it is hard to work out why one person is restored after a fall and another isn't. Is it because some sins are worse than others? For example, King Saul disobeyed God by breaking the Law and was not restored; David broke the Law and was. As we shall see below, Saul broke the Ceremonial Law; David broke the Moral Law. And yet David's sin – certainly in some ways – seems worse than Saul's. The sins of adultery and murder seem worse than the wrong person offering a burnt offering. But there was one *big* difference between the two: David truly repented and Saul didn't.

This is so encouraging. When there is a genuine, uncontrived and unfeigned repentance, it shows there is hope – and that God is at work.

But why David repented and not Saul – and why people like Samson have been granted repentance in the end and others apparently have not – remains a mystery. Moreover, why are some found out – and others seem to get away with their sin? We will have to wait until the Final Judgment for the complete answer. In the meantime I appeal to Paul's glorious submission to the inscrutable and sovereign will of God: 'Oh, the depth of the riches of the wisdom and knowledge of God! How unsearchable his judgments, and his paths beyond tracing out! Who has known the mind of the Lord? Or who has been his counsellor?' (Romans 11:33–34). Remaining in awe of this aspect of God's ways should keep us on our knees and make us profoundly thankful when we are granted true repentance.

Second Chance

'My son, do not make light of the Lord's discipline,
  and do not lose heart when he rebukes you,
because the Lord disciplines those he loves,
  and he punishes everyone he accepts as a son.'

Hebrews 12:5–6

The Greek word for disciplining or chastening (AV) means *enforced learning*. God has a way of getting our attention – to teach us a lesson. Chastening is not a case of God 'getting even'; God got even at the cross! 'As far as the east is from the west, so far has he removed our transgressions from us' (Psalm 103:12). Chastening is essentially preparation; it is because God has not finished with us yet. 'No discipline seems pleasant at the time, but painful. Later on, however, it produces a harvest of righteousness and peace for those who have been trained by it' (Hebrews 12:11).

There are three kinds of chastening: (1) internal chastening – when God speaks to us through his word. That is the best way to have God discipline you – internally, through the word and the Spirit. If only we would listen! (2) external chastening – Plan B. It is when people will not listen to him when he speaks clearly. It is what happened to Jonah; he was found out and God subsequently sent the fish to swallow him up. Plan B is God making a further effort to get our attention. It is like getting caught. Being exposed. Losing everything. But one can still hear God speak. (3) terminal chastening is when it is *over*. Sometimes God brings about death, as in 1 Corinthians 11:30 (those who abused the Lord's Supper) or 1 John 5:16 (the sin that leads to premature physical death).

There are therefore two kinds of terminal chastening: (a) that which leads quickly to physical death, and (b) that which results in becoming inwardly stone deaf to the Spirit – but the person lives on. The latter was what happened to King Saul.

There are probably those with a fairly high profile in business and professional positions today – not to mention the ministry – whose gift functions but who no longer hear God. If in business, they continue to make money. If they are professionals, they do their jobs well. If in ministry, like Saul, whose prophetic gift functioned for a while, they manage to keep vast followings and supporters behind them.

Second Chance

'"For this son of mine was dead and is alive again; he was lost and is found." So they began to celebrate.'

Luke 15:24

Although the word 'backsliding' is not found in the New Testament, the Parable of the Prodigal Son surely shows, among other things, that a true child of God can go off the rails and then come back to the Lord. Our heavenly Father loves to welcome the backslider home. We must never forget too that the older brother in this parable was indignant when the prodigal son got so much attention. I don't mean to be unfair, but a returning backslider can anticipate some older brothers and sisters in the church who may not be too welcoming!

When this present book was nearly finished, a ministerial friend of mine (who has had a fall) told me of a book that argues that a fallen person in the ministry cannot be restored. I have not read it, but he had read it almost in desperation, hoping for a word of encouragement that he could be used again. He said that the book he had read gave him no hope. It might even have demoralised him completely. I cannot imagine that an inflexible approach that gives no hope for future usefulness to fallen Christians – ministers or laymen, high-profile or unknown – could be in the spirit of Jesus.

The truth is, God can use *anybody* who has truly repented. He can open doors that would normally be closed, break down barriers that would normally preclude usefulness again, open people's hearts that had previously been cold and prejudiced. To the fallen person I say: your task is to repent fully; God's job is forgiving, restoring and opening doors. It dignifies the blood that Jesus shed on the cross that a fallen saint can be forgiven and used again.

Second Chance

Even if I caused you sorrow by my letter, I do not regret it. Though I did regret it – I see that my letter hurt you, but only for a little while – yet now I am happy, not because you were made sorry, but because your sorrow led you to repentance. For you became sorrowful as God intended and so were not harmed in any way by us. Godly sorrow brings repentance that leads to salvation and leaves no regret, but worldly sorrow brings death.

2 Corinthians 7:8–10

There are basically two Greek words used in the Bible that may be translated 'repentance': *metanoia* and *metamelomai*. The main one is *metanoia*. It means 'change of mind' – meaning the change of *nous*, 'mind' or 'understanding'. The original Greek idea in *metanoia* was 'later knowledge', 'subsequent knowledge', often with the implication lest it be 'too late'. It is said that we all have 20/20 hindsight vision. To be granted repentance, a true change of mind, is to have 20/20 vision *now* rather than later.

In other words, to repent means to see and do *now* what you will wish you had seen and done *later*. So if one is granted repentance, it is a marvellous mercy of a sovereign God. It is being able to do what you will be glad you did, especially when you stand before God at the Judgment Seat of Christ. If one is given a true *change of mind* – in time before it is too late – we have only to thank God and his undeserved mercy for this marvellous privilege.

The second word, *metamelomai*, means 'to experience remorse'. Whereas *metanoia* implies that you have arrived at a different view of something, *metamelomai* indicates that you have a different feeling about it. This is the word used in 1 Samuel 15:35, that 'the LORD was *grieved* that he made Saul king over Israel'. It is used in Psalm 110:4: 'The Lord has sworn and will not change his mind' (cf. Hebrews 7:21) – that is, he will not regret his sworn oath. However, Paul uses both *metanoia* and *metamelomai* interchangeably in 2 Corinthians 7:7–10, which shows that you must not press the distinction of these meanings too far.

Second Chance

March

'This, then, is how you should pray . . .'

Matthew 6:9

In the Sermon on the Mount, the Lord's Prayer emerged not in answer to the disciples' request but in the context of Jesus' teaching how not to pray. He had been telling the disciples *not* to pray like the hypocrites who love to pray 'standing in the synagogues and on the street corners to be seen by men' (Matthew 6:5).

We deduce from this that Rule Number One in how not to pray is praying to be seen by people. If your motive to pray is to make sure others see you pray or know that you do a bit of praying, your approach to prayer is quite wrong. It violates one of the most consistent principles of Jesus' teaching. He says the same thing about giving and fasting; if things like this are done to be 'seen' by people, then you do get your reward, yes – but that reward is merely *that people know* you prayed, gave or fasted. In a word: a pretty shabby reward (if you ask me) compared to what would have come from God alone had one done it entirely for his glory (John 5:44).

The Lord's Prayer is a prayer to be prayed – whether individually or together. It is a corporate prayer. We pray, '*Our* Father'. Not only that, the command is how 'you' (second person plural) should pray. I might add that it is a correct prayer; we are told exactly what to say. This is a prayer approved of by God; praying this prayer is at least one time you can be sure that you pray in the will of God. Moreover, it is a complete prayer. It contains six petitions that include everything we may rightly wish from God.

Let the Lord's Prayer be your model, follow its petitions, its order; you can never outdo praying along these lines – whether in private or in public.

Did You Think to Pray?

2 March

'"Our Father"'

Matthew 6:9

The prayer we normally pray should be addressed to God the Father. There is nothing wrong with addressing a prayer to Jesus (Luke 23:42; Acts 7:59), or to the Holy Spirit (otherwise, a lot of our hymnody got it wrong, as in 'Come, Holy Ghost, all-quickening fire'). But our praying, speaking generally, should recognise God the Creator and Redeemer as Father.

Some have objected to praying the Lord's Prayer because it does not end in Jesus' name. My reply: the moment we address God as *Father* we pray in Jesus' name. This is because we have no right to call God Father except that we have been brought to him through his Son, Jesus Christ.

Be careful about popular talk – 'Fatherhood of God'. It is absolutely true that the Fatherhood of God is essential Christian teaching, but there are those who take a 'universalist' perspective that is alien to Scripture. They would say that God is Father to everybody, whether or not they come to him through Jesus. Wrong. God is Father only through Jesus; hence the Lord's Prayer is to be prayed because it *assumes* Jesus is God's only Son and our Saviour. Furthermore, Jesus gave this prayer to the Church, not the world.

It also means that God is *personal*. The late Paul Tillich, a universalist, would call God 'the ground of all being'. This is very like pantheism ('everything is God'), although some prefer to call it panentheism – 'everything, all creation, is in God'. In any case, it makes God impersonal. In ancient times even the Jews would not address God as Father, but rather Sovereign Lord, King of the universe or, simply, *Adonai* – 'Lord'. But you and I are invited to call him *Father*, because that is what he is and who he is to those who come to God through Jesus.

Did You Think to Pray?

'"in heaven"'

Matthew 6:9

Why does Jesus add these words, 'in heaven'? In a word: it puts us in our place. I connect this phrase 'in heaven' to these words: 'Do not be quick with your mouth, do not be hasty in your heart to utter anything before God. *God is in heaven and you are on earth*, so let your words be few' (emphasis mine, Ecclesiastes 5:2–3). Psalm 115:3 also comes to mind: 'Our God is in heaven; he does whatever pleases him.' These words 'in heaven' remind us of how big and how great God is. It is a word also given partly to ensure that we never become overly familiar with him.

It also means that the Father is invisible – out of sight. You cannot see him; faith is required. When you can see the person you are talking with, you don't need to exercise faith that he or she is before your eyes. So although God is personal ('Our Father'), he is also Spirit (John 4:24). He cannot be seen.

His being in heaven also means he is independent. When one is as high as the heavens are above the earth, you know you can't snap your finger at the person, expecting immediate service. You are in your place. You, instead, are on the begging end – waiting for him to grant us mercy. According to the writer to the Hebrews, the first thing we ask for when we pray is *mercy* (Hebrews 4:16). Or as it is put in one of the psalms of ascents, 'As the eyes of slaves look to the hand of their master, as the eyes of a maid look to the hand of her mistress, so our eyes look to the LORD our God, till he shows us his mercy' (Psalm 123:2–3). Never forget that the God of the Bible continues to say, 'I will have mercy on whom I will have mercy' (Exodus 33:19; Romans 9:15). Never forget too that God can give or withhold mercy and be equally just either way.

Did You Think to Pray?

'"hallowed be your name"'

Matthew 6:9

The first petition of the Lord's Prayer is a petition of praise and worship. Note: it is not 'holy is your name'; God's name is holy anyway. It is a petition, 'hallowed *be* your name' – a prayer that the Father's name will be *treated as holy*.

There are two essential things in a name. The first is identity. In ancient times a person's name was revelatory – in other words, it was closely related to one's calling. God's name was *Yahweh*: 'I AM WHO I AM', 'I will be who I will be' (Exodus 3:14). In the Lord's Prayer we pray that the Father will be universally recognised for who he truly is.

The second essential thing in a name is reputation: 'A good name is more desirable than great riches' (Proverbs 22:1). As Jesus was jealous for his Father's name, so should you and I be.

What Jesus wants you and me to pray is that *all* will respect his Father's name. Everything we do must bring honour and glory to his name. We should want the whole world to revere the Father's name. It is the first petition we put to him: that we – and everybody else on the planet – will participate in the awesomeness of the Father's name.

You may not have realised it, but when you pray the Lord's Prayer you pledge to be accountable to that name. You cannot pray, 'hallowed be your name' and then live in a manner that is contrary to his honour. You cannot pray that all will recognise the awesomeness of that name when you do not mirror this plea yourself by a life that shows reverence for that name. You do not want people to misuse or abuse that name, neither will you ever drag God's name into your life in a way that does not reflect his holiness.

To pray 'hallowed be your name', then, is a pledge to treat his name as holy as you represent him to the world. You are the nearest that some will ever come to seeing the Father's face.

Did You Think to Pray?

'"your kingdom come"'

Matthew 6:10

The phrase 'kingdom of God' (kingdom of heaven) is used in more than one way, however, in the New Testament. In the Sermon on the Mount it mainly refers to the internal reign and rule of the Holy Spirit in our hearts. Whether you take its meaning in the Sermon on the Mount or in Luke's account of the Lord's Prayer (Luke 11:2), the kingdom refers primarily to the inner testimony of the Spirit – not an outward, visible kingdom. The kingdom of heaven refers to God's sovereign and gracious occupation in the *hearts* of his people.

Having said so much about the kingdom, Jesus therefore counsels us to pray 'your kingdom come'. We are to pray that the kingdom would be our living experience and possession. That is what interests God and that is what should interest us. All of the theological principles Jesus taught about the kingdom of heaven are assumed in this petition, 'your kingdom come'.

The new birth, being 'born again', is the prerequisite to seeing the kingdom (John 3:3). But presumably anybody praying the Lord's Prayer has already been born again since this prayer was given to Jesus' own disciples. However, I would simply say that if a person who is not born again prays this prayer, then he or she is *praying* to be born again.

But when the Christian prays for the coming of the kingdom, it means an utter submission to the total rule of God over that person. It may mean suffering. After all, we enter the kingdom of God through hardship and suffering (Acts 14:22).

Did You Think to Pray?

'"your will be done on earth as it is in heaven"'

Matthew 6:10

When we pray 'your will be done', we acknowledge that *God has a will*. We don't give him input and help him to see what he ought to want to do. He already has a will of his own. Therefore when I pray 'your will be done', in that moment I acknowledge that he has already decided what he has willed to do. We don't advise him on what we think it should be.

By God's 'will' it means that God is independent from us; he has a will of his own. It means that he thinks for himself; he has a mind of his own. In a word: God has a plan.

And yet God's will is also understood as his Word (Holy Scripture) – which is his revealed will. The Word of God is the revealed will of God. If you want to know God's will, get to know his Word. The Bible contains all we need for knowing God, how to live a life that is pleasing to him. Therefore when we pray 'your will be done', we pledge to live according to his Word – what he has already revealed. The same God who gave us his Word is not going to lead you in a direction contrary to it.

Did You Think to Pray?

'"Give us today our daily bread."'

Matthew 6:11

Does it surprise you that the first petition of the Lord's Prayer that focuses on us has to do with our food? We may have thought that God would bring in the spiritual petitions first! But no. The first petition we ask for ourselves is for our daily bread. He regards this as what we are to pray for first. He begins with the body. God chose to give us bodies, and he deals with this first.

I reckon the reason for the order is partly because it is extremely difficult to cope spiritually when we are hungry, thirsty, tired, or deep in debt. This petition is a reminder that God knows our situation and what we are like; that we have to eat to live. Therefore God made this petition a priority over the spiritual need.

'Daily bread' does not only mean food in the literal sense, however. It is a phrase that covers all our *essential needs*. 'Bread' in Hebrew means all kinds of nutriment. But more than that, it refers to everything non-spiritual that is essential to life: physical needs, emotional needs, material needs, financial needs. This petition covers everything that God knows to be essential for us: food, shelter, clothing, having a job, income – even sleep. Try praying effectively without sleep! This petition includes all that is essential – the ability to work, having strength, intelligence, peace.

There is a further purpose in this petition: to warn against greed and to teach us gratitude. This petition does not hint at comforts and luxuries – only what is essential. As for gratitude, God loves gratitude; he hates ingratitude. This petition should make us thankful for the way God supplies our daily needs. It should make us realise our debt to God every single day.

Did You Think to Pray?

'"Forgive us our debts, as we also have forgiven our debtors."'

Matthew 6:12

I suppose this petition has made liars out of more people than any document in history. I say this because it is a *plea* and a *promise*. The plea is for forgiveness of our own sins; the promise is a statement that we also *have* forgiven those who have sinned against us. I fear that untold millions have prayed this petition and either didn't know what they were saying, didn't want to know, or didn't mean it.

In Luke's rendition we are to say, 'Forgive us our sins, for we also *forgive* everyone who sins against us' (emphasis mine, Luke 11:4). Note that the promise we make to God is in the present tense; we *forgive* everyone who sins against us. In Matthew's account we declare that we *have forgiven* our debtors. In other words, we claim that we have already done it. Have you?

Jesus assumes that: (1) we will need to be forgiven of all we have done, and (2) there will be those we must forgive (no matter what they have done to hurt us). In my book *Total Forgiveness* I elaborate on how you know you have forgiven others totally – it means you don't repeat what they did, or let them feel afraid of you or guilty; in other words, you let them save face, you protect them from their darkest secret and you keep on forgiving – as long as you live. (Obviously if the 'darkest secret' involves something that is actually *illegal*, this is a different matter.) You forgive to enjoy the rule and reign of the Holy Spirit – which is inheriting the kingdom of heaven. By the way, the greater the suffering (or hurt you feel), the greater the comfort, blessing or, in some cases, anointing that is promised to you (if you dignify the trial and totally forgive the person/persons).

Did You Think to Pray?

'"And lead us not into temptation, but deliver us from the evil one."'

Matthew 6:13

The classic rendition of the Lord's Prayer (AV) is 'deliver us from evil'. But the majority of scholars believe that the Greek word *ponerou* with the definite article really means 'the evil one', a reference to Satan. It is a prayer that we will not get caught in the devil's snare, but be spared of any success on his part. What is more, dignifying the trial is the best way to be delivered from the evil one. If we don't accuse God ('why me?') or if we don't complain the whole time, but rejoice in all circumstances, *Satan will utterly fail with us.*

Keep in mind too that the devil will take full advantage of any bitterness in us. This is why total forgiveness is essential if we are to be delivered from his power. Satan exploits bitterness and grudges. Paul said, 'I have forgiven in the sight of Christ . . . in order that Satan might not outwit us. For we are not unaware of his schemes' (2 Corinthians 2:10–11). As the New Living Bible puts it, 'A further reason for forgiveness is to keep from being outsmarted by Satan.'

Remember the 'three Rs' of spiritual warfare: recognise, refuse, resist. Recognise the devil – that is, when an evil thought comes, a thought that God would not have put there, see it at once as the devil. Refuse. That means do not entertain the thought. Refuse to give the evil thought any attention whatever. Resist. If the devil keeps coming back, resist him! We have the promise, 'Resist the devil, and he will flee from you' (James 4:7).

The devil knows his end; he knows that his time is short (Matthew 8:29; Revelation 12:10–12). The next time the devil reminds you of his past, remind him of his future (Revelation 20:10)!

Did You Think to Pray?

'For if you forgive men when they sin against you, your heavenly Father will also forgive you. But if you do not forgive men their sins, your Father will not forgive your sins.'

Matthew 6:14–15

Having just finished the Lord's Prayer Jesus says, 'For *if* [my italics] you forgive men when they sin against you, your heavenly Father will also forgive you' (Matthew 6:14). It is almost as though that is why he gave us the prayer in the first place!

Why does Jesus add this? Obviously it shows which of the petitions was the most important. But there are other reasons too, for we can never get enough of this kind of teaching. I know I need to be reminded of this all the time. The most natural tendency in the world is to want to get your own back. It is as natural as eating or sleeping; you instinctively want to get even. But what Jesus is telling us to do here is something that is not natural, but supernatural – totally forgiving people (sometimes those closest to us) for what they have done to us. I have to tell you I still struggle here, and have to keep reminding myself. But when I truly and totally forgive, I have crossed over into the supernatural. One may not have experienced much of signs and wonders and miracles, or experienced many of the gifts of the Holy Spirit. But if we have totally forgiven those who have unjustly hurt us, in that moment we have crossed over into the supernatural realm – an accomplishment equal to any miracle.

Total Forgiveness

And do not grieve the Holy Spirit of God, with whom you were sealed for the day of redemption. Get rid of all bitterness, rage and anger, brawling and slander, along with every form of malice. Be kind and compassionate to one another, forgiving each other, just as in Christ God forgave you.

Ephesians 4:30–32

The manifestation of God's glory in this life will tend to be temporary. Why? First, me. Us. We grieve the Spirit. The chief way we grieve the Spirit seems to be bitterness. I do know that in my own case bitterness and an unforgiving spirit crept in and the powerful sense of God's presence subsided.

But the second reason is the sovereignty of the Spirit. He chooses to stay for a while, but not indefinitely in the sense he had been manifesting himself. Why? You tell me. I only know that the Holy Spirit is sovereign and, whether he is grieved or if it belongs to his inscrutability, he doesn't stay around indefinitely. Sometimes it is for years and sometimes it is for days. One hopes the immediate sense of his power will last, but eventually the Holy Spirit seems to withdraw the feeling of awe.

My point is this. We need to come to terms with what may suddenly become yesterday's anointing. It will do us no good to pretend that what happened yesterday is happening today if it isn't.

The Anointing

The LORD said to Samuel, 'How long will you mourn for Saul, since I have rejected him as king over Israel? Fill your horn with oil and be on your way; I am sending you to Jesse of Bethlehem. I have chosen one of his sons to be king.'

1 Samuel 16:1

In this verse I see three types of ministry: yesterday's man or woman – King Saul; today's man or woman – Samuel, to whom God was speaking; tomorrow's man or woman – David, whom Samuel was led to anoint.

King Saul, yesterday's man, lost God's approval but still wore the crown. Tomorrow's man, David, got the anointing but without the crown. Today's man had to break with yesterday's man and cast his lot with tomorrow's man. It was a hard and painful word which Samuel was having to receive. It shows the sobering responsibility on the shoulders of the one who is truly today's man or woman.

In recent years I have found myself using the expression 'yesterday's man'. I'm not sure where I heard it first. I have understood it to mean a person who ceases to be relevant. He or she may continue to minister and say things. But such a person has somehow 'lost' it – they are out of touch. They are saying the same old thing they have uttered in years gone by when it probably had some impact if not power. But it has ceased to carry weight today. Such a person often struggles to prove him- or herself, trying to show their relevance. But the power has gone. In a word: such is a has-been although they are still around.

The Anointing

*This is what the LORD says: 'Out of your own household I am
going to bring calamity upon you. Before your very eyes I will take
your wives and give them to one who is close to you, and he will
lie with your wives in broad daylight. You did it in secret, but I will
do this thing in broad daylight before all Israel.'*

2 Samuel 12:11–12

Being yesterday's man or woman may be a temporary state. It may
mean a time of severe chastening, or disciplining (Hebrews 12:6). God
may set one on his 'back burner' until he deems us ready to be used
again. Many have returned to a high profile in ministry having learned
their lesson.

The obvious question is, what determines the difference? The answer,
in a word: our attitude towards his rebuke. Saul was defensive and
unteachable. Jonah and Samson prayed with all their hearts for another
chance – and God gave it.

David got caught for his adultery and murder after Nathan the
prophet revealed the sin to him. What he did was reprehensible. But
when Nathan nailed him to the wall, David took the word with both
hands.

What Nathan said was not a very pleasant thing to hear. But David's
immediate reaction was what Saul came up with too late. For David
said, 'I have sinned against the LORD' (2 Samuel 12:13). David paid
dearly for his sin but God wasn't finished with him. He still had a
future.

The Anointing

How long, O LORD? Will you forget me forever?
  How long will you hide your face from me?
How long must I wrestle with my thoughts
  and every day have sorrow in my heart?
How long will my enemy triumph over me?

Psalm 13:1–2

Another indication that one is yesterday's man or woman may be that success has come too soon. Everybody wants success but it can be dangerous, even leading to our becoming yesterday's man or woman – especially if it has come too soon.

If you are tomorrow's man or woman you must have the patience to wait for your time to come. The anointing is on you now, but you have no platform, no people, no authority or opportunity. All you can do is to wait. You have a vision that you *will* be used. But you must wait. You may have a message burning in you but your time has not come. 'Like the trampling of a mighty army,' said Victor Hugo, 'so is the force of an idea whose time has come.' That could be paraphrased: like the trampling of a mighty army so is the power of one's anointing whose time has come.

Tomorrow's man or woman has the anointing but not the platform. He or she has no basis of power in terms of recognition. They may have to await further training, further preparation and further disciplining under God's hand. Spurgeon said, 'If I knew I had twenty-five years left to live, I'd spend twenty of it in preparation.' Most people today spurn further preparation; they think they are ready now.

The Anointing

When David had fled and made his escape ... he and Samuel went to Naioth and stayed there. Word came to Saul: 'David is in Naioth at Ramah'; so he sent men to capture him ... So Saul went to Naioth at Ramah. But the Spirit of God came even upon him, and he walked along prophesying until he came to Naioth. He stripped off his robes and also prophesied in Samuel's presence.

1 Samuel 19:18–24

Let me share some of my deep fears with you. I am not talking about a 'spirit of fear' (2 Timothy 1:7) – that is, a dread, timidity or terror engendered by the devil. No, I am talking about honest concerns that trouble me when I think about ending well.

My first concern is that *God might take his hand off me – and leave me alone*. I am reminded of those ominous words, 'Ephraim is joined to idols; leave him alone!' (Hosea 4:17). I cannot think of anything worse than for God to leave me alone. It can't get worse than that. But it is exactly what happened to King Saul, as I said earlier. Let me remind you: here was a man who was chosen of God (1 Samuel 9:15–16), who had a brilliant beginning (1 Samuel 10:9–10), who lost the anointing of God's approval (1 Samuel 16:1; 18:12), and yet whose prophetic gift flourished simultaneously with his shameful behaviour (1 Samuel 19:18–24). This was Saul on his way to kill young David, because David was such a threat; and yet Saul prophesied as if he still had God's total favour.

In other words, King Saul's gift flourished as if all was well and as though his relationship with God was as it once had been; as if nothing bad had happened in the meantime.

It is so easy for either a God-given natural ability or a gift of the Holy Spirit, as in 1 Corinthians 12: 7–11, to camouflage our true, secret relationship with God.

Second Chance

'But I tell you that men will have to give account on the day of judgment for every careless word they have spoken.'

Matthew 12:36

My second fear is that *I might teach what is not exactly true.* I cannot bear the thought that I would pass on any measure of theological error. I suppose some people do not worry too much about whether they hold to sound theology. But I do. It is my life. I want to get it right in my thinking before I stand in a pulpit or take a pen in my hand. One day I will have to give an account of every sentence I have written, every word I have uttered (in and out of the pulpit), including every 'careless' word.

What is my assurance that I will not accept or teach heresy? I answer: one thing – my obedience to the Holy Spirit. Not my training, my mentors, my reading or my level of intelligence; it is unconditional obedience to the will of God. I put all my eggs into this basket – Jesus' words: 'If any man will do his will, he shall know of the doctrine, whether it be of God, or whether I speak of myself' (John 7:17, AV). I think this verse promises to keep us from any *serious* theological error when our relationship with God is right.

If I have not grieved the Holy Spirit through bitterness (or whatever else grieves him – see Ephesians 4:30–5:7), I can expect to have the full benefit of the promise from Jesus that the Holy Spirit will guide me into 'all truth' (John 16:13). When I grieve the Spirit, the anointing temporarily lifts and I cannot think so clearly during this time or enjoy the benefits of the promises that pertain to the Holy Spirit, as given in chapters 14, 15 and 16 of John's Gospel. But when I am granted repentance and am changed from glory to glory (2 Corinthians 3:18), I am given insights that are good, solid and true. To be honest, it is what I live for. Nothing – absolutely nothing – thrills me more than a fresh insight that comes from the immediate and direct work of the Holy Spirit.

Second Chance

Thinking he was in their company, they travelled on for a day.
Then they began looking for him among their relatives and friends.

Luke 2:44

Third, I fear that *I could be out of the will of God and not know it.*
If this could happen to Joseph and Mary, it could happen to you or
me. They went an entire day without Jesus, but assumed the whole
time 'he was in their company'. It is so easy to take the will and presence of God for granted.

I am sobered when I recall that God is no respecter of persons, that
he will not bend the rules for any of us. If he didn't bend the rules
for Joseph and Mary, he won't do it for you or me! If we proceed
without him, we too are *on our own.*

The only prevention I know of is to develop an intimate knowledge of the *ways* of the Holy Spirit. The more familiar I am with his
Presence and his ways, the more likely it is that I will *instantly sense
his absence* when I move ahead without him.

To be fair, I don't think anyone of real faith can get seriously out
of God's will for very long without his or her heart longing for his
Presence. But I do not want to go a day, not even an hour, knowingly,
without his conscious Presence.

Second Chance

These things happened to them as examples and were written down as warnings for us, on whom the fulfilment of the ages has come.
1 Corinthians 10:11

Fourth, I fear that I might discover that I could have had much more of God and been used in a greater manner but for my stubbornness to recognise his warnings. I have made so many mistakes over the past fifty years, and I would give anything to have a second chance in certain areas (especially with my family). I know I am a forgiven man, though. I have forgiven myself – totally. Furthermore, I put my trust in Romans 8:28: 'And we know that in all things God works for the good of those who love him, who have been called according to his purpose.' I believe in that promise with all my heart.

But I admit at the same time that I sometimes wonder how much better it might have been had I listened to clear cautions from the Lord over the years. This is why I am so keen not to brush aside any loving word from a friend or stranger – lest I miss all that God would do with me. The older you get, the more you want to avoid any past mistakes.

Second Chance

Be all the more eager to make your calling and election sure. For if you do these things, you will never fall, and you will receive a rich welcome into the eternal kingdom of our Lord and Saviour Jesus Christ.

2 Peter 1:10–11

Fifth, I fear that *I might not hear God say to me, 'Well done'.* You may say that all Christians get that very same commendation when they get to heaven, but I don't agree. A 'rich welcome' is promised on certain conditions. This is one of several reasons I believe that not everyone who goes to heaven will get the same reward, or even that everyone will get *some* reward.

As for those people who say, 'I don't care about a reward, I just want to make it to heaven', I know what they mean by that. After all, the difference between heaven and hell is infinite and incalculable. Those who are spared eternal punishment and make it to heaven have a debt to God that can never be paid. It was paid by the blood of Jesus and we can never take any credit for it. But God wants all of his children not only to have an eternal home in heaven, but to be awarded the *crown.* It is therefore pleasing to God that we show gratitude *now* by living disciplined, God-honouring lives that will be rewarded. Yes, *rewarded.* Paul could say just before the end that the Lord would 'award' him 'the crown of righteousness' (2 Timothy 4:8).

How do you think you will feel on that Day if you have no crown to cast before the throne? If those around you have the inestimable privilege of taking off the crowns from their heads and then laying them before King Jesus? I should think it would be a most horrible, embarrassing and even shameful feeling to be seen without a crown.

Second Chance

Endure hardship with us like a good soldier of Christ Jesus.

2 Timothy 2:3

It is sometimes God's will for the Christian to experience suffering for a while. Suffering and endurance lead to character building. Paul said that it is given to us not only to believe but also 'to suffer' for Christ's sake (Philippians 1:29), that there are trials which are 'destined' (1 Thessalonians 3:3). God has given us the promise that no trial is allowed to fall our way but what is 'common to man'. 'And God is faithful; he will not let you be tempted [Greek: *peirasmos* means either 'trial' or 'temptation'] beyond what you can bear. But when you are tempted [or tried], he will also provide a way out so that you can stand up under it' (1 Corinthians 10:13).

When a trial comes, it is assumed that we will suffer. In other words, it hurts. God has allowed this. When suffering comes we may wish for a 'pill' to give relief, but sometimes we are simply called to endure suffering. All suffering the Christian undergoes is with a purpose and therefore will do us good not harm. Whatever the suffering is, it will work together for good (Romans 8:28). But while it lasts, it hurts.

Totally Forgiving Ourselves

Our fathers disciplined us for a little while as they thought best; but God disciplines us for our good, that we may share in his holiness. No discipline seems pleasant at the time, but painful. Later on, however, it produces a harvest of righteousness and peace for those who have been trained by it.

Hebrews 12:10–11

Some people hastily assume that their pain, or even disappointment, is punishment from God. They therefore connect pain with guilt, thinking it is something they have done to cause this pain. God can do this; he may indeed roll up his sleeves and judge us.

On the other hand, not all chastening is traceable to actual sin which we have committed. Chastening is essentially preparation – not God doing a 'tit for tat' or getting even with us; he got even at the cross! 'As far as the east is from the west, so far has he removed our transgressions from us' (Psalm 103:12). Chastening is meted out by a loving Father for this reason, 'that we may share in his holiness'. God begins doing this early on in the life of the believer, not because of any sin committed but because we all need correction along the way.

Totally Forgiving Ourselves

The LORD said to Samuel, 'How long will you mourn for Saul, since I have rejected him as king over Israel? Fill your horn with oil and be on your way; I am sending you to Jesse of Bethlehem. I have chosen one of his sons to be king.'

1 Samuel 16:1

Samuel was ordered to move outside his comfort zone. When God says, 'How long will you mourn?' the implication is that Samuel has been in that state for a good while. And too long. But after a while, even though we are mourning, we can get used to it – and begin to live with it. Even to like it. What was once upsetting can become comfortable. We get used to it. This is why some people coming out of prison, which they hated at first, want to return.

It is like the Leaning Tower of Pisa in Italy. Were it not for the historic tower there most of us would never have heard of Pisa. But a few years ago it was discovered that the tower was, although very slowly, beginning to lean too much. The city fathers had an emergency meeting – what were they to do? There was only one thing to do: bring in architects and professional builders who would ensure that the tower did not topple over. But this injunction came to the professionals: keep the tower from falling over but don't correct the tilt! In other words, make sure it stays like it is.

We are all like that. We want to stay as we are. After many years of pastoral experience I think perhaps I have learned at least one thing: people don't want their problems solved, they want them understood.

The Anointing

But Samuel said, 'How can I go? Saul will hear about it and kill me.'

1 Samuel 16:2

Samuel was now on the spot. He had to break with yesterday's man, Saul, whom he had discovered and put in power, and at the same time find and anoint tomorrow's man, David. In seeking tomorrow's man Samuel was at considerable risk.

I sometimes wonder which is more painful: being yesterday's man or woman, today's man or woman or tomorrow's man or woman. Yesterday's man endures the pain of irrelevance, having known what it was to be used of God. And yet if he *thinks* he is still under the same anointing he once had, he still suffers by knowing in his heart of hearts he is struggling with great effort to convince himself and others he is still on the cutting edge of what God is doing today.

The pain of being tomorrow's man or woman is that you have to wait – sometimes much longer than you thought. The preparation is hard, God having to mould and shape you for your usefulness at the proper time. 'How long, O Lord?' you cry as David did (Psalm 13:1). We are never quite prepared for the rigid disciplining God puts us through for the calling he has destined us for.

The pain of being today's man or woman largely comes from the degree of courage required with the job. We never feel up to it. 'Who is equal to such a task?' (2 Corinthians 2:16).

The Anointing

At that time Jesus said to the crowd, 'Am I leading a rebellion, that
you have come out with swords and clubs to capture me? Every day
I sat in the temple courts teaching, and you did not arrest me. But
this has all taken place that the writings of the prophets might be
fulfilled.' Then all the disciples deserted him and fled.

Matthew 26:55–56

The paramount stigma of being today's man or woman is probably
that of being misunderstood. Nothing is more painful than this. We
can cope with a lot that people say against us – as long as they are
fully in the picture and still disagree. But what *hurts* is when they
aren't in the picture and form judgments and perceptions that are
based on limited information.

I sometimes think that much of Jesus' pain at the crucifixion was
through his being misunderstood. Nothing made sense. It didn't add
up that the same man who raised Lazarus from the dead a few days
before was now hanging on a cross. Why didn't Jesus *stop* the proceed-
ings that led to the crucifixion? Anybody who could control the wind
and storm on the Sea of Galilee could surely have intervened before
Herod or Pilate. When a detachment of soldiers fell back (John 18:6)
Jesus could have fled. There were any number of ways in which he
could have stopped being crucified. Common sense told everybody
this. So why was he being crucified? The disciples couldn't figure it
out – they all forsook him and fled (Matthew 26:56). Never once did
Jesus explain himself. It must have been almost unbearable emotional
pain for Jesus to see Mary Magdalene sobbing her heart out at the
scene of the cross and not be allowed to whisper to her, 'It's OK, Mary,
all is going according to plan, I'm atoning for the sins of the world
by my blood.' But there was no hint of this. He had to bear the further
stigma of being misunderstood, even by those closest to him.

The Anointing

*Do not take revenge, my friends, but leave room for God's wrath,
for it is written: '"It is mine to avenge; I will repay," says the Lord.'*

Romans 12:19

'*R*.T., *you must totally forgive them. Until you totally forgive them
you will be in chains. Release them and you will be released.*'

Those words came to me during the greatest trial I had ever experienced up until then. I had not felt able to tell anybody at all about
it, but because my friend, Josif Tson, was from Romania and would
never tell, I told him everything.

It was the hardest thing I had ever been asked to do.

An unexpected blessing emerged as I began to forgive: a peace came
into my heart that I hadn't felt in years. It was wonderful; I had
forgotten what it was like. Now, though, it was beginning to come
back – the peace and the sense of Jesus' nearness. All because I was
setting those people free, forgiving them; letting them off the hook.

However, as I found myself once again thinking about 'what they
did' I would get churned up inside. I would say to myself, 'Those
people are going to get away with this. This is not fair. They won't
get caught. They won't be found out. Nobody will know. This is not
right.' And that sweet peace left again.

When we are bitter we delude ourselves into thinking that those
who hurt us are more likely to be punished as long as we are set on
revenge. We are afraid to let go of the feelings of revenge. After all,
if we don't make plans to see that justice is done, how will justice be
done? We make ourselves believe that it is up to us to step in.

This is a lie – the devil's lie. We only hurt ourselves when we dwell
on what has happened to us and fantasise about what it will be like
when 'they' get punished. Most of all, we grieve the Holy Spirit of
God. This is why we lose that inner peace.

Total Forgiveness

*When Mary reached the place where Jesus was and saw him, she
fell at his feet and said, 'Lord, if you had been here, my brother
would not have died.' When Jesus saw her weeping, and the Jews
who had come along with her also weeping, he was deeply moved
in spirit and troubled.*

John 11:32–33

It was a painful moment for Mary. There was a manipulative element
present, yes, but her hurt was real. The tears were real. Her dilemma
was real. It made no sense whatever to her that the Lord would come
to see her days after the funeral when he could have come so easily
while Lazarus was still alive – to heal him.

Yet what a wonderful thing it is to be able to cry. Tears can be
medicinal. As sweat pours from our bodies on a hot day to keep us
cool so do tears pour from our eyes to keep our souls from falling
apart. God grants to all of us the privilege of crying when we are
hurt, lonely, dismayed, under pressure and feeling that there is
absolutely no hope left. Tears are God's own gift for such a time as
this. He shows us that he cares by inviting us to cry.

In my pastoral experience I have watched people in agony who
could not shed a tear. I have seen them want to cry but couldn't. There
have been a few occasions when I actually sought to encourage them
to cry. When I succeeded they *always* felt better. I saw one person who
finally let himself go. When he began to sob his shoulders shook, his
voice trembled and his emotional display was almost frightening; but
after about ten minutes he looked across at me and simply said,
'Thanks.'

Does Jesus Care?

Hear my prayer, O Lord,
  listen to my cry for help;
  be not deaf to my weeping.
For I dwell with you as an alien,
  a stranger, as all my fathers were.

Psalm 39:12

Do you want to get God's attention? Try tears. Why? Because tears are one thing God cannot stand to watch for very long. It is a strain that runs right through the Bible. Nothing moves the heart of God like tears. It is as though the one thing he cannot bear is our tears.

One day Jesus happened to notice a funeral procession. It turned out that a widow was following the coffin in which her only son lay. That was more than Jesus could take. 'When the Lord saw her, his heart went out to her and he said, "Don't cry." Then he went up and touched the coffin, and those carrying it stood still. He said, "Young man, I say to you, get up!" The dead man sat up and began to talk, and Jesus gave him back to his mother' (Luke 7:13–15).

Tears move God's heart. If you are brought to tears, be encouraged. You are getting God's attention.

Tears reflect a humble state which God also wants to see in us. 'For everyone who exalts himself will be humbled, and he who humbles himself will be exalted' (Luke 14:11). 'God opposes the proud but gives grace to the humble' (James 4:6). 'Humble yourselves, therefore, under God's mighty hand, that he may lift you up in due time' (1 Peter 5:6). Tears may be evidence that a real humbling process has taken place in our hearts. This may be why God says, 'They who sow in tears will reap with songs of joy' (Psalm 126:5).

Does Jesus Care?

Jesus entered the temple area and drove out all who were buying and selling there.

Matthew 21:12

Everything hinged upon a direction Jesus took, once he entered the city of Jerusalem. It was a turning that surprised and disappointed everybody. Once he entered Jerusalem, he had two choices:

1 to turn to the left: temple area;
2 to turn to the right: governor's palace.

Picture Jesus coming down from the Mount of Olives: he walks through the eastern gate. A turn to the right meant that he would confront Rome. A turn to the left meant that he would confront religious people. And end up dying on a cross. He turned to the left, to confront the religious people. Has it occurred to you to thank God that Jesus made the 'left turn'? What Jesus did at that very juncture gave shape to his destiny and ours and the content of the gospel we believe.

What did this left turn mean? Five things:

1 Jesus was more concerned about religious leaders than about politicians.
2 Jesus was more concerned about lost souls than about political injustice.
3 Jesus was more concerned about true prayer than about political action.
4 Jesus was more concerned to obey his Father than to fulfil the expectations of men.
5 Jesus was more concerned about his death and resurrection than about overthrowing the Roman authorities.

The people had to cope with the fact that Palm Sunday did not come up to expectation. The truth can be disappointing at first but this truth turned out to be transforming. One week later, Jesus' followers had no regrets – that is, after he was raised from the dead. God always does it like this. He sanctifies to us our deepest distress. Thank God for Palm Sunday. The people then did, even though they didn't know its significance! But we do understand, so we should be the most thankful of all.

Thanking God

So then he told them plainly, 'Lazarus is dead, and for your sake I am glad I was not there, so that you may believe. But let us go to him.'

John 11:14–15

Jesus' decision to not immediately answer the call of Mary and Martha to heal Lazarus did not make sense to anybody at the time. But it gave the disciples an opportunity to exercise faith when otherwise they would not have that opportunity. In other words, had Jesus hearkened to the call of Mary and Martha to come and heal their ailing brother, it would have made complete sense to the Twelve. They all knew that Jesus was fond of Lazarus. Moreover, it did not cross the minds of Mary and Martha that Jesus would do anything but come like a shot to Bethany and keep their brother from dying.

But Jesus showed up four days after the funeral. Martha was perplexed. '"Lord," Martha said to Jesus, "if you had been here, my brother would not have died"' (John 11:21). Mary, too, was really upset: 'When Mary reached the place where Jesus was and saw him, she fell at his feet and said, "Lord, if you had been here, my brother would not have died"' (John 11:32). Neither of these two sisters could make sense of Jesus' deliberate and conscious decision to let Lazarus die.

There were two reasons Jesus let Lazarus die. The first was that Jesus thought that raising Lazarus from the dead was a better idea than keeping him from dying. The second was that all the parties concerned might have the chance to demonstrate true faith – that is, to show they still trusted the Lord when nothing added up. This is why Jesus said, 'This sickness will not end in death. No, it is for God's glory' (John 11:4).

According to Hebrews 11:1, faith, to be faith, is believing without empirical evidence. 'Now faith is being sure of what we hope for and certain of what we do not see' (Hebrews 11:1). When you see the total evidence, then, it ceases to be true faith. 'Seeing is believing,' says the world. But the Bible says that if you see, it isn't faith any more.

Thanking God

They devoted themselves to the apostles' teaching and to the fellowship, to the breaking of bread and to prayer.

Acts 2:42

It is interesting to note here the order of these things: doctrine, fellowship and then the Lord's Supper and prayer. This indicates that we have no right to partake of the Lord's Supper when we are out of fellowship with others who are present. We will not be able to worship God if we have not made an attempt to put things right. We grieve the Holy Spirit if it is within our power to release another person by what we say and yet we do nothing about it.

I know there are times when we just can't sort things out. We can talk to some people for hours and get nowhere with them. But at least we have followed the New Testament pattern and tried. Paul said, 'If it is possible, as far as it depends on you, live at peace with everyone' (Romans 12:18) – our heavenly Father loves all of us equally. However, what is important is that we ourselves should not be harbouring animosity and bitterness.

Worshipping God

In the same way, after supper he took the cup, saying, 'This cup is the new covenant in my blood; do this, whenever you drink it, in remembrance of me.'

1 Corinthians 11:25

Before his death on a cross, Jesus gave a liturgy to his disciples. This was to be kept by the Church until his Second Coming. The word 'liturgy' comes from the Greek word *leitourgia*. It is translated 'service' (Luke 1:23, Philippians 2:17), 'help' (Philippians 2:30) and 'ceremony' (Hebrews 9:21). The word 'liturgy' usually means a certain form of worship, 'ceremony', an order of service, or ritual. Some churches are known as liturgical because of a predictable pattern of worship; others have overreacted to this and claim that spontaneity is the only acceptable way to worship God.

The truth is that, like it or not, all churches have some form of liturgy. Those that fancy themselves as anti-liturgical may be just as predictable in their pattern of worship as any so-called 'liturgical' church.

When Jesus introduced what we call the Lord's Supper he instituted a liturgy. The ultimate reason: 'This do in remembrance of me.' It was remembering to show gratitude for Jesus' death. Some remembering is spontaneous. But the Lord's Supper is ensured to enforce a sense of gratitude – by a certain form of worship. Gratitude must be taught, and Jesus gave us Holy Communion in order that we never forget why he was sent by the Father into the world in the first place.

Thanking God

April

By faith Abraham, when called to go to a place he would later receive as his inheritance, obeyed and went, even though he did not know where he was going.

Hebrews 11:8

How's that for trying to impress your friends? 'What are you up to, Abraham?' 'Not sure!' 'What do you mean, not sure, what's happening in your life?' 'Well, I am obeying God!' 'Where are you going?' 'Not sure!' That was it. In fact, 'The LORD had said to Abram, "Leave your country, your people and your father's household and go to the land I will show you"' (Genesis 12:1). What kind of mission is that? Yet Abraham became one of the greatest men in all history. He's known as the father of the faithful. He had no idea what it would lead to. Jesus said, 'Whoever can be trusted with very little can also be trusted with much, and whoever is dishonest with very little will also be dishonest with much' (Luke 16:10).

Do you feel that life is passing you by although you've kept your eyes on the Lord? He's led you to this place and to that place, and you can see that he did lead you there, but you think to yourself, 'This is not what I had in mind!' But it's not over yet! There was a lot for Abraham to discover.

The Thorn in the Flesh

And being found in appearance as a man, he humbled himself and
became obedient to death – even death on a cross!

Philippians 2:8

Much of Jesus' suffering was keeping in his heart how much he knew.
He knew that he would be crucified – and why. But the implications
of this were known to him alone. When he was summoned to Herod's
palace the king had hoped to see a miracle performed by Jesus. What
did Jesus do? Nothing (Luke 23:8–9). He just stood there. That infu-
riated Herod. But Jesus was taking his cue the whole time from the
Father. It meant suffering.

Jesus knew the possible disillusionment of his followers when he
allowed himself to be crucified. What would those who had been
healed think? What about those who were present when he turned five
loaves of bread and two fish into enough food to feed five thousand?
When Jesus went to the cross he told nobody why. He was never given
permission to say, 'I'm doing this for you. I'm dying in your place. I'm
making atonement for the sins of the world.' He allowed people to
think what they would. It, too, was a part of his suffering.

Our Lord's consolation is keeping his own eye on the ultimate event.
What kept him going, humanly speaking, was knowing all would end
well. Otherwise there would be nothing but despair for us all.

This is how he can allow suffering. He sees the end from the beginning. However much it hurts him to let things happen and watch us
weep in our perplexity, he waits in order that he might see our joy
later.

Does Jesus Care?

He who did not spare his own son, but gave him up for us all – how will he not also, along with him, graciously give us all things?

Romans 8:32

God 'did not spare his own son'. We may well keep this in mind when we are tempted to question God for allowing one of our loved ones to die. God did not spare his one and only son. God could have stopped his son from dying. But that would have meant that none of us could be saved.

When one of our loved ones is taken from us it is extremely difficult to see things objectively. But God knows that. This is why he does not shame us or lecture us in our moments of sorrow. Mary would eventually see how wrong she was to accuse Jesus as she did. But she could never forget that Jesus let her get things off her heart. He did not rebuke her once.

God knows how we feel when a loved one is taken from us. Fortunately he does not take us too seriously in our bitterness. 'For the wrath of man worketh not the righteousness of God' (James 1:20, AV). God overlooks our bitterness. That is how much he cares.

Does Jesus Care?

No temptation has seized you except what is common to man. And God is faithful; he will not let you be tempted beyond what you can bear. But when you are tempted, he will also provide a way out so that you can stand up under it.

1 Corinthians 10:13

We are to rejoice 'always'. Why? Because circumstances change. Therefore, if we are found rejoicing at all times, we are showing gratitude. If we make a commitment to gratitude, it means we must be prepared for the unexpected trial and dignify that trial when it comes. Dignifying the trial means:

- refusing to complain;
- accepting that the trial is from God;
- letting God end the trial his way.

Every trial has a built-in time-scale. It *will* end! God will see to that. This word translated 'temptation' or 'tempted' is the same as for 'trial'. God knows how much we can bear. If we will truly believe that, we can keep our commitment to be grateful – and show it by the choice to rejoice – no matter what the circumstances.

If we wait for circumstances to change before we heed God's command to rejoice, we may wait a long time! If then we begin rejoicing only when circumstances change – but only then – what kind of gratitude is that? If we promise to show gratitude, we can only make good that promise if we maintain a positive sense of being thankful no matter how adverse the circumstances.

Thanking God

For what I received I passed on to you as of first importance: that Christ died for our sins according to the Scriptures.

1 Corinthians 15:3

'How *can* I believe that God exists?' you ask. I answer: can you not begin by agreeing with him on what you *know* is true? Consider what God has said about *you*. You know that you are a sinner, don't you? Only God has told you that. No other source in the whole world would come up with 'God talk' like that. Sin. This three-letter word would not be known were it not for the God of the Bible. It is 'missing the mark' (that is what *hamartia*, the Greek word for 'sin', means). It is falling short of God's 'glory' (Romans 3:23). It is 'lawlessness' (1 John 3:4). It is knowing what you ought to do and not doing it (James 4:17).

Where in the world would you get the best explanation for what man's condition is but in the Bible? Despite our advancement in technology, learning, expertise, culture and wonderful achievements, is not man the same as ever? Why is it that a politician can be brilliant in surgery but a failure as a husband? Why is it that a scientist can be brilliant in a laboratory but still prone to jealousy, greed, pride, lust and all those things that keep him an unhappy and frustrated man? Why? Answer: sin.

Only the Bible explains man's plight. Only the Bible explains how man can be helped. It is by sending his one and only son into the world to die on the cross. Why did Jesus die? '. . . for our sins.'

Does Jesus Care?

Preach the Word; be prepared in season and out of season; correct, rebuke and encourage – with great patience and careful instruction.

2 Timothy 4:2

Disciplined prayer arises from two things: first, a good general knowledge of God's word; second, a strong desire to please him. In other words, I am talking here about praying as an act of sheer obedience whether we feel like it or not. And it is the mature Christian who follows this way. If you think the spontaneous impulse is the only kind that matters, you show yourself to be a superficial Christian. If you only respond to God when you are carried along by feeling, then you are an immature Christian.

There are times when the spontaneous impulse is at work: this corresponds to what Paul describes as being 'in season'; there are also times when we feel nothing: this is being 'out of season'. It is what the members of a church do when they are 'out of season' that testifies to their maturity. And it is this that demonstrates their commitment to God and each other.

You may decide to spend more time in prayer, but then you find that everything seems to militate against it. So you think, 'These things which are stopping me praying are providential.'

That's what Jonah said. He ran from God, and wanted to get a ship to Tarshish. Lo and behold – when he got to the dock, there was a ship going to Tarshish! And he said to himself, 'This is providential.' We can call any sin or temptation providential.

So don't be surprised if, when you commit yourself to prayer, everything seems to be hindering you. There must be discipline.

Worshipping God

One day Peter and John were going up to the temple at the time of prayer – at three in the afternoon.

Acts 3:1

This is one of the forgotten verses of the Bible. The chapter goes on to describe how Peter and John healed a crippled man, but what is interesting is that it happened when they were on their way to the temple to pray. This was three o'clock in the afternoon, described in the Authorised Version as 'the hour of prayer'. So we see that even when the Spirit was present in great power, these early disciples were not afraid to go by a schedule. At this high peak in the history of the Church it would seem that the first Christians still observed set times for prayer.

The principle is that if you live by the disciplined impulse you will get the spontaneous impulse as well, and this is why I urge each Christian to pray for thirty minutes a day, and to attend the weekly church prayer meetings. Here were Peter and John on their way to the temple, when the lame beggar held out his hand to them, expecting to receive some money. But Peter just turned to him and said, 'Silver and gold have I none; but such as I have give I thee: In the name of Jesus Christ of Nazareth rise up and walk.' And the man was healed.

Worshipping God

8 April

'If I were hungry I would not tell you,
for the world is mine, and all that is in it.'

Psalm 50:12

One May evening, while I was going through my reading for the day,
I came across this verse in Psalm 50. And something happened to me
then. That verse did more to convict me to pray than any book on
prayer I have read. You may think that it has nothing to do with prayer,
but this verse showed me that God will not necessarily tell us when
we are doing it wrong. We may justify ourselves when we don't have
time to pray, and our reasons may sound perfectly good and right to
us. But God has said, 'If I were hungry, I would not tell you.' None
of us is so spiritual that we can assume that God will tap us on the
shoulder and let us know every time we are doing it wrong. This
convinced me that it is my job, not only as a Christian minister, but
as a child of God, never to excuse myself again for what I haven't
done regarding time spent in prayer.

Worshipping God

But God chose the foolish things of the world to shame the wise;
God chose the weak things of the world to shame the strong. He
chose the lowly things of this world and the despised things – and
the things that are not – to nullify the things that are, so that no-
one may boast before him.

1 Corinthians 1:27–29

God always has looked for what will offend sophisticated people, possibly because he wants to put obstacles in our way to see if we will believe in his Word only. This is because faith – to be faith – is believing God without evidence for that belief. Only God's Word. 'Faith is being sure of what we hope for and certain of what we do not see' (Hebrews 11:1).

In other words, that which makes faith *faith* is when you keep trusting what God says although you are not able to prove your point. When people ask, 'Why does God allow evil when he has the power to stop it?', I answer: to make room for faith. We wouldn't need faith if we could supply the answer to the problem of evil. Neither would we need faith if we could make ourselves look good before our accusers – whether they be sophisticated or not.

It isn't fun when respectable, intelligent people roll their eyes heavenward when they see our 'foolish' stubbornness and adherence to God's chosen manifestation of his glory. The crowning blow among the 'hard sayings' of Jesus came when he said, 'Whoever eats my flesh and drinks my blood has eternal life' (John 6:54). Jesus made no attempt to explain himself; he just let people vent their feelings – which they did. A very interesting and fruitful study is tracing the miracles of Jesus and how many times he waited for the Sabbath to arrive in order to offend the religious people of the day (e.g. John 5:9; 9:14).

Out of the Comfort Zone

Now on his way to Jerusalem, Jesus travelled along the border between Samaria and Galilee. As he was going into a village, ten men who had leprosy met him. They stood at a distance and called out in a loud voice, 'Jesus, Master, have pity on us!' When he saw them, he said, 'Go, show yourselves to the priests.' And as they went, they were cleansed.

Luke 17:11–14

John Wesley said that God does nothing but in answer to prayer. What is certainly true in the account of the ten lepers being healed is that they prayed first – and the Lord heard them. 'Jesus, Master, have pity on us' (verse 13). Asking the Lord for pity, or mercy, is always the right approach to God. 'Let us then approach the throne of grace with confidence, so that we may receive mercy and find grace to help us in our time of need' (Hebrews 4:16). Therefore, they got it right when they called out to Jesus for mercy.

It is amazing how we get it right in prayer when we are desperate. They not only asked for 'pity' but called out in a 'loud voice'. Why this? Is God deaf? No. But he responds to us when we are desperate.

The ten lepers recognised that Jesus had the power to heal them. They wanted to be sure he felt what they felt. They cried with loud voices – and asked for mercy. If you asked, 'What is more important – to ask for mercy or to cry with desperation?' I think I would answer, 'When you are desperate you are very likely to pray to God in the right manner – and ask for mercy.' Let me quote it again: 'Let us then approach the throne of grace with confidence, so that we may receive *mercy* and find grace to help us in our time of need' (Hebrews 4:16). Many people read this verse hurriedly and miss one of the main points: the very first thing we are commanded to pray for when we approach God is mercy.

Thanking God

One of them, when he saw he was healed, came back, praising God in a loud voice. He threw himself at Jesus' feet and thanked him – and he was a Samaritan. Jesus asked, 'Were not all ten cleansed? Where are the other nine? Was no-one found to return and give praise to God except this foreigner?' Then he said to him, 'Rise and go; your faith has made you well.'

Luke 17:15–19

Part of the reason for this story being recorded was also that the one who came back to express his thanks was a Samaritan. It would seem that the others were Jews.

Samaritans were hated by the Jews. The people called Samaritans were what was left of the ten lost tribes of Israel that settled in a part of the land called Samaria. John wanted his readers to know (in case they didn't know already) that 'Jews do not associate with Samaritans' (John 4:9). Thus, for a Samaritan to be healed by Jesus may have made this man immeasurably more thankful. But that does not excuse those who didn't come back to thank Jesus.

For Jesus' immediate comment was: 'Were not all ten cleansed? Where are the other nine?' (verse 17).

God notices gratitude – and ingratitude.

Do you want to get God's attention? Have you had difficulty getting his attention? Here are two things you can do: first, ask for mercy when you approach the throne of grace; second, say 'thank you' when God answers prayer.

Jesus added, 'Was no one found to return and give praise to God except this foreigner?' (Luke 17:18). For God notices gratitude – and ingratitude.

Thanking God

'Suppose one of you had a servant ploughing or looking after the sheep. Would he say to the servant when he comes in from the field, "Come along now and sit down to eat"? Would he not rather say, "Prepare my supper, get yourself ready and wait on me while I eat and drink; after that you may eat and drink"? Would he thank the servant because he did what he was told to do? So you also, when you have done everything you were told to do, should say, "We are unworthy servants; we have only done our duty."'

Luke 7:7–10

The striking phrase 'we have only done our duty' is followed by the healing of the ten lepers; but only one of them did his duty by thanking God. Jesus did not *commend* the leper for doing his duty by showing gratitude. His response to the thankful person was: 'Were not all ten cleansed. Where are the other nine?' (Luke 17:17).

Therefore we must never – ever – forget that our thanking God does not deserve us his further blessing. For gratitude is a duty. 'So you also, when you have done everything you were told to do, should say, "We are unworthy servants; we have only done our duty"' (Luke 17:10).

Here is the irony: though thanking God is our duty and does not deserve to be further commended by God, he nonetheless *notices* when we thank him – and loves to show it! The lesson for us here is not to look over our shoulder at God and say, 'I hope you noticed that I thanked you.' That would be letting our right hand know what our left hand is doing – the opposite of Jesus' command (see Matthew 6:3).

In a word: thanking God is both a privilege and a duty. Never forget it. But do not be surprised how such heart gratitude is recorded and blessed. Our heavenly Father can't seem to help it!

Thanking God

Joseph had a dream, and when he told it to his brothers, they hated him all the more. He said to them, 'Listen to this dream I had: We were binding sheaves of corn out in the field when suddenly my sheaf rose and stood upright, while your sheaves gathered round mine and bowed down to it.'

Genesis 37:5–7

The man or woman who takes himself or herself *too seriously* is a ripe candidate for becoming yesterday's man or woman. One reason I took myself too seriously back in 1956 was that I received visions that indicated I would be used of God. I assumed these visions would be fulfilled soon. They weren't. But because I had them and believed they were truly from the Holy Spirit I assumed I was special. I became arrogant. I was not unlike Joseph, who not only strutted around in his coat of many colours but flaunted his prophetic dreams to his brothers. Those dreams *were* from God. There was nothing wrong with Joseph's gift but there was a lot wrong with Joseph. God had earmarked Joseph for a wonderful ministry down the road, but he *also* earmarked Joseph for a long era of preparation and being refined. Because Joseph was not ready. I was not ready. If you put me under a lie detector today I would have to admit I'm still not sure I'm ready for the anointing I pray for. I am still being dealt with. Like peeling the layers of an onion, so I see so much about myself that is not right.

The Anointing

Samuel said to Saul, 'I am the one the LORD sent to anoint you king over his people Israel; so listen now to the message from the LORD.'

1 Samuel 15:1

Despite Saul's folly in not waiting for Samuel and going outside his anointing, a second chance was on offer. Notice how it was put: *'listen now'*. Had the king truly been sorry and repentant he would have taken that word from Samuel with both hands. He should have been able to see that God was still on speaking terms with him.

If God gives us a word of rebuke we should welcome it. It may come from reading the Bible, when we least expect it. It may come through preaching. It may come from a trusted friend. 'Wounds from a friend can be trusted' (Proverbs 27:6). It may come from a person with a true prophetic gift.

But what if we reject – or neglect – a word given to us and later wish we had listened? I answer: should God speak *at all* after that, take it to heart with all your being. How kind God was to come again to Saul, speaking to him with dignity. It was Saul's second opportunity after he blew it the first time. Any word from the Lord is a test. We should treat it as though we may never hear him again *just in case* we have not been fully obedient previously.

The Anointing

*Let us fix our eyes on Jesus, the author and perfecter of our faith,
who for the joy set before him endured the cross, scorning its
shame, and sat down at the right hand of the throne of God.*

Hebrews 12:2

Joy is a fruit of the Holy Spirit (Galatians 5:22), but a smile on one's
face may have more to do with one's natural temperament and personality. I know people who have a smile on their faces all the time, but
it is hardly the joy of the Lord, for these people I am talking about
aren't even Christians! I know one Christian lady who always seems
to have a smile on her face. One day I asked her about this beautiful
smile and she graciously admitted that it actually camouflaged a very
sad heart, and that she was not the cheerful, happy person her smile
suggested.

A Christian who has a radiant smile – whether in church or out
shopping – is indeed a wonderful witness to the Christian faith. There
is little doubt about that. And those of us who by nature look sad or
depressed all the time are not good testimonies. That's me. I seldom
smile. I'm a photographer's nightmare. Any picture you see of me
smiling is the result of the hard work of people saying 'cheese', and
standing on their heads or something like that!

But joy is inward. Our Lord Jesus was a man of sorrows (Isaiah
53:3), but he could speak of his joy (John 15:11, 17:13). I doubt he
had a great smile on his face when he was on the cross crying out,
'My God, my God, why have you forsaken me?' (Matthew 27:46), but
he endured it all because of the joy that was set before him (Hebrews
12:2). We therefore are not required to look cheerful or buoyant when
in a deep trial, but we can still have pure joy the whole time simply
because we know what is waiting for us down the road if we don't
give up.

Pure Joy

Woe to those who go to great depths to hide their plans from the
LORD, *who do their work in darkness and think, 'Who sees us?*
Who will know?'

Isaiah 29:15

One of the devil's devices is to try to make us believe that God doesn't pay attention to things here on earth, that he doesn't notice us and that he won't even register if we are disobedient to him. The greatest folly in the world in that connection is to say to ourselves, 'God doesn't notice, God doesn't see.' God does notice, he does see. Isaiah not only warned God's people in this matter but used the same concept to encourage them:

> Why do you say, O Jacob,
> and complain, O Israel,
> 'My way is hidden from the LORD;
> my cause is disregarded by my God'?   (Isaiah 40:27)

The moment we say 'thank you' to the Most High God we have his undivided attention. Therefore, whenever we sense God is hiding his face from us, it is a precious opportunity not only to get his attention but to please him more than ever.

Showing gratitude when we are happy is easier to do, even if it is an inconvenience or a bit of a sacrifice, than when we are sad. God likes it when we thank him in a happy mood, make no mistake about that. But he likes it even more when we keep saying 'thank you' even though we are in a melancholy state. It is truly a 'sacrifice of praise' (Hebrews 13:15) when we manage to praise him in adverse circumstances. Moreover, it is then when we make the greatest spiritual progress in our Christian life.

Thanking God

Paul and his companions travelled throughout the region of Phrygia and Galatia, having been kept by the Holy Spirit from preaching the word in the province of Asia.

Acts 16:6

Flowing in the Spirit means to honour God's 'no' as well as his 'yes', the red light as well as the green light. Paul and his companions were 'kept by the Holy Spirit' ('forbidden', AV) from preaching the word in the province of Asia. Really? Are we to believe that the *Holy Spirit* – not the devil – would actually stop people from preaching the gospel? It seems to me that this would take both supernatural discernment and considerable courage to act on a word from the Spirit like that. This seems to fly in the face of our mandate to preach the gospel to every person (Mark 16:15). But that is what was happening. Did not these people need the gospel? Yes. Then why were they forbidden by the Spirit from preaching in Asia at this time? You tell me. I only know they listened to the Spirit and obeyed. It must have taken as much courage to obey not to preach as it did to preach it. How did they know? I only know that they knew. To flow in the Spirit is to have intimacy with him and to feel what he wants.

Not only that; when they came to the border of Mysia and tried to enter Bithynia, 'the Spirit of Jesus would not allow them to' (Acts 16:7). Had this been a providential hindrance – or opposition – Luke would have said so. Paul wanted to come to Rome, but said he was prevented many times (Romans 1:13) and claimed to be stopped by Satan from coming to Thessalonica (1 Thessalonians 2:18). But both incidents in the book of Acts attribute their course of direction to the Holy Spirit. Paul and his companions walked in the Spirit because they knew his *ways*.

Pure Joy

Since we live by the Spirit, let us keep in step with the Spirit.

Galatians 5:25

What does flowing in the Spirit mean? It is moving along with him, keeping in step with him, and missing nothing he may be wanting to do through us. The joy of flowing in the Spirit is equal to anything God may ever do for us and in us. There is such a thrill in flowing in the Spirit. You feel what you are doing is worthwhile; you feel authenticated, you feel loved; you know you are a part of something very important — the kingdom of God. It happens to me when I am preparing a sermon, witnessing to an unsaved person, helping my wife clean the house, doing the shopping, or anything else in life that is either necessary or a blessing to people. You feel this when visiting a sick person or resisting temptation; when you walk to work or do work in the office. It is a twenty-four hour a day possibility.

Pure Joy

But you, dear friends, build yourselves up in your most holy faith
and pray in the Holy Spirit.

Jude 20

Flowing in the Spirit is praying in the Spirit. Praying in the Spirit is praying in the will of God. It is the only kind of praying that matters because it is only when we ask in God's will that we are heard. We are fools if we think we can upstage God's will, as if our idea would be better than his. Here is a principle you can count on for the rest of your life: God always gives his best to those who leave the choice with him. The reason is this. He already has a plan for you. It has been carefully thought out. The same wisdom that entered into God's plan for creation and redemption is the brilliance and care that lay behind his thoughts towards you. He has lavished the riches of his grace with wisdom and understanding (Ephesians 1:7–8). As David put it: '*How precious to me are your thoughts, O God! How vast is the sum of them! Were I to count them, they would outnumber the grains of sand*' (Psalm 139:17–18).

God's plan for us was designed before we were born, while still in our mother's womb (Psalm 139:13); indeed, from the foundation of the world (Ephesians 1:4, 11). This is why only a fool would try to come up with a better idea than the one already conceived in God's heart and mind. Therefore to pray in the will of God is the best thing we can do when it comes to prayer. To flow in the Spirit is to flow in God's will and to pray in God's will.

Pure Joy

When they heard this, they raised their voices together in prayer to God. 'Sovereign Lord,' they said, 'you made the heaven and the earth and the sea, and everything in them.'

Acts 4:24

Unity is of vital importance in worship. The people here had achieved their unity by coming together against a common enemy. But this unity also required magnanimity. You can be sure that they had differences among themselves – everybody does. (And the less you have of the Spirit, the more important will those differences seem.) But they knew that the devil was against them so they put their differences aside. Would to God that the Church at the present time would do the same.

The issue at stake here was that the witnessing should not stop. The authorities had told Peter and John that they would not be put in prison for what they believed, but that they were to keep it to themselves. If these early Christians had been like some of us today, someone would have stood up and said, 'Look here, Peter and John, we think you're carrying this a bit too far. We've done our piece. We've done a bit of witnessing and shown that we could do it. But now we've upset the Sanhedrin, and they are learned and respected men. So let's cool it for a while.'

But not one person said anything like that. Instead, they lifted up their voices to God with one accord. If the Church had become divided at that point, the book of Acts would have ended right there. There is no substitute for witnessing.

Worshipping God

When they heard this, they raised their voices together in prayer to God. 'Sovereign Lord,' they said, 'you made the heaven and the earth and the sea, and everything in them.'

Acts 4:24

These people uttered their longings. They put their words on the line. It is easy to keep one's thoughts to oneself. Other people can't hold us accountable for what we've not said. But these early Christians shared what was in their minds.

'They raised their voices.' I don't think I've ever heard that in our church meetings. I never hear more than one person pray at a time. Are we afraid to speak out all at once?

In Korea the Christians are seeing God at work, and a film has been made about the revival there. In this film we see the minister of a church lead in prayer, and everyone starts praying. I don't suppose the people even knew what the minister was saying. It's a noisy meeting.

Could it be that revival has come to the Third World and passed us by because we are too sophisticated? In those churches in Korea they are not ashamed to cry aloud to God. Most of our praying is shameful: 'Heavenly Father, we come to you ... we pray for your blessing upon us and ... to have your way ... in our hearts and lives ... and ... and ...'

There is no indication in our language that we expect to see God do anything. I'm not saying that this would bring revival. I'm only saying that this is what they knew in Acts, when the Spirit was present. Perhaps our problem is that we're just too comfortable.

Worshipping God

The LORD said to Job: 'Will the one who contends with the Almighty correct him? Let him who accuses God answer him!' Then Job answered the LORD: 'I am unworthy – how can I reply to you? I put my hand over my mouth.'

Job 40:1–4

Self-righteousness is the last thing we tend to see in ourselves, not realising how heinous it is in God's eyes. And yet we *never will* see it in ourselves unless God intervenes – as he did in the case of Job.

Righteous people need to see their self-righteousness. I know a lot of so-called 'good' people – great examples of holy living in so far as their being outwardly blameless is concerned. They are, for all practical purposes, sinless – in that they, like the Pharisees in Jesus' day, do not outwardly break any of the Ten Commandments. The trouble is, so many people like this assume that their righteousness is what gives them an entrance to heaven. The sobering thing about such people is that they are still unconverted – for they are trusting their own good works rather than Christ's blood and righteousness on their behalf. They do not have a 'sense' of sin that comes when they examine themselves before God or in the light of Jesus' interpretation of the Law, neither do they see that their righteous acts are like 'filthy rags' in God's sight (Isaiah 64:6).

It is only the Holy Spirit that will help you and me see that we are guilty sinners and need the atoning grace of the Lord Jesus Christ to make it to heaven. We are by nature loath to trust his blood to wash away our guilty past. Furthermore, just because we become Christians it does not follow that we have no self-righteousness left in us. Quite the contrary! It is something we must guard against all our lives.

Totally Forgiving Ourselves

Elijah was afraid and ran for his life. When he came to Beersheba in Judah, he left his servant there, while he himself went a day's journey into the desert. He came to a broom tree, sat down under it and prayed that he might die. 'I have had enough, LORD,' he said. 'Take my life; I am no better than my ancestors.'

1 Kings 19:3–4

We saw that Job eventually realised he was self-righteous. But parallel with this sin was his self-pity: 'Although I am blameless, I have no concern for myself; I despise my own life' (Job 9:21).

Elijah, one of the most spectacular prophets in the Old Testament, was also filled with self-pity. He wanted to die! Why? Believe it or not, it was because he was 'no better' than his ancestors. Why should this bother him? Who ever said he was better than those who preceded him? Who ever required that he be better than those who went on before? The answer is, Elijah imposed a standard and a wish upon himself that God did not put there. He wanted to be the best there ever was!

Self-pity, like self-righteousness, is always counterproductive; it doesn't do any good, it gets us nowhere. It never achieves its goals; we only hurt ourselves. Foolishly we tell ourselves that we don't deserve Christ's atonement – we are so pitiful and unworthy – that we should pay for our own sin. Therefore self-pity, like its twin, will lead us away from totally forgiving ourselves by trusting Christ's blood, and make us wallow in our sorry state indefinitely.

Totally Forgiving Ourselves

'For God so loved the world that he gave his one and only Son, that whoever believes in him shall not perish but have eternal life.'

John 3:16

If Christ did not die for everybody, one can understand why some people lack assurance of salvation. For the view that Christ did not die for all leads to the question, 'However can I believe he died for *me*?' For this reason the poor seeker of assurance cannot look directly to Christ, for they may be trusting in one who never died for them in the first place. The only place to look in such a case is towards your own good works, or their sanctification. The problem here is, how can you be sure you have amassed a sufficient number of good works to be sure? Or how can you know that your sanctification is now adequate? People who seek assurance of salvation in this manner tend to be in perpetual doubt. But to the question, 'How do we know that Christ has *interceded* for us?' the reply is simple: Christ ever lives to make intercession for those who come to God by him (Hebrews 7:25). If you come to God through Jesus it is because he has interceded for you!

Martin Luther is often quoted as saying, 'I'm so glad that John 3:16 says that God so loved the *world* that he gave his only begotten Son that whoever believes in him shall not perish but have eternal life. Because if it said that God so loved Martin Luther that if Martin Luther believes, Martin Luther will not perish but have eternal life, I would be afraid it referred to another Martin Luther.'

But Christ died for all. Therefore anybody can avoid the endless pain of doubt if they take the free offer of the gospel on board. Assurance of salvation for all believers and the premises that Christ died for everybody are bound together.

In Pursuit of His Glory

It was not through law that Abraham and his offspring received the promise that he would be heir of the world, but through the righteousness that comes by faith. For if those who live by law are heirs, faith has no value and the promise is worthless.

Romans 4:13–14

I was brought up in a Christian denomination that taught that you could be genuinely converted but could nonetheless forfeit the promise of going to heaven when you die by sinning. As to what sin you could commit to disqualify you from heaven, this ranged from wearing make-up and smoking to committing adultery.

My own assurance of eternal salvation came after my conversion. For until I was blessed with that immediate and direct witness of the Spirit I simply tried to live the best Christian life I knew how to live and walked as close to the Lord as one could imagine. I was not looking to Christ, but to having 'met the condition' which, as far as I could tell, meant not committing any known sin. However, when I was given assurance of my own salvation I went for a while with the belief that this was true in *my own* case but not necessarily anybody else's.

Until I read Romans 4. I then knew that what was true of me is true of anybody to whom the righteousness of Christ has been imputed. I then realised that all who embrace the promise are as saved as I was!

I have sought to spread this joy to anybody who would listen to me ever since. It is, to my mind, foundational. For those who can't believe that they are eternally saved – apart from works – invariably and ultimately are trusting in their own works to some extent. They may not realise it, but they do. They cannot, at the end of the day, sing with total confidence 'My hope is built on nothing less than Jesus' blood and righteousness' if they equally believe they could be lost – somehow.

In Pursuit of His Glory

So I say, live by the Spirit, and you will not gratify the desires of the sinful nature.

Galatians 5:16

The mistake many good Christians make, in my opinion, is to allow the keeping of the Law to be the basis of assurance of salvation. This is a precarious thing to do. First, you would be leaning on a temporary measure. The Law was actually a parenthesis, or interlude, between the promise to Abraham and its fulfilment in Christ. The Law came in aside – 'added' (Galatians 3:19) – but was only a temporary measure to enforce righteousness through fear of punishment because of the transgressions of the ancient people of God. The Law was fulfilled when Jesus died on the cross and said, 'It is finished' (John 19:30). This is why our Lord said that Abraham saw Jesus' day and was 'glad' (John 8:56). We get our assurance from Christ because we are under his blood. The moment one looks to the Law and not Christ for assurance, that assurance will be very shaky.

But when we walk in the Spirit, showing all the fruits of righteousness (Galatians 5:22f), we manifest the godliness that truly glorifies God – and keep the Law without trying! And yet none of us is without sin (1 John 1:8), and we are frail children of dust who don't always walk in the Spirit as we should. But the motive to please God comes not from fear (2 Timothy 1:7) but love – which is the fulfilling of the Law. This results in an unselfrighteous and non-legalistic morality that honours God and the gospel.

In Pursuit of His Glory

... because the Lord disciplines those he loves, and he punishes everyone he accepts as a son.

Hebrews 12:6

The Greek word for disciplining means 'enforced learning'. God has many ways of teaching us a lesson. It can be very painful. No Christian is without it.

Why does God chasten us? To keep us on the straight and narrow. We all need it from time to time and to some degree. 'If you are not disciplined (and everyone undergoes discipline), then you are illegitimate children and not true sons' (Hebrews 12:8).

There are three levels of chastening: internal, external and terminal. Internal chastening comes through the Word, preaching and good teaching. It is God working form *within* us. This is the best way to have our problems dealt with. This is God's Plan A. It is when his two-edged sword operates on our hearts and we say 'Yes, Lord.' It is listening to the Holy Spirit who says, 'Do not harden your hearts' (Hebrews 3:8).

External chastening is Plan B. It is God working from outside us. It is when we did not heed God's Word and he must now work from without, as it were. He may use sickness. He may put us flat on our backs. It could be financial reverse. It could be being found out – as Jonah was (Jonah 1). It may be the withholding of vindication. In a word: whatever it takes for God to get our attention. Plan B usually works.

But there is a third stage: terminal chastening. And this normally takes shape one of two ways (or occasionally both!). It may be a case of spiritual stone deafness setting in, when the child of God can no longer hear God speak, is no longer being changed from glory to glory (2 Corinthians 3:18) and therefore cannot be renewed again to repentance (Hebrews 6:4–6). It is terminal chastening because God no longer uses his Word (Plan A) or situations (Plan B) to get our attention. But in some cases God may say, 'Your time is up.' This is the death some Corinthians experienced (1 Corinthians 11:30). John calls it the sin that leads to death, namely, premature physical death (1 John 5:16). This is also why I call it terminal.

In Pursuit of His Glory

God, who has saved us and called us to a holy life – not because of
anything we have done but because of his own purpose and grace.

2 Timothy 1:8–9

At the bottom of all, I believe, is the sovereignty of God. Not all who believe in God's sovereignty believe as I do about election and predestination. But these principles have been absolutely foundational to me. I could not have coped over the years had I not believed as I do regarding the sovereignty of God.

I believe that God has predestined the elect he chose – not on the basis of foreseen faith or good works but according to his own purpose and grace from the foundation of the world (2 Timothy 1:9). The only way we can know for sure that God will triumph in the end is because he has predestined it.

Predestination is the *a posteriori* explanation why some believe and others do not. Why God chose to do it this way is a mystery to me, but I accept it. Why does he not choose all but only some, I do not know. I only know that 'those he predestined, he also called; those he called, he also justified; those he justified, he also glorified' (Romans 8:30). God said a long time ago to Moses, 'I will have mercy on whom I have mercy, and I will have compassion on whom I have compassion' (Romans 9:15). I live with this because God does nothing wrong and everything right.

In Pursuit of His Glory

Jesus replied, 'You are in error because you do not know the Scriptures or the power of God.'

Matthew 22:29

There has been a silent divorce in church, speaking generally, between Word and Spirit. When there is a divorce sometimes the children stay with the mother, sometimes with the father. In this divorce it is a case of either 'Word' churches or 'Spirit' churches. What is the difference? Those on the Word side emphasise expository preaching and sound teaching. They say, 'We must get back to the theology of the Reformation and to the God of Jonathan Edwards and Charles Spurgeon.' What is wrong with that emphasis? Well, very little – it is *almost* right.

Those on the Spirit side emphasise the gifts of the Spirit – signs, wonders and miracles. They say, 'We must get back to the book of Acts and see a demonstration of the Spirit's power as they experienced it.' What is wrong with that emphasis? Well, very little – it is *almost* right.

While the Sadducees Jesus spoke to in Matthew 22 were ignorant of both, it seems to me that we today are at home with one or the other. What is needed is *both* – simultaneously.

The problem is, you cannot get many in a Word church to admit they don't have much openness to the Spirit. 'Of course we are open to the Holy Spirit,' they will say in all honesty. And you can't get very many in a Spirit church to admit they don't emphasise the Word and teaching enough. 'What do you mean that we don't teach the Word? That is all we believe.' Thus the great gulf is fixed and neither will become vulnerable, be willing to learn and to cross over into the area of their neglect.

In Pursuit of His Glory

30 April

All Scripture is God-breathed and is useful for teaching, rebuking, correcting and training in righteousness.

2 Timothy 3:16

Behind all I preached and taught for twenty-five years in Westminster Chapel was my firm conviction in the total inspiration, utter reliability and truthfulness of the Bible.

There are two ways we come to believe in the full inspiration of the Bible: the external witness and the internal witness. The former lies within the realm of apologetics whereby various 'proofs' of Scripture are given that uphold the reliability of the Bible. I do not dismiss this at all, but as the old saying goes, 'A man convinced against his will is of the same opinion still.' The external witness of Scripture will convince no one unless there is an effectual application of the Spirit.

For this reason I have emphasised the internal witness of the Spirit. It is by the 'internal testimony' of the Spirit that we come to believe the Bible is the inspired Word of God.

What has possibly convinced me most is having to preach through a book of the Bible at a time, as I have consistently done. When I came upon the most difficult verses and was tempted to move on to the next one, what held me and caused me to stay with such a verse was my persuasion that the Holy Spirit actually wrote those words. The result was rewarding beyond my wildest expectations. I came up with the most refreshing and illuminating insights as a consequence of this conviction. There are a lot of verses I still don't understand, but I have yet to preach through a book in which the Holy Spirit did not rescue me regarding what I needed to know at the time.

In Pursuit of His Glory

May

God made him who had no sin to be sin for us, so that in him we might become the righteousness of God.

2 Corinthians 5:21

Jesus was and is the God-man. He was God as though he were not man and man as though he were not God. The same writers who stress his deity (as in John and Hebrews) equally emphasise his being human to such a degree that it sometimes seems incredible that the same author is still writing about the same Jesus. The second person of the Trinity is the Creator (John 1:3; Hebrews 1:1–3) but very much a man who could be physically tired (John 4:6), could be thirsty (John 19:28) and was even made perfect by the things he suffered (Hebrews 2:10; 5:8).

There are those Christians who believe in his deity but are sometimes shocked when they hear preaching that demonstrates how human Jesus really was. And yet the Apostles' Creed was designed to show Jesus' humanity!

This same Jesus died on the cross to pay our debt. Charles Spurgeon used to say that there is no true gospel without *substitution* and *satisfaction*. Jesus died as our substitute – taking our place and suffering God's wrath. Not only that; he satisfied the divine justice by his blood. Therefore when we trust Christ's blood and not our good works (however sincere or commendable they may be) we are promised a full pardon of all our sins. We are saved by confessing that Jesus is Lord and believing in our hearts (not head knowledge) that God raised him from the dead (Romans 10:9).

After Jesus rose from the dead he ascended to God's right hand (Hebrews 1:4) where he intercedes for us as our great high priest (Hebrews 4:14–15) and remains capable of sympathising with our temptations because he never forgot what it was like. He is coming again (Hebrews 9:28) and will judge the living and the dead.

In Pursuit of His Glory

For therein is the righteousness of God revealed from faith to faith: as it is written, 'The just shall live by faith.'

Romans 1:17 (AV)

Even the righteousness of God which is by faith of Jesus Christ unto all and upon all them that believe: for there is no difference: For all have sinned, and come short of the glory of God.

Romans 3:22–23 (AV)

When Paul said that the righteousness of God is revealed 'from faith to faith' (Romans 1:17) he tells exactly what he meant by that when he mentions the righteousness of God in Romans 3:22. Faith to faith means Christ's faith and our faith. Thus Paul said that we have believed *in* Christ in order that we might be justified *by* the faith *of* Christ. It is our faith in Christ's faith that justifies.

As a man Jesus had faith (Hebrews 2:13), a perfect faith. He was given the Spirit without measure (John 3:34) which is why he had a perfect faith. You and I have a measure, or limit, to our faith (Romans 12:3). But not Jesus. His faith is what lay behind his perfect obedience. Hence Jesus was our substitute as a man throughout the whole of his life. He believed perfectly on our behalf, which is why he is the only person who could fulfil the Law (Matthew 5:17). Therefore we are not only saved by his death but also by his life! Our imperfect faith is covered because his righteousness – which he produced by a perfect faith – is put to our credit (Romans 4:5). You and I are not required to produce a perfect faith to be saved, only faith in a perfect Saviour.

When Paul says, 'I live by the faith of the Son of God' (Galatians 2:20, AV) – the Greek literally being translated is, 'I live by faith, viz. that of the Son of God' – he is showing how he continues to trust not his own faith but that of Jesus. This perfect faith continues because Jesus intercedes for us in no degree of unbelief or doubt whatever. That is why we can trust his intercessory work at God's right hand. No wonder, then, that Paul could testify that he lives by the faith of the Son of God. No one should rely on their own faith but you can certainly rely on his – both that by which Jesus lived before he died and by his intercessory faith in heaven now.

In Pursuit of His Glory

Just as man is destined to die once, and after that to face judgment ...

Hebrews 9:27

Of all the doctrines I have taught, the Judgment Seat of Christ is possibly the one that has affected my personal life the most. Once I saw how real and true this is, my life was to be governed by a different kind of motivation deeper than anything else I hold dear. In a word: I shall face the Lord himself, probably with everybody watching, and give an account of my life on earth. It will be then and only then that all who have known me will know for sure whether I have walked in integrity or have been a phoney.

This judgment that faces us all will be comprised of two phases: the separation of the saved from the lost, and the judgment of the saved. Concerning the former, one's eternal destiny is either heaven or hell; as to the latter, some Christians will receive a reward and others will not.

The same man who had the most to say about justification by faith alone also said: 'For we must all appear before the judgment seat of Christ, that each one may receive what is due him for the things done while in the body, whether good or bad' (2 Corinthians 5:10). In other words, the imputed righteousness of Christ fits us for heaven, but not necessarily for a reward at the Judgment Seat of Christ. Some will receive a reward, others will be saved only by fire (1 Corinthians 3:15) and the fire will reveal whether we have built a superstructure of wood, hay and straw or one of gold, silver and precious stones (1 Corinthians 3:12ff.).

Some Christians say, 'I don't care about a reward, I just want to make it to heaven.' I can understand this. But it is not a very spiritual outlook. The truth is, receiving a reward, prize or crown (these words are used interchangeably) was very important to Paul. 'I beat my body and make it my slave so that after I have preached to others, I myself will not be disqualified for the prize' (1 Corinthians 9:27).

In Pursuit of His Glory

From the sixth hour until the ninth hour darkness came over all the land.

Matthew 27:45

This verse has been regarded by some as either an eclipse of the sun or just a dark cloud that hid the sun. But I believe the darkness was not only supernatural but the very glory of God.

In Leviticus 16 we have the instructions from God regarding the Day of Atonement; the chapter is introduced with words that show the glory of God would be manifested by a *cloud* over the 'atonement cover' – meaning the mercy seat.

There is no indication at this juncture that the cloud – which came to be called the Shekinah glory – would be dark. But Solomon somehow knew it was dark. This became obvious when Solomon had finished building the temple and brought the ark into it. The ark of the covenant was an oblong chest that had a lid on top called the mercy seat. When the ark was brought into the temple the priests could not do their work 'because of the cloud, for the glory of the LORD filled his temple' (1 Kings 8:11).

'Then Solomon said, "The LORD has said that he would dwell in a dark cloud"' (1 Kings 8:12). I used to wonder with surprise that the cloud was a 'dark cloud', for I had always taken the Shekinah to be described as a golden haze, if not brightness. All I know is that Solomon said it was 'dark'.

On Good Friday God manifested his glory in the land by putting his undoubted seal on Jesus' work. For Jesus' crucifixion was *atonement*. The blood of the cross was about to be sprinkled on the *real* mercy seat. What was brought into the temple was but a copy of the real thing (Exodus 25:40; Hebrews 8:5). What Solomon witnessed was but a taste of things to come. The darkness therefore was the Shekinah glory, showing God's redemptive work.

These events indicated that God was in Christ reconciling the world to himself (2 Corinthians 5:19). The smoke that filled the temple – the 'dark cloud' – was probably far greater on Good Friday, when Jesus atoned for our sins, than ever it was when Solomon saw it a thousand years before.

In Pursuit of His Glory

Men swear by someone greater than themselves, and the oath
confirms what is said and puts an end to all argument. Because
God wanted to make the unchanging nature of his purpose very
clear to the heirs of what was promised, he confirmed it with an
oath. God did this so that, by two unchangeable things in which it
is impossible for God to lie, we who have fled to take hold of the
hope offered to us may be greatly encouraged.

Hebrews 6:16–18

For many years I was puzzled by this reference in Hebrews to 'two unchangeable things'. Fortunately *The Living Bible* makes it clear: these two things in which it is impossible for God to lie are the *promise* and the *oath*. But what is the difference? They are both equally truthful and reliable, but why the two?

The oath was not sworn by God to him until Abraham became totally willing to sacrifice Isaac. But what kind of communication had existed between God and Abraham for all those years prior to that event? Between Genesis 12 and Genesis 22 there were several promises given to Abraham, all much the same. But one day God swore an *oath* to Abraham. What was the difference? What Abraham had believed by faith was now confirmed by the oath – which, as Hebrews 6:16 says, put an end to the argument. The oath was much more powerful.

The oath is almost always unconditional. When you are given a promise there is usually a condition attached; but once the oath comes you know beyond any doubt that what God promised *will indeed happen* – no matter what. Before the oath came Abraham believed, yes; but he often struggled. But once the oath came Abraham knew without any doubt that his seed would be as the sand on the seashore and the stars of heaven. Abraham never doubted again as he used to do.

God wants to do that for each of us. What we have believed but which still admits to a lot of struggle can be transcended by God's oath – when little room for doubting is left. The writer of Hebrews wanted to assure his readers that God's oath is worth waiting for. It will put an end to all argument! God will become so real that we can hardly believe we ever doubted.

In Pursuit of His Glory

6 May

It is impossible for those who have once been enlightened, who have tasted the heavenly gift, who have shared in the Holy Spirit, who have tasted the goodness of the word of God and the powers of the coming age, if they fall away, to be brought back to repentance, because to their loss they are crucifying the Son of God all over again and subjecting him to public disgrace.

Hebrews 6:4–6

The key to this passage is found in the context that began with the warning of Hebrews 3:7: 'So, as the Holy Spirit says: "Today, if you hear his voice"', and was then introduced in Hebrews 5:11: 'We have much to say about this, but it is hard to explain because you are slow to learn.' 'Slow to learn' is not a good translation. We must get to the original Greek, which the Authorised Version correctly translates 'dull of hearing'. It means being hard of hearing. In other words, these Jewish Christians were already, spiritually speaking, barely able to hear the Holy Spirit's voice. The warning of Hebrews 6:4 therefore means that, if this hardness of hearing continues, there is the possibility that they can never hear God speak at all – and will therefore be unable to be renewed again to repentance.

Are these people genuine Christians? Yes. But they do not lose their salvation. They lose the spiritual acumen to hear God speak again. It is so sad. It has already happened at that time, for the Greek literally reads that they *have* fallen away, as the Revised Standard Version translates it. These people were not only converted but had developed to considerable maturity.

I do not believe one falls away by the sins of the flesh, as in the case of King David, because David was restored (Psalm 51). The sin described in Hebrews 6:4–6 refers to repeatedly rejecting the warnings of the Holy Spirit. The sins of the flesh may certainly come alongside, but the immediate danger is the Christian not taking the call to intimacy with God seriously enough, so that they cease to hear God speak at all.

The proof that it has not happened to you or me is that we are still gripped by God's Word, that we can still hear him speak and that we want more of the Holy Spirit than we want anything on earth.

In Pursuit of His Glory

Then he will say to those on his left, 'Depart from me, you who are cursed, into the eternal fire prepared for the devil and his angels.'

Matthew 25:41

It should not give anyone one bit of pleasure to preach on hell. I only know it is what I am required to believe – if I accept *all* the teachings of Jesus – and what I must preach.

Many of my friends and some of the most valued servants of Christ I know have opted for the teaching of annihilation – the view that hell ultimately and completely annihilates the individual so that they are given non-existence. I could defend this position intelligently and probably convincingly. Those who accept annihilation are not God-haters or people who deny the Word of God. They believe this is what the Bible actually teaches. I believe they are wrong.

To teach annihilation is to present a theological rationale to the unbelievers on a silver platter of precisely what they hope is true anyway. The motivation to evangelise is considerably diminished, and I doubt many preach annihilation in an evangelistic meeting; it would cut across a solid motivation to flee from the wrath of God.

If pushed to summarise briefly why I believe there is a hell and that it is conscious and never-ending punishment, I would say: (1) a natural reading of the texts that refer to hell would lead the unbiased reader to believe that it is conscious and eternal (e.g. Mark 9:43–48; Matthew 13:49; Revelation 14:11); (2) the same God who alone has immortality also chose to bestow this on human beings when he created man and woman in his own image (Genesis 1:28), and this forms part of the basis for conscious existence beyond the grave for the lost; (3) since Jesus said it would be better if Judas Iscariot had never been born (Matthew 26:24), annihilation must not have awaited Judas (since he was lost – John 17:12) because the very point of annihilation is to render someone without existence as if they'd never been born in the first place; (4) Revelation 20:10 could not be clearer that the devil will not be annihilated: therefore those who are punished must expect not to be annihilated (Matthew 25:41).

In Pursuit of His Glory

I have set the LORD always before me.
  Because he is at my right hand,
  I shall not be shaken.

Psalm 16:8

One of the greatest things you can ever learn as a Christian is to remember that you have the presence of God. A verse that has meant the world to me is Psalm 16:8. Why does it say he 'set the LORD' before himself? It means that he had to remind himself that the Lord was there. You see, setting the Lord before him didn't mean that by doing this the Lord managed to get there on time. No, the Lord was already there, because David went on to say, 'because he is at my right hand'. 'I have set the LORD' means he put himself in a frame of mind to *remind* himself the Lord was already there. 'I have set the LORD always before me.' And if you can do this in the toughest moment, in the loneliest moment, then you know that he is there. Remind yourself, he is there.

I wish I could explain how much comfort this gives me when I am praying. Sometimes when I am praying, I feel the Lord is not listening and I think, wait, hold it – Wow! He is listening and, in fact, he is right here; I remember Psalm 16:8, 'I have set the LORD always before me.' All of a sudden, I begin to feel him and it is so wonderful to know that he and the angels are watching. The presence of God. What compensation! The presence of God also means protection: 'You will not fear the terror of night, nor the arrow that flies by day, nor the pestilence that stalks in the darkness, nor the plague that destroys at midday. A thousand may fall at your side, ten thousand at your right hand, but it will not come near you' (Psalm 91:5–7).

The Thorn in the Flesh

Do not be anxious about anything, but in everything, by prayer and petition, with thanksgiving, present your requests to God.

Philippians 4:6

I began my quiet time this morning (with a cup of coffee), as always, by welcoming the Holy Spirit. I always do this. 'Welcome, Holy Spirit' I say each morning. I then ask for the sprinkling of the blood of Jesus to be applied to my mind and heart by the Holy Spirit. I have my own little routine in this connection that I have followed for many years. The next thing I do is to turn to my journal. I go through every item I have written down, thanking the Lord for everything from the previous day, one by one. As it happens, today, as I write this, it is 25 January 2008, and this is what happened yesterday that I thanked the Lord for: (1) some impressions I put down in my journal – which I found edifying, (2) the particular prayer requests I felt good about (I almost always write down any fresh request), (3) a lovely breakfast with a bluegrass singer from my state of Kentucky (who phoned and welcomed me to our new town in Tennessee – he is a neighbour), (4) the CDs and the DVD he gave us – which Louise and I played and enjoyed, (5) the progress I made in writing this very book, (6) helping us shop as we went to the grocery store, (7) the good supper we ate, (8) the television we enjoyed last evening, (9) another powerful insight I was given during the afternoon, (10) a good night's sleep. That's it. That is what literally happened yesterday and what I thanked the Lord for on this very day. It took just half a minute to thank the Lord for these things.

You don't need to keep a journal; this is just something that I choose to do. But I would urge you to remember to thank the Lord for everything you should be happy about. *Everything.* If you don't keep a journal, then thank him before you go to bed! Don't wait – we all forget so easily! But learn to be thankful and *tell* God what you are thankful for. Don't say to yourself, 'He already knows I'm thankful.' Tell him.

Did You Think to Pray?

The sacrifices of God are a broken spirit;
* a broken and contrite heart,*
* O God, you will not despise.*

Psalm 51:17

Many readers will have heard of Joni Eareckson Tada. Her diving accident as a teenager that left her paralysed for life from the neck down could have driven her to bitterness and despair. But by the grace of God she chose to dignify her extreme suffering and God has made her a legend in her own time and an incalculable blessing to thousands of hurting people. I haven't suffered anything like Joni. But I can say nonetheless that the adversities I have encountered have been worth more than gold. I have no complaints whatever. I pray that you will join me in doing what was put many years ago like this:

Count your blessings, name them one by one,
Count your blessings, see what God has done;
Count your blessings, name them one by one,
And it will surprise you what the Lord has done.   (Anon)

Thanking God

Saul was afraid of David, because the LORD *was with David but had left Saul.*

1 Samuel 18:12

Perfect love casts out fear; when we are afraid we are not made perfect in love (1 John 4:18). Why would anybody be afraid of another's anointing? It is God who gave it. We should affirm the anointing in another. If we are afraid of it, it suggests a rival spirit has crept in. Or we are afraid people will be influenced and think more of them than of us. We *may* be afraid that God will use that person to bring revival! We say we want revival – until, that is, it appears it won't come through us, via our party line or through those who agree with us.

The fear of another's anointing is a dead give-away that we are not right in ourselves. It characterised Saul who was already yesterday's man by that time. May God give us such objectivity about ourselves that we truly and unfeignedly confess our sin. I say again, I can think of nothing worse than for God to be in something or someone and for me not to see it. Fear keeps us from seeing the obvious.

The Anointing

I am bound both to Greeks and non-Greeks, both to the wise and the foolish.

Romans 1:14

I once listened to a friend of mine read aloud a statement that gripped him. I replied, 'I like that – read it again.' He did. 'Who said that?' I asked. When he told me my stomach churned. I began to see what I could find that was *wrong* with what was said. It was by a person whose views on so many issues are those I reject categorically. Then I realised how childish I was being. Either I will recognise truth for its own sake or I am going to embrace the thoughts only of those who adhere to my way of thinking. I felt convicted to my fingertips. I vowed then and there to be a seeker of truth, no matter who says it. If Paul can express a debt to the foolish, surely I can accept truth, even if it is stated by my enemy!

Joseph Tson once asked me, 'How far are you willing to go in your commitment to Christ?' We must be willing to follow truth no matter where it leads us. This is the only way you and I can recognise and experience today's anointing.

The Anointing

Jesus Christ is the same yesterday and today and for ever.

Hebrews 13:8

One of the paradoxes of church history is that the anointing has been characterised by both continuity and discontinuity.

Continuity. The tremendous statement of Hebrews 13:8 was placed in the context of the warning: 'Remember your leaders, who spoke the word of God to you. Consider the outcome of their way of life and imitate their faith' (Hebrews 13:7). For there is absolute continuity with the message. So Jude began his brief epistle: 'Dear friends, although I was very eager to write to you about the salvation we share, I felt I had to write and urge you to contend for the faith once delivered to the saints' (Jude 3). This message must never change. It was the message of Athanasius, the message of Augustine, the message of the Reformers, the message of Wesley and Whitefield. Continuity. Today's anointing will have an unbroken continuity with the past, linking with that scarlet thread.

By discontinuity I mean the manifestation of God's anointing that may have no obvious precedent. It may appear and disappear. That it had no precedent does not invalidate its authenticity. That it may not last long does not mean it wasn't right at the time. An example of this is the strange phenomenon in the early Church when all the believers 'had everything in common. Selling their possessions and goods, they gave to anyone as he had need' (Acts 2:44–45). Many of us find this very odd. It didn't last. But the seal of God on this practice became apparent when Ananias and Sapphira acted as though they were in on it but lied. God struck both of them dead in the space of three hours (Acts 5:1–10). There is no biblical principle that states that Christians are to do what the early Church did for a time. But there is equally no doubt that this is what happened for a while. I am sure it seemed natural to those who did it at the time. Discontinuity.

The Anointing

'Do not be like them, for your Father knows what you need before you ask him.'

Matthew 6:8

Do you show how thankful you are? How could you best build in a daily opportunity to thank the Lord?

'He knows I'm thankful,' you may say. Please tell him. Tell him. Do you not appreciate it yourself when people thank you for something? Even though God can see my heart while people can't, we need to tell him. God also knows what things you need before you ask him, says Matthew 6:8, but he still wants you to tell him, and when we pray that's what we should do.

We have a curious way of *asking* the Lord for what we need (even though he knows the need). We should also remember to *thank* him (even though he may well know we are thankful).

How can we be so sure we are thankful if we do not go to the trouble to remember to say 'thank you' to the one 'who has blessed us in the heavenly realms with every spiritual blessing in Christ' (Ephesians 1:3)?

We all know people who annoy us by their lack of gratitude and appreciation. It is surely true that those who remember to say 'Thank you' are more thankful than the ones who forget to say 'Thank you'. God loves to hear us say 'Thank you' to him and to each other.

Thanking God

Then God said, 'Let us make man in our image, in our likeness, and let them rule over the fish of the sea and the birds of the air, over the livestock, over all the earth, and over all the creatures that move along the ground.' So God created man in his own image, in the image of God he created him; male and female he created them.

Genesis 1:26–27

Sanctification is the process by which we are made holy. It is becoming more and more like Jesus. But why be sanctified? Answer: to show we are thankful. This is why the reformed doctrine of sanctification has been called, literally, the doctrine of gratitude. We are not saved by our sanctification; we are not going to heaven because we are becoming more and more like the Lord Jesus Christ. We are saved by sheer grace. 'For it is by grace you have been saved, through faith – and this not from yourselves, it is the gift of God – not by works, so that no one can boast' (Ephesians 2:8–9).

Gratitude must be taught. Sanctification shows gratitude by holy conversation and godly living. Living a holy life – when you know you are saved wholly by faith in Jesus' blood – shows that you are grateful. Is that not enough? Just living a godly life?

No. God wants more. Not only for us to show gratitude by obedience; he wants us to learn to *tell* him, to *hear* us say 'thank you'. He wants to hear it all the time.

We are made in the image of God (Genesis 1:26–27). This is a profound teaching that means many things. For example, it shows us that we, as God's created people, like to be thanked and praised because that is how we are *made*. God made us like himself. He wants to be thanked and praised, and made us to want this if only to send a hint to us that he wants it just the same as we do. I might want you to thank me for something nice I did for you, and in the same way God wants *me* to thank *him* for the things he has done for me.

Thanking God

It is impossible for those who have once been enlightened, who have tasted the heavenly gift, who have shared in the Holy Spirit, who have tasted the goodness of the word of God and the powers of the coming age, if they fall away, to be brought back to repentance, because to their loss they are crucifying the Son of God all over again and subjecting him to public disgrace.

Hebrews 6:4–6

I often think of how I came across a 'revelation' concerning Hebrews 6:4–6, arguably one of the most difficult passages in the New Testament. It talks about falling away and not being able to be renewed to repentance – a pretty awful state. I am not wanting to get into a controversial theological debate here but just want to say that when I saw clearly what it meant I was stunned and thrilled. But my point for mentioning it is this: I am so deeply thankful that I myself have not sinned so as to be in a Hebrews 6:6 situation. It is the sheer grace of God that has kept me from becoming stone deaf to the Holy Spirit – which is what Hebrews 6:6 means.

Therefore we must thank him if we 'hear his voice' (Hebrews 3:7). As long as we have maintained a sensitivity to the Holy Spirit we are not in danger of falling so as to be unteachable or unreachable. It is something to be very, very thankful for. When I contemplate this for very long I am all the more moved. I have given God cause to put me to one side many times – by my pride, stubbornness, greed and impatience. But *he* has stayed with me. Has this been the case with you? Have you thanked him?

Thanking God

'And when you stand praying, if you hold anything against anyone, forgive him, so that your Father in heaven may forgive you your sins.'

Mark 11:25

The truth is, we have all got away with a lot. We all have skeletons in the cupboard. God has been gracious to all of us. So pray for your enemy. I repeat: don't pray that God deal with them! Say, 'God forgive them!' That means God releases them. That means that you are telling God that he doesn't have to deal with them, only forgive them and let them go! Then add: 'Forgive me for the way I feel about that person.' Prove that you really do mean this by employing the following principles: (1) Let nobody know what that person has done to you. (2) Don't allow the person to be intimidated or afraid of you. (3) Don't let the person feel guilty. (4) Let the person save face. (5) Protect that person from their deepest fear. This is the way Joseph forgave his brothers (Genesis 45:1–15).

One day all will be revealed: 'Therefore judge nothing before the appointed time; wait until the Lord comes. He will bring to light what is hidden in darkness and will expose the motives of men's hearts. At that time each will receive his praise from God' (1 Corinthians 4:5). That will happen. We will know who was right, whether we have truly forgiven and prayed for our enemies (Mark 11:25). And after you have done everything, as long as the Holy Spirit in you is ungrieved, that very enemy will turn out to be the reason you began to grow by leaps and bounds and began to love, and to experience unusual power. You will thank God for that thorn in the flesh that would not go away.

The Thorn in the Flesh

In all the travels of the Israelites, whenever the cloud lifted from above the tabernacle, they would set out; but if the cloud did not lift, they did not set out – until the day it lifted. So the cloud of the LORD was over the tabernacle by day, and fire was in the cloud by night, in the sight of all the house of Israel during all their travels.

Exodus 40:36–38

Israel was locked into this manner of direct guidance from God. They could only move when the cloud lifted. If the cloud did not lift, they stayed. No matter how tedious and tasteless that particular place in the wilderness might have been, they had to 'stay put' until they were released to move on. The cloud did not adjust to the Israelites; they had to adjust to the cloud.

It often takes as much courage to stay as it does to move. It may take even more faith sometimes to remain where you are than to explore a new geographical area. It may not be mere boredom, however, that tempts one to move on; sometimes it is opposition. Paul went into Corinth to preach the gospel. His custom was to offer the gospel to Jews first (Romans 1:16). This he did in Corinth. 'But when the Jews opposed Paul and became abusive, he shook out his clothes in protest and said to them, "Your blood be on your own heads! I am clear of my responsibility. From now on I will go to the Gentiles"' (Acts 18:6). Paul left the synagogue where he had been preaching and went next door. He had some spectacular conversions (Acts 18:7–8), but the persecution was so fierce that Paul *wanted* to move on. 'One night the Lord spoke to Paul in a vision: "Do not be afraid; keep on speaking, do not be silent. For I am with you, and no one is going to attack and harm you, because I have many people in this city"' (Acts 18:9–10). The consequence was that Paul stayed for a year and a half. A great church was formed and we all have the benefit of 1 and 2 Corinthians as a result. All because Paul stayed.

Whenever God says, 'Stay,' it is with a definite purpose. We will never be sorry when we remain where we are if God says we must. We may not know the reasons at the time.

The Sensitivity of the Spirit

In all your ways acknowledge him,
    and he will make your paths straight.

Proverbs 3:6

This is a wonderful proverb and a wonderful promise. 'All your ways' must refer to anything that pertains to us. Some people worry that they should bother God with small things. But as Pastor Jim Cymbala puts it, 'Don't worry about bringing small things to God, for with God everything is small!' After all, Jesus said, 'Whoever can be trusted with very little can also be trusted with much, and whoever is dishonest with very little will also be dishonest with much' (Luke 16:10). It is much easier to bring the more difficult requests to God when we are in a daily habit of bringing *everything* to him already.

One of the sadder moments in the life of Joshua was the way in which he and Israel were lied to and deceived by the Gibeonites. Moses had warned them before he died, 'Make no treaty' with any of the inhabitants of Canaan (Deuteronomy 7:1–2). But the Gibeonites ingeniously manipulated their way into Joshua's good graces and, before he realised what was happening, 'Then Joshua made a treaty of peace with them to let them live, and the leaders of the assembly ratified it by oath' (Joshua 9:15). Soon afterwards they realised they had been tricked. 'But all the leaders answered, "We have given them our *oath* by the Lord, the God of Israel, and we cannot touch them now"' (Joshua 9:19). And yet all this happened because they, incredibly, 'did not inquire of the Lord' (Joshua 9:14). At their fingertips were the faithful means of knowing God's will, and they bypassed them.

The Sensitivity of the Spirit

Our gospel came to you not simply with words, but also with power, with the Holy Spirit and deep conviction.

1 Thessalonians 1:5

I can never forget something Alex Buchanan said to me once concerning preaching: 'We must communicate God as well as his word.' That shook me rigid. I always assumed that if I preached the word – God's word – that was enough. That, surely, was my calling. Wrong. If God *himself* is not experienced in the hearers I preach to, I have failed to do my job well. It is possible to preach the word without the Spirit. When Paul said that his gospel came not in word only he meant that it is very possible indeed to preach with just words. I fear I have been as guilty as they come at this point.

Some of us are determined to 'make' God speak, even when he is clearly saying nothing. We do it with the Scriptures. We make them say what they are not saying in order to fit them in with our own theological bias.

The old saying, 'Where the Scriptures speak, we speak; where the Scriptures are silent, we are silent,' is good sense. God doesn't answer the question regarding the origin of evil – why he made the world knowing man would sin and suffer. It is a mystery. Moses wanted to unravel the mystery as to how a bush could be on fire and that bush not burn up. So he said to himself,

> 'I will go over and see this strange sight – why the bush does not burn up.' When the Lord saw that he had gone over to look, God called to him from within the bush, 'Moses! Moses!' And Moses said, 'Here I am.' 'Do not come any closer,' God said. 'Take off your sandals, for the place where you are standing is holy ground.' (Exodus 3:3–5)

God's silence is holy ground. We must take off our shoes, and worship.

The Sensitivity of the Spirit

'If I were hungry I would not tell you,
  for the world is mine, and all that is in it.'

Psalm 50:12

This is one of the most stunning lines I have come across. One evening when our children were sitting on the floor in front of me watching television, not being too interested in what they were watching, I found myself reading that verse. I began to feel very uneasy. I thought to myself, 'I wish the Lord would tell me if he were hungry.' I began to wonder, what if God wanted me to spend more time with him than I had been giving him, would he tell me? I kept reading it, 'If I were hungry I would not tell you.' I couldn't shake it off. I read it again. And again. I began to get the definite feeling that by saying this God was telling me after all he needed and wanted me.

The context of this verse in Psalm 50 is that, though the world is his and although he has cattle on a thousand hills, God is hungry for me. Though he has countless angels – millions and billions – not to mention other people all over the world worshipping him and spending time with him, he wanted me. I seized the moment, for some reason. I decided to fast the next day. I sought his face as I had not done before. The curious thing was, God was hinting the very opposite of what he was saying in Psalm 50:12.

Out of the Comfort Zone

22 May

Once, having been asked by the Pharisees when the kingdom of God would come, Jesus replied, 'The kingdom of God does not come with your careful observation, nor will people say, "Here it is," or "There it is," because the kingdom of God is within you.'

Luke 17:20–21

Are you aware that there is a sense in which a main issue in both the Old Testament and the New Testament has to do with living conditions? The Old Testament stresses again and again the matter of living conditions. Moses and the people of Israel lived in a desert, and they were looking for a land flowing with milk and honey. The thrust of the Law was: if you obey, certain happy living conditions will follow. If you disobey, the opposite will follow (see Deuteronomy 28:1–61). In the New Testament, sadly, the Jews' messianic expectations had to do entirely with living conditions. They thought that when Messiah came, he was going to change living conditions for them and set them free from Rome. This is why they couldn't cope with the thought that their Messiah would end up on a cross. Jesus warned them, for he knew exactly what they were thinking. Jesus put it as he did in Luke 17 so that they would understand that this present world is not all there is.

The Thorn in the Flesh

'But you will receive power when the Holy Spirit comes on you.'

Acts 1:8

I am sometimes asked if we can manifest the fruits of the Spirit without having received the baptism of the Spirit. Answer: yes. This is because we are all responsible for showing the fruits of the Spirit in our lives. '. . . the fruit of the Spirit is love, joy, peace, patience, kindness, goodness, faithfulness, gentleness and self-control' (Galatians 5:22–23). We all have the potential to manifest the fruits of the Spirit because we have the Holy Spirit. Every Christian has the Spirit of Christ. If one does not have the Spirit of Christ it is because he or she does not belong to Christ (Romans 8:9). Therefore let no one say, 'I cannot demonstrate the fruits of the Spirit because I have not received the baptism of the Spirit.' All of us have not only the potential to show the Spirit's fruits, but have a mandate from the Lord to do so.

I have been equally asked if we can witness for the Lord if we have not received the power promised in Acts 1:8, 'But you will receive power when the Holy Spirit comes on you; and you will be my witnesses . . .' Again the answer is: yes. We are responsible for sharing the gospel with others whether or not we have received the same kind of power given to the 120 in the upper room. The woman of Samaria was excited to tell the people in her area about Jesus. 'Come, see a man who told me everything I ever did. Could this be the Christ?' They came out of the town and made their way towards him. There is no indication that she had unusual power, only the joy of having met the Lord.

Pure Joy

24 May

For it is by grace you have been saved, through faith – and this not from yourselves, it is the gift of God – not by works, so that no-one can boast.

Ephesians 2:8–9

Are you saved? Do you know for certain that if you were to die one hour from now you would go to heaven? One of the reasons that the Bible was written was that you may 'know that you have eternal life' (1 John 5:13). *Do* you know this? Moreover, suppose you were to stand before God and he were to ask you, 'Why should I let you into my heaven?' what would you say? If you have never thought about a question like this, why not lay this book aside for a moment and write on a slip of paper what your answer to this last question is – then come back to the book, continue reading and compare your answer with what I submit below.

Perhaps you would like to know what many others have said in answer to that question. 'I have tried to live a good life.' 'I believe in the Ten Commandments.' 'I try to keep the Golden Rule.' 'I have never hurt anybody.' 'I walked forward at a Billy Graham crusade.' 'I was baptised.' 'I joined the Church.' 'I was brought up in a Christian home.' 'I'm as good as the next person.' 'I believe in God.' 'I like going to church.' 'Please God, let me in.' 'I love you.' 'I've tried to be a good husband/wife/parent.' 'I knelt at an altar.'

Nearly all of the above answers begin with 'I' and stress what the person has done to *earn* his way into heaven. If your own answer is similar to one of those above, you are like most people in thinking that we get to heaven by our good works. But now for the good news. That is what the word 'gospel' means – good news! Heaven is a *free gift*. It is not earned or merited by anything we have done. 'For the wages of sin is death, but the *gift* of God is eternal life in Christ Jesus our Lord' (Romans 6:23).

Stand Up and Be Counted

Jesus said, 'Father, forgive them, for they do not know what they are doing.' And they divided up his clothes by casting lots.

Luke 23:34

It is very, very hard to forgive those who have hurt us directly, especially when they feel not the slightest twinge of conscience. When we can see they are sorry it makes it a lot easier.

But no one seemed very sorry at the cross of Jesus. There was no justice at his 'trial' – if you could call it that. There was glee in the faces of the people who got what they wanted: '"Crucify him!" they shouted' (Mark 15:13). Furthermore, 'Those who passed by hurled insults at him, shaking their heads and saying, "So! You who are going to destroy the temple and build it in three days, come down from the cross and save yourself!"' (Mark 15:29–30). They shouted, 'Let this Christ, this King of Israel, come down now from the cross, that we may see and believe' (Mark 15:32). And what was Jesus' response?

He might have said, 'I forgive you', but such words would have been misinterpreted and wasted. It would also have been casting his pearls before pigs (Matthew 7:6). Instead, Jesus asked the *Father* to forgive them. That was a far grander gesture in any case. By asking the Father to forgive them it showed *he* had forgiven them; he released all of them from their guilt. He likewise set the Father free from having to punish them by asking him not to take revenge on them. It was not a perfunctory prayer; Jesus meant it. And it was gloriously answered! They were among the very ones Peter addressed on the Day of Pentecost (Acts 2:14–41) and who were converted.

It must be our response as well.

Total Forgiveness

'Do not judge, or you too will be judged.'

Matthew 7:1

The motivation to forgive often has a natural explanation. For Jesus speaks to us in a way that gets our attention – if only by appealing to our self-interest. A motive for not judging others is to stop ourselves from being judged. If a person's chief desire is for a greater anointing, and he is told that this anointing will come in proportion to the degree that he forgives others, then he is more motivated to forgive.

For example, I unexpectedly saw a person in one of our services who had severely hurt one of our children. It was just before I was scheduled to preach. I felt like Corrie ten Boom must have felt. In a flash the Lord seemed to say to me: 'You say you want revival in this church. What if revival hinges on whether you totally forgive this person?' I felt awful. I felt selfish. I felt trapped. But I had to make a decision on the spot – at least it felt that way – as to whether I really wanted revival in our church. In other words, which meant more to me: getting even with one who had hurt one of our children or the blessing of the Spirit? I opted for the latter, but my prayer still had a natural explanation. I did not want it on my conscience that I was obstructing the blessing of the Spirit when all around me there were those who were earnestly praying for this. I still struggle in this area and think – just maybe – I have totally forgiven this person. I have asked the Lord to bless this person and let them off the hook, but it hasn't been easy. Totally forgiving somebody doesn't necessarily mean we will want to go on holiday with them.

Total Forgiveness

And we, who with unveiled faces all reflect the Lord's glory, are being transformed into his likeness with ever-increasing glory, which comes from the Lord, who is the Spirit.

2 Corinthians 3:18

The Christian faith launches someone on a new journey, and this is because you have been given a new life. You have been 'born again' – by the Holy Spirit (John 3:3–7). But God does not say to you at your conversion, 'Nice to meet you – see you in heaven.' No. It is the beginning not only of a relationship with him, but of an *ongoing* changing of your life.

Paul calls it being changed from 'glory to glory', which means being transformed into Christ's image 'from one degree of glory to another' (English Standard Version). It is being renewed again – and again – to repentance, which means that our minds are continually being changed. Repentance (Greek: *metanoia*) means 'change of mind', so as we get to know God we get to know ourselves. Like a loving, wise parent who does not tell us all he or she knows, so our heavenly Father – who sees our flaws and defects long before he lets us see them – patiently leads each of us by the hand one day at a time.

It is through prayer that the Bible comes alive and we are given to see not only insights into Holy Scripture but also into ourselves. I am seventy-two as I write, and I would blush to tell you how much changing I still have to do. It is embarrassingly wonderful! My first reaction is, 'Lord, why didn't you show me this before?' or 'Lord, how could you keep loving me so much when you knew all the time what horrible faults I have?'

When I retired from Westminster Chapel in 2002 at the age of sixty-six, I was not prepared for how much I would learn about God and myself in what are supposed to be my 'retirement' years.

In other words, we never stop learning and we never stop growing.

Did You Think to Pray?

'If you are pleased with me, teach me your ways so I may know you and continue to find favour with you. Remember that this nation is your people.'

Exodus 33:13

I had a surprising awakening not long ago when I was reading Exodus 33:13, which shows Moses' first reaction to the knowledge that he had found favour with God – a verse I have read a thousand times, but had not really grasped: 'If you are pleased with me, teach me your ways.' When I saw what this was saying, I was shaken rigid.

Think about this for a moment, and put yourself in Moses' shoes. Moses is handed on a silver platter a knowledge that is more extraordinary than any knowledge that could be wished for here below – namely, that God was pleased with him. I have to tell you, it doesn't get better than that! Exodus 33:13 tells us how Moses handled this sublime information: 'If you, Lord, are truly pleased with me, teach me your ways.'

Would you have responded that way? Would I? I doubt it, I am ashamed to say. I have asked myself, if God said that to me – that he is pleased with me – and I could consequently ask for anything, what would I ask for?

What was it Moses asked for? He did not hesitate: 'If you are pleased with me, *teach me your ways*.' That immediate reply convicted me no end. I would like to think this would have been the answer I would have given, but I doubt it. But that is not all; Moses asked for this, '*so I may know you and continue to find favour with you*' (Exodus 33:13). Moses' request absolutely sobered me. I don't honestly think I would have asked for that. I would probably have asked for a greater anointing – which, you might say, is a spiritual request. Perhaps you are right – but Moses' reply shows how well he knew God already, and my own wish suggests I have a long way to go.

Did You Think to Pray?

As Saul turned to leave Samuel, God changed Saul's heart, and all these signs were fulfilled that day. When they arrived at Gibeah, a procession of prophets met him; the Spirit of God came upon him in power, and he joined in their prophesying.

1 Samuel 10:9–10

Spiritual or ministerial gifts are sovereignly bestowed on a person – not because of one's good works or sanctification. This explains how King Saul – whom God had chosen but later had clearly rejected (1 Samuel 10:1; 16:1; 18:12) – still prophesied. Saul had been given a change of heart along with the gift of prophecy. But later, strange as it may seem, *on his way to kill young David*, 'the Spirit of God came upon him' and the people were still saying, 'Is Saul also among the prophets?' (1 Samuel 19:23–24; cf. 1 Samuel 10:11). God's approval had been withdrawn, but not Saul's gift.

But having an irrevocable gift does not mean that one is exempt from God's severe displeasure and judgment. A gift from God is bestowed upon the assumption that one will not abuse such a privilege. That person should be utterly grateful to God for his or her talent, anointing, natural ability, and his or her calling and following. If the person is not full of gratitude – which is demonstrated by words and deeds – then he or she will sooner or later be found out, and will also discover that the effectiveness of that gift diminishes.

As for King Saul, he eventually lost everything – including any connection with anything prophetic. 'God has turned away from me. He no longer answers me, either by prophets or by dreams', lamented Saul near the end of his life (1 Samuel 28:15). I would suspect therefore that a person's gift can flourish for a while despite his or her conduct, but that eventually that gift will begin to disappear if the person is not finally granted unfeigned repentance. Therefore the irrevocability of one's gift should not be regarded as meaning that it will be *effective* for ever.

Second Chance

30 May

*Now the earth was formless and empty, darkness was over the
surface of the deep, and the Spirit of God was hovering over the
waters.*

Genesis 1:2

From a letter to Rabbi David Rosen, former Chief Rabbi of Ireland:

Thank you for bringing up the subject of the Trinity. I can understand your comment that the idea that 'God is somehow exclusively
incarnate in one human being' as being totally beyond your compre-
hension. I cannot grasp this either. Who can? Your namesake King
David could not fully take in the matter of God creating and loving
humankind: 'What is man that you are mindful of him?' (Psalm 8:4)
and felt much the same as he reflected on God's care and omniscience,
'Such knowledge is too wonderful for me, too lofty for me to attain'
(Psalm 139:6).

As for the Trinity, I am not about to tell you anything you don't
know already, that we Christians do not remotely believe in three gods,
for God is *one* (as in the *Sh'ma*): 'Hear O Israel: The LORD our God,
the LORD is one' (Deuteronomy 6:4). God is *one*, his name is the Lord
(or Yahweh, known to you as *HaShem*). His Son the Messiah is the
very image and reflection of God and he touches us and speaks to us
by his Spirit – the same Spirit who participated in creation (Genesis
1:2). The word 'Trinity' is not in the New Testament, as you know.
Tertullian (*c.* 200) coined the Latin word *trinitas* and was the first of
our Church Fathers to refer to the Father, Son and Spirit as *personae*.
And yet I must tell you that one thing we are not willing to give up is
the biblical teaching that God is one – it is not negotiable. Trinity is
also an *a posteriori* explanation of our Church Fathers of how best
to understand that God is manifest as Father, Son and Holy Spirit.

The Christian and the Pharisee

'But I tell you that men will have to give account on the day of judgment for every careless word they have spoken.'

Matthew 12:36

This is perhaps my most 'unfavourite' verse in the Bible.

A careless word. 'Idle word' (KJV). 'Useless word' (TEV). 'Thoughtless word' (NEB). Oh dear. I am in serious trouble. This does not make me look forward to the Day of Judgment.

I cannot think of anything scarier than having every careless word, idle word, useless word or thoughtless word thrown up at me on that Day. Imagine this: you are standing before the Lord with him looking on, but also everybody else (this is also why it hurts so much). I don't know how it will happen – whether God gives earphones to everybody to eavesdrop our conversations – in secret and in public. I only know this is a word that I take seriously, and so should you. Were we to believe it literally, I can assure you that it would go a long way in helping us to control our tongues!

Your Words Have Power

June

'Whoever believes in me, as the Scripture has said, streams of living water will flow from within him.'

John 7:38

I want to look at three possible approaches to the Holy Spirit in our worship.

The first approach is *hiring the Spirit*, that is, engaging his services for temporary use. We decide what we want to include in our services and what our aim is to be and then tell the Holy Spirit to take us there. When we hire the Spirit in this way we manipulate him to serve our own ends, and that is a great abuse.

The second approach is *hindering the Spirit*. One way of doing this is to hem him around with our own preconceived ideas and prejudices. This happens when we come to worship after having already decided on the form the worship should take. Nothing quenches the Spirit like prejudice of this sort. And as a result many people never have any idea of what God can do in them and through them.

The third approach is *honouring the Spirit*. We do this by releasing him. Many of us think only in terms of the Spirit coming down, but he can flow out from a well deep within us (John 7:38).

How do we release the Spirit in ourselves? It will happen when we keep peace in our hearts with everybody we know. Sometimes we play games with ourselves, and pretend we are at peace and that all is fine. It is like someone who loses his temper and then says, 'I'm not mad.' We can justify ourselves until we are a hundred, but the Spirit will never be himself in us as long as we are unforgiving or judgmental, prejudiced, or speaking evil of anyone. He will not be himself in us as long as we are preoccupied with what others are going to think of what we do. It may mean apologising to someone, or it may be a little thing like raising your hand in worship. But obeying his impulse is all part of honouring the Spirit and releasing him in ourselves.

Worshipping God

And do not grieve the Holy Spirit of God, with whom you were sealed for the day of redemption. Get rid of all bitterness, rage and anger, brawling and slander, along with every form of malice. Be kind and compassionate to one another, forgiving each other, just as in Christ God forgave you.

Ephesians 4:30–32

Now bitterness can be directed towards God, towards others or towards ourselves. We are bitter towards God if we get angry about what he has allowed to happen. This prevents us worshipping by the Spirit, because we can't worship God very well if we are angry with him.

Bitterness towards others comes when we are hurt over what they have done to us, and we feel bitterness towards ourselves when we cannot forgive ourselves for what we have done. This shows that we have not accepted the promise, 'If we confess our sins, he is faithful and just to forgive us our sins and to cleanse us from all unrighteousness' (1 John 1:9). We are trying to dictate to God when we refuse to forgive ourselves when he has forgiven us.

I know what it is to be bitter – and to be bitter for a long time. And I know what it is to justify myself all the time by saying, 'God understands.' He does. But all the time we are being bitter, the Holy Spirit is being grieved, and we will not know his impulse within us.

Worshipping God

They devoted themselves to the apostles' teaching and to the
fellowship, to the breaking of bread and to prayer.

Acts 2:42

Form this verse you can see the importance of fellowship in the worshipping life of the early Church. If fellowship is not present, worship ceases. But what constituted fellowship? The answer is that two things were shared: a common faith and a common enemy. Three thousand people may seem like a good number, but compared to the hundreds of thousands who were in Jerusalem at that time, it was a very small minority.

These three thousand all believed in the resurrection of Jesus. They had all just been baptised and were full of the Holy Spirit. And they were hated by the religious and secular leaders. But, in the face of this opposition, they had each other.

We know that the world has nothing in common with us and we come together to be with people who share what we believe. In the early Church no one was at odds with anyone else at first. There was such power present that they were actually detached from their worldly possessions (Acts 2:44).

The world looked on and sensed that something special was happening. Acts 5:13 says, 'And of the rest durst no man join himself to them.' The non-Christian Jews were in awe of Christians at the time, and they could not join them unless the Holy Spirit brought them in.

That is what is needed today, but it is impossible when people in church avoid each other.

Worshipping God

For we must all appear before the judgment seat of Christ, that each one may receive what is due to him for the things done while in the body, whether good or bad.

2 Corinthians 5:10

The saddest thing of all is the loneliness of sin and its consequences. Sin results in the greatest loneliness that ever was. You know the expression, 'You ain't seen nothing yet.' You may well feel lonely, but sin will ultimately result in the greatest loneliness there ever was. You can blame others and circumstances for so long, but 'be sure that your sin will find you out' (Numbers 32:23). As Billy Graham said, 'When you die you will die alone.'

When you stand before the Judgment Seat of Christ, you will stand alone to give an account of the things done in the body. You won't have your parents, you won't have a friend who will stand there with you, you will stand alone. It may be our loneliest moment. One of the things that will make hell into hell is loneliness. You will pray and weep, but there will be none to help you, and sadly it will last for ever.

I thought I should say this: is there a reader who needs this? Have you come to terms with your sin? There is one way and only one way God will deal with your sin. It will not be by making him promises. It will not be by you saying, 'Well, from now on I am going to be better!' It will be only by your affirming his Son as the only way to heaven, whose death on the cross paid your debt by the shedding of his blood. Then your sins will be washed away. There's no other name by which we can be saved. It means affirming that Jesus died and paid your debt, and if you haven't yet put your trust in Jesus Christ, do it! Do it now! Be sure that heaven will be your home because there will be no loneliness in heaven.

The Thorn in the Flesh

About the ninth hour Jesus cried out in a loud voice, 'Eloi, Eloi, lama sabachthani?' – *which means, 'My God, my God, why have you forsaken me?'*

Matthew 27:46

Consider the loneliness of Jesus. The loneliest person that ever was, was Jesus. Think about that time, at the Last Supper, when all of a sudden the disciples were arguing among themselves, who is the greatest? You can almost sense Jesus looking up to the Father, as if to say, 'Hasn't anybody listened to me here?' After three years of spoon-feeding them, teaching them, here they are, arguing among themselves, who's going to be the greatest? They haven't really heard Jesus. Then in the Garden of Gethsemane, he took his closest friends, Peter, James and John, and said, 'Would you wait with me one hour?' But they fell asleep. He pleaded with them to stay with him for just one hour! He came back, and there they were asleep; one of the most moving ways of translating it is in the Authorised Version: Jesus just looked at them and said, 'Sleep on now . . . the hour is come' (Mark 14:41). He just wanted some close empathetic companionship there at the end. He knew he would die alone. On the cross, he cried out, 'My God, my God, why have you forsaken me?' (Matthew 27:46). The loneliest person that ever was, was our Lord.

But there is a value in loneliness. Loneliness isn't for nothing. If you are in a situation of enforced solitude, there is a reason. God does not send the thorn in the flesh for nothing. Moreover, it is not punishment. Don't say, 'Oh, I am getting my dues!' Wrong!

God got even at the cross. The thorn in the flesh is not punishment. It is preparation.

The Thorn in the Flesh

And the scripture was fulfilled that says, 'Abraham believed God, and it was credited to him as righteousness,' and he was called God's friend.

James 2:23

The value of loneliness is also to remind you that your real home is heaven. Abraham, I believe, was a very lonely man. We are told that he spent a lifetime living in tents, but the writer of Hebrews said, 'For he was looking forward to the city with foundations, whose architect and builder is God' (Hebrews 11:10). Abraham, the great man of faith, was a lonely man, but he was on his way to a better place. There will be no loneliness in heaven. So don't look at your heavenly Father and shake your fist, but rather say, 'Lord, you know me. You know what I need and I accept that you know what I need.' Jim Bakker was unfairly put in prison. He has since been vindicated, but do you know what Jim Bakker now says? 'I deserved to go to prison for other things, not for the things that they got me on.' He said, 'God put me there, God did it, God meant it for good!' And if you can look at loneliness like that, though it's not fun, you can recognise that the Lord knows what you are like, and what you need.

Is there a victory in loneliness? I don't say victory over it, but victory in it. Yes! You become aware of the presence of Jesus. I repeat, he wants you to himself. He loves your company, but are you giving it to him? He wants to be real to us. But he wants us to want it so much that we will take advantage of the enforced solitude and just be with him. I do not say that it totally takes the place of friends, but his presence compensates. You get to talk to him as a friend. Abraham was God's friend (James 2:23). Moses talked to the Lord face to face as a man talked to his friend (Exodus 34:11). Your victory is that you feel his presence, you become more like him. After all, Jesus walked alone. He forgave everybody, there was not a trace of bitterness in him, he never gave in to self-pity.

The Thorn in the Flesh

'Bring the whole tithe into the storehouse, that there may be food in my house. Test me in this,' says the LORD Almighty, 'and see if I will not throw open the floodgates of heaven and pour out so much blessing that you will not have room enough for it.'

Malachi 3:10

Perhaps you will know that the Bible makes no attempt to prove God. This may seem a little strange to some at first. Surely, one may want to say, since the Bible is God's own book and God's own word, he would prompt at least one of the writers of the sixty-six books to prove to the reader that he exists! But he never does. 'The greatest liberty is having nothing to prove,' says my friend Pete Cantrell, and God is totally free in himself. He has no need to prove himself to the most sceptical person.

The nearest he ever comes to proving himself, however, is in Malachi 3:10. And the way it is done is by giving him what is due to him (10 per cent of our income). It is our duty. And yet he promises to bless the tither so much he or she can hardly contain it. And it is true!

My point is this. In the same way that we cannot out-give the Lord so also can we never out-thank the Lord! He blesses us more than ever! This is why I say that thanking God, as with giving to him, can almost become a selfish thing.

Thanking God

No, I beat my body and make it my slave so that after I have preached to others, I myself will not be disqualified for the prize.

1 Corinthians 9:27

The older I get, the faster times flies; the older I get, the more I cry out to God, 'Let me end well.'

The Apostle Paul ended well. He said so in what was almost certainly his last epistle, when he wrote to Timothy: '. . . I have finished the race, I have kept the faith. Now there is in store for me the crown of righteousness, which the Lord, the righteous Judge, will *award* to me on that day' (2 Timothy 4:7–8). Paul did not have such confidence early on; his letter to the Corinthians, quoted above, was written around AD 50. But some fifteen years later he could say to Timothy, just before he was beheaded in Rome, that he would receive the crown he aspired to. He was not worried about whether he was saved when he wrote those words in 1 Corinthians 9:27; he was very concerned that he not be rejected for the prize – a reward that is on offer in addition to salvation.

As we will see, rewards will be handed out at the Judgment Seat of Christ. I have heard people say, 'I don't care about getting a reward after I die, I just want to make it to heaven.' I don't mean to be unfair, but I have never thought a comment like this reflected a very deep spirituality. It sometimes even smacks of false modesty, as in the old song I heard as I grew up, 'Lord, build me just a cabin in the corner of glory land' – as if one did not want a spectacular mansion, only a cabin! The truth is, although I don't know precisely what a reward in heaven entails (other than God saying 'Well done'), I know it was of deep concern to Paul, who wanted it almost more than anything – and who could say in the end that he *got* it.

Second Chance

*If what he has built survives, he will receive his reward. If it is
burned up, he will suffer loss; he himself will be saved, but only as
one escaping through the flames.*

1 Corinthians 3:14–15

I find it so interesting that the same Apostle Paul who spent much of
his life stressing justification by faith alone and salvation by sheer
grace also had the most to say about a 'reward' at the Judgment Seat
of Christ! That is why Paul said, 'I beat *my body* and make it my
slave.' Why? Not because he thought he had to do that to make it to
heaven. After all, salvation is by grace, not works (Ephesians 2:8–9).
Paul's fear was not missing out on heaven, but being rejected for the
'prize'. In other words, he was not talking about whether he would or
would not get to heaven; he was speaking about something *in addition* to going to heaven – or, you could say, *in advance* of getting to
heaven: a reward at the Judgment Seat of Christ on the Last Day.

The word 'prize' (Greek: *brabion* – used also in Philippians 3:14)
is used interchangeably with 'crown' (Greek: *stephanos* – used eighteen
times in the New Testament) and 'reward' (Greek: *misthos* – used
twenty-nine times), and often with 'inheritance' as well (Greek:
kleronomia – used at least seventeen times to mean 'reward', as in
Colossians 3:24).

One of the clearest but most neglected teachings in the New
Testament is the distinction between salvation and *reward*. All who
rest on the foundation, namely, Jesus Christ (1 Corinthians 3:11), will
be saved. They are assured of heaven. That is *given* to us – it is a free
gift (Romans 6:23). But not all who are saved will receive a *reward*
(see above).

It was the *reward*, then, that Paul was after. He could not bear the
thought of seeing others get a reward, but finding himself being rejected
for this reward, crown or prize. But he knew that this was possible,
and he dreaded the shame of being openly rejected for this prize more
than anything.

Second Chance

10 June

If you, O LORD, kept a record of sins,
O Lord, who could stand?
But with you there is forgiveness;
therefore you are feared.

Psalm 130:3–4

God never approved of our sin; he hates sin. Jesus forgave the adulterous woman, but he did not approve of what she did. He told her, 'Leave your life of sin' (John 8:11). God was angry with our first parents, Adam and Eve, but made garments of skin for them and clothed them (Genesis 3:21). This immediately showed that he had forgiven them. The garments of skin meant the sacrifice of blood that pointed towards the Redeemer who was to come. So God did not approve of what they did – or approve of our sin today.

So too with us. Forgiving people does not mean approval of their evil. We forgive what we don't approve of because that is the way God is with each of us.

Total Forgiveness

'In accordance with your great love, forgive the sin of these people, just as you have pardoned them from the time they left Egypt until now.'

Numbers 14:19

Forgiving someone does not mean excusing what they did. We do not cover up for them. We do not point to circumstances that explain away their behaviour. It is true that 'every person is worth understanding', as Dr Clyde Narramore says, but that does not excuse them.

Moses was offered a 'new deal'. God said to him – in so many words – 'You have a sorry lot of people to lead, and they aren't following you very well. They have been stubborn and unteachable. I am going to wipe them off the face of the earth and start all over again – with a new nation' (see Numbers 14:11–12). But Moses rejected the offer; he interceded for them. However, he did not excuse their behaviour, but instead appealed to God's mercy. And God forgave them.

To justify means to make right or just. The *Oxford Dictionary* says it means 'to show (a person or statement or act, etc.) to be right or just or reasonable'. There is no way that evil can be justified; God never justified evil and does not require us to do so.

In the above incident regarding Moses and the Israelites, Moses did not offer a hint of justification for their behaviour. Instead he pointed out to God that the Egyptians would not think very highly of God's power or name if they were obliterated. Therefore when we are required to forgive we are not required to make what is wrong look right.

Total Forgiveness

12 June

*All this is from God, who reconciled us to himself through Christ
and gave us the ministry of reconciliation: that God was reconciling
the world to himself in Christ, not counting men's sins against
them. And he has committed to us the message of reconciliation.*

2 Corinthians 5:18–19

Forgiveness and reconciliation are not always the same. Reconciliation takes two people, and the person you forgive may not want to see you. They may even be dead. Moreover, you may not want to be the best friend of the person you forgive.

Reconciliation means a restoration of friendship after a quarrel. When a husband and wife totally forgive each other it will usually mean a reconciliation – but not always. The bitterness and the desire to punish may be gone, but the wish to have things as they were may not necessarily be so strong. If one's spouse is unfaithful and sleeps with one's best friend, that friendship will probably never be the same again, although the bitterness and desire for revenge need to go. An injured person can forgive an offender without reconciliation. It is wonderful indeed should reconciliation follow, but this must not be pressed in some cases. Some things can never be the same again. It takes two to reconcile, a total willingness on both parts.

God was in Christ, reconciling the world to himself (2 Corinthians 5:19). But we still implore people on Christ's behalf: 'Be reconciled to God' (2 Corinthians 5:20). Why? The reconciliation doesn't really exist unless both parties agree.

Total Forgiveness

Love . . . is not rude, it is not self-seeking, it is not easily angered, it keeps no record of wrongs.

1 Corinthians 13:5

Wilful blindness is slightly different from repression. Blindness is a conscious choice to pretend; repression is usually unconscious and involuntary.

Both are wrong and can be psychologically damaging, because when we play games with ourselves like this, though the motive may be to forgive, we delay coming to terms with our responsibility. In some cases the same person who meant to forgive explodes one day – all because they were not being true to themselves – and everybody is shocked. It is not total forgiveness until you admit to *seeing* what they did – and *then* you set them free.

Paul said that love keeps no record of wrongs, but he did not mean that you are blind to those wrongs. Some think that a way of forgiving is to pretend that no wrong is there. The Greek word *logizetai* means to 'reckon' or 'impute'. It means essentially that 'love does not store a wrong', – that is, the wrong doesn't go into our 'mental computer' to be reckoned with later on. We would say today: love doesn't allow a wrong to be computed. But that there *is* wrong staring you in the face is not to be denied. In fact, the Greek word translated 'wrong' is *kakon*: evil. The wrong – the evil – is acknowledged; we are not blind to it; we are not required to pretend it didn't happen. This is not what total forgiveness means.

Love is never blind to the hurt. If the person who hurt us is an authority figure or, let us say, known to be very 'godly', we say to ourselves, 'I didn't see this. I didn't hear this. This could not have happened; therefore it didn't.' The truth is, sometimes the people we admire most can be very mean and do hurtful things. It is of no value to pretend that we didn't see.

Total Forgiveness

14 June

For I will forgive their wickedness and will remember their sins no more.

Hebrews 8:12

When someone says we must 'forgive and forget' I understand what they mean. But literally to forget may not be realistic; it might even be impossible. We may, owing to a deep trauma, temporarily forget things. But the only way back to sanity is to try to remember everything – in detail.

Love doesn't erase our memories. Furthermore, it is a demonstration of great grace when we are fully aware of what they did – and still choose to forgive totally. Deep hurts may not be eradicated as though they never happened. The truth is, they *did* happen. We cannot easily forget them. We certainly must not dwell on them but we cannot always forget them.

Even God doesn't literally forget our sins: he *chooses* to overlook them. He knows full well what we have done and what he has forgiven us of – every sordid detail. But he chooses not to remember, so that he doesn't hold them against us. That is precisely what *we* are to do, choosing not to remember while maybe not forgetting.

Total Forgiveness

Remember this: Whoever sows sparingly will also reap sparingly, and whoever sows generously will also reap generously. Each man should give what he has decided in his heart to give, not reluctantly or under compulsion, for God loves a cheerful giver. And God is able to make all grace abound to you, so that in all things at all times, having all that you need, you will abound in every good work.

2 Corinthians 9:6–8

Most Christians don't tithe simply because they have not been taught to do so. When they are taught they are usually grateful for the 'discovery' and most keep it up. My dad was a tither. He was never wealthy, to put it mildly, but he tithed even in the hardest times. When he earned eight dollars a day he made sure that eighty cents went to his church. So I was taught it as a boy. I have learned that if people are gently taught they will take this on board with cheerfulness.

A few people, however, do not tithe for 'theological' reasons. They reckon that tithing is going back to the Law. Wrong. It is going back to Abraham who, as far as we know, was the first tither. He was the Old Testament example of justification by faith (Genesis 15:6) and also the example of a tither (Genesis 14:20). The Law came in 430 years *after* Abraham. The Law was a 1,300-year parenthesis during which people were motivated by fear of punishment (Genesis 3:17–19). The Law enforced what Abraham did voluntarily. We are not under a legal mandate to tithe but nonetheless are told to give cheerfully.

In 2 Corinthians 9:6–8, Paul wants us to know we cannot outgive the Lord.

But giving 10 per cent of our income to the 'storehouse' (Malachi 3:8–10), which I take to be one's local church, must be taught and continually encouraged. For we all could easily spend the money elsewhere. It is true that God has no needs (Psalm 50:10) and yet he invites us to join with him in using our material possession to extend his kingdom. There is the incredible idea in Scripture of 'lending to the Lord'. We may well have many regrets when we stand before the Lord at the Judgment Seat of Christ, but not one of us will regret a single penny given to the Lord – for it is the only money we keep!

In Pursuit of His Glory

16 June

Consider it pure joy, my brothers, whenever you face trials of many kinds, because you know that the testing of your faith develops perseverance.

James 1:2–3

It is not every day that I can remember where I was when 'the penny dropped' with regard to understanding a particular verse in the Bible, but I do when it comes to James 1:2. It came not at the end of a forty-day fast or an all-night prayer meeting. It was when I came to myself after losing my temper in a pizza shop in Kissimmee, Florida, in the summer of 1979. I had *so* looked forward to a pizza in this particular place and regarded such as a measure of compensation for having to return to Disney World a second year in a row. But when the time came, everything went wrong: as a result of driving rain, my pizzas fell out of a wet paper bag into a puddle of water, and now I had to face the same manager of the pizza shop – to which I returned – after telling him off for taking forty-five minutes in the first place. 'How could all this happen?' I asked myself.

But James 1:2 had already been on my mind for weeks since I had planned to start preaching on the little book of James at Westminster Chapel in the autumn. As I drove back to the pizza shop that evening, I said to myself, 'Either James 1:2 is true or it isn't, and if I plan to preach on it shortly I had better begin practising what I preach.'

Jesus taught us that they who are faithful in that which is least – or in little things – are the ones who will be faithful in much – bigger things (Luke 16:10). That is why that pizza story is so important to me. I decided then and there to *dignify* that situation by accepting the entire matter as something God sent. It was a divine set-up. I not only repented to the Lord, but thanked him for the whole thing. I apologised to the manager and cheerfully waited for another pizza (for some reason, he wouldn't let me pay) and returned to my family at the motel a different person.

Pure Joy

Consider it pure joy, my brothers, whenever you face trials of many kinds, because you know that the testing of your faith develops perseverance.

James 1:2–3

Who enjoys the feeling of disgrace? It would, after all, be abnormal to enjoy this. Unless, that is, one had a definite reason for feeling this way. Moses did. He considered disgrace as more valuable than earthly luxury – all because it put him in good stead for the future. Jesus endured the cross because of the joy set before him (Hebrews 12:2). The Apostle Paul used *heegeomai* when he referred to the 'pluses' of his background – being circumcised the eighth day, being of the stock of Israel and of the tribe of Benjamin, being a Pharisee, and faultless as to legalistic righteousness. He *considered* these things not pluses, but minuses – all because of the dazzling privilege of knowing Jesus. That is simply the way he regarded those things that most people would love (Philippians 3:5–8).

This is what James wants us to do when we face trials of many kinds: consider them pure joy. It doesn't make sense! And yet it does! He tells us to consider trials as pure joy because of what they do for us *if* we believe and apply these words. It will be seen to make very good sense indeed. James wants us to see it now – by faith. Moses did what he did – regarding disgrace for the sake of Jesus of inestimable value – by faith; and he was never sorry he made that choice. Neither will any of us be.

Pure Joy

'How can you believe if you accept praise from one another, yet make no effort to obtain the praise that comes from the only God?'
John 5:44

Imagine a congregation of 100 people. Suppose we could hear each person's story of hardship. Some of those stories might relate to a deep hurt – of a misdeed or injustice done to them; some might have lost a fortune; some have been lied about; some have suffered physically, or mentally; some cry out for vindication. Let us say we all vote on the 'top ten' – those who in our estimation suffered the most out of the 100 people present. Let us then say we narrow the list down to three. Finally, we pick the person we believe has suffered the most out of the 100 present. Now imagine that you were in that congregation and not only got short-listed, but were voted to be the person in the congregation who, by all accounts, had suffered more than anyone else in that room.

How would you feel? What do you suppose you would say? Perhaps you would say, 'See, I told you I had suffered more than anybody else.' And suppose we all agreed, that you have suffered more than anybody we have ever met? What would you expect then? Would you want us to gather around you and say, 'We are very sorry for you. We had no idea how much you have suffered. I don't know how you managed'? Is that what you would want? Would you feel somewhat compensated so you could say to us, 'I told you how much I have suffered'? What would this do for you? Would you be any better off? You may say, 'At least I would feel better, that all those people around me realised how much I have suffered.' I can appreciate that. But are you *really* better off? The truth is, it does feel good when others are sympathetic – but only to a degree. Suppose someone says 'Congratulations!' But the danger is that we could become insatiable in wanting people to know what we have gone through. If all we want is for *people* to know, *that* is all the 'reward' we will get. But if we get our joy from knowing *God* knows, we qualify for the honour that only he can bring.

Pure Joy

And they were calling to one another: 'Holy, holy, holy is the LORD Almighty; the whole earth is full of his glory.'

Isaiah 6:3

Angels talk to one another about God, and their conversation reveals great wonder and reverence. Never let us be flippant or familiar when we talk of God or to God. If we are superficial or off-hand, we reveal merely how far we are from God and true worship.

I wish with all my heart that Christians would talk to one another about God. We talk about the weather, about sports, about our work, about television programmes, about other people and what is happening to them, yet how strangely silent we are about God, even after the church services! Surely this is one of the greatest of all indications that our lives are empty of God, and we know nothing of true worship? 'Out of the abundance of the heart the mouth speaketh,' said Jesus (Matthew 12:35). And if our mouths are silent about God in our day-to-day conversation, what does that say about our hearts?

Worshipping God

20 June

Be prepared in season and out of season.

2 Timothy 4:2

Many years ago I felt somewhat prompted to arise at a certain hour to pray. I said, 'Lord, if you really want me to get up at this hour, you wake me up. That way I will know you really want me to do it.' I can tell you that the very next morning I found myself wide awake. My first reaction was to try to go back to sleep. I looked at my watch. It was dead on the exact hour I had asked to be awakened. As a matter of fact it was the time that made me remember that I had asked the Lord to wake me up at that hour! I was actually surprised. So I got up and spent the time in prayer. On the same evening as I was getting ready to go to bed I prayed, 'Lord, do it again. Wake me up at the same hour.' I can tell you, I slept past that hour by two hours! I tried for several successive nights to get the Lord (rather than the alarm clock) to wake me up, but it never happened again. I now use a good alarm clock. Always.

Spontaneity is often the way God begins something which he wants to continue. But if it is right, then it is worth doing regularly and with effort. If I waited until I felt 'led' to pray, I doubt I'd pray very much. 'Every time I feel the Spirit moving in my heart I'll pray,' says the old spiritual. But it isn't spiritual people who adopt that line of thinking. We should do something because it has a valid biblical precedent, not because we are given the 'luxury' of spontaneity to do the same thing. If it is right to do when there is 'much' (power, spontaneity and effort-lessness), then it is right to do when there is 'least' (struggle, effort and self-control).

Stand Up and Be Counted

*If you do away with the yoke of oppression, with the pointing
finger and malicious talk, and if you spend yourselves on behalf of
the hungry and satisfy the needs of the oppressed, then your light
will rise in the darkness, and your night will become like the
noonday.*

Isaiah 58:9–10

A husband may say to his wife in a moment of anger, 'I'll remember that.' And he does! She may say to him, 'I can never forget this.' And she doesn't! So many marriages could be healed overnight if *both* parties would stop pointing the finger. Pointing the finger, a common problem in human history, shows that one has kept a record of wrongs.

Love is a choice. Total forgiveness is a choice. It is not a feeling – at first – but an act of the will. It is the choice to tear up the record of wrong. As we observed above, we clearly see the evil that was done, but we erase it – or destroy the record – before it becomes lodged in the heart. This way, resentment does not have a chance to grow. But when we say, 'I'll remember that', when we have been hurt or maligned, we fertilise the soil then and there for an abiding resentment. When we develop a lifestyle of total forgiveness we learn to erase the wrong rather than file it away in our mental computer. When we do this all the time – that's what I call a lifestyle – we not only avoid bitterness, but experience total forgiveness as a feeling. It is not initially a feeling; it is a painful choice at first. But *later* we feel it – and it is a good feeling.

Total Forgiveness

There is no fear in love. But perfect love drives out fear, because fear has to do with punishment. The one who fears is not made perfect in love.

1 John 4:18

Our refusal to punish is the essence of total forgiveness. It is when we give up the natural desire to see them 'get what's coming to them'. By nature we cannot bear the thought that they have got away with what they have done; it seems so unfair. Therefore we want vengeance – namely, their just punishment. The fear that they won't get punished is the opposite of perfect love.

When perfect love – the love of Jesus and the fruit of the Holy Spirit – enters, the desire for our enemy to be punished leaves. When the desire for one to be punished gains entrance, the anointing of the Spirit subsides.

Therefore total forgiveness is refusing to punish. It is refusing to cave into the fear that this person or those people won't get their 'come-uppance' – the punishment or rebuke we think they deserve.

I have long been intrigued by the phrase in the New International Version that fear 'has to do with punishment' (1 John 4:18). This means many things, but partly it means our fear that God won't step in and give 'them' their just deserts. But if one gives into this fear we will be trespassing on God's territory, and he doesn't like that. Vindication is God's prerogative and God's prerogative alone. Deuteronomy 32:35 – 'It is mine to avenge; I will repay' – is quoted twice in the New Testament (Romans 12:19; Hebrews 10:30). Vindication is what God does best. He doesn't want our help. So when we refuse to punish – and God likes that – it sets him free to decide what should be done. But if we manoeuvre our way into his expertise he may well let us do it, but neither divine vengeance nor true justice will be carried out – only our personal grudge.

It is therefore important that we examine ourselves in this area. We must ask ourselves, how much in what I am about to say or do is but an attempt to punish? If it is, we grieve the Holy Spirit however much right may be on our side.

Total Forgiveness

'Blessed are the merciful, for they will be shown mercy.'

Matthew 5:7

There is a sense in which the Bible basically says two things about God: (1) that he is merciful, and (2) that he is just. The heart of the gospel is related to these two characteristics of God. The greatest question we can ask when it comes to the gospel of Christ is: how can God be just and merciful at the same time? By merciful, it means that God does not want to punish us; by just, it means he must punish us because we have sinned against him. So how can he be both simultaneously? Answer: he sent his Son Jesus Christ – the God-man – who died on a cross for us. 'We all, like sheep, have gone astray, each of us has turned to his own way; and the Lord has laid on him the iniquity of us all' (Isaiah 53:6). Because God punished Jesus for what we did, he can now be true to himself and still be truly merciful to us. That is the heart of the gospel.

But when we are told to be godly – which means being like God – it does not follow that we can be like him in every sense. After all, God is omnipotent (all-powerful) and we are not commanded to be that. He is omnipresent (present everywhere) and we can never be that. So too when it comes to carrying out punishment, *this belongs to God alone*, as we must continually emphasise, and never, never underestimate.

When it comes to being merciful, this is our Lord's command: 'Be merciful, just as your Father is merciful' (Luke 6:36). In the Greek language this is the opposite of wrath or justice. Being merciful is not giving justice, but the opposite. One difference between grace and mercy is that grace is getting what we *don't* deserve (favour) and mercy is not getting what we *do* deserve (justice). So when we show mercy we are withholding justice from those who have injured us. That is godliness.

Total Forgiveness

'For out of the overflow of the heart the mouth speaks.'

Matthew 12:34

Total forgiveness must take place in the heart for otherwise it is worthless. If we have not truly forgiven, in our hearts, those who have hurt us, then it will come out – sooner or later. But if forgiveness has indeed taken place in the heart, our words will show it. When there is bitterness, it will eventually manifest; when there is love, 'there is nothing in him to make him stumble' (1 John 2:10), even in our words.

It is for this reason that reconciliation is not always essential to total forgiveness. If it takes place in the heart, one does not need to know whether one's enemy will reconcile. If I have forgiven him or her in my heart of hearts, and he doesn't want to speak to me, I can still have the inner victory. It is true that it is far easier to forgive when we know that those who maligned or betrayed us are sorry; but if I must have this before I can forgive, I may never ever have a victory.

If someone tells me that I am not required to forgive unless the other person repents first and says, 'I'm sorry', then I answer: Jesus' example on the cross is good enough for me. 'Jesus said, "Father, forgive them, for they do not know what they are doing." And they divided up his clothes by casting lots' (Luke 23:34). If he had waited until they felt any guilt or shame for their words and actions, then Jesus would never have forgiven them.

Total Forgiveness

And we know that all things work together for good to them that
love God, to them who are the called according to his purpose.

Romans 8:28 (AV)

Only a fool would claim to know the full answer to the question 'Why does God allow evil and suffering to continue when he has the power to stop it?' But there is a partial answer: namely, in order that we may believe. There would be no need for faith if we knew the answer concerning the origin of evil and the reason for suffering. I only know it is what makes faith possible.

God does turn evil into good. He causes things to work together for good. God did not send his Son into the world to explain evil, but rather to save us and to exemplify suffering. Jesus who was, and is, the God-man suffered as no one else has. One day God will clear his name from the charge of being unjust. In the meantime, we need to trust him and take him at his word that he is just and merciful.

As for all the unhappy things he has allowed to happen to me, I affirm his justice. He is God. He knows exactly what he is doing and why; he knows why he allows things to take place that he could have stopped.

For those who struggle with God's right to allow evil – and we have all done this – there still must be a genuine forgiveness on our part, for any bitterness grieves the Spirit. We therefore must forgive him – but not because he is guilty, but for allowing evil to touch our lives. But if we will lower our voices and patiently wait for God's purposes to be fulfilled, then one day – and this is a guarantee – we will say that he has done all things well, even in what he permitted. He was never guilty in the first place, but because he sometimes appears to us to have been unfair, we must set him free before we can effectively move on in our lives.

Total Forgiveness

But a man who commits adultery lacks judgment;
whoever does so destroys himself.

Proverbs 6:32

It may surprise you how closely wisdom and understanding are connected to sexual purity. You see it again and again in the book of Proverbs. Early on in this amazing book of Scripture we learn that 'the fear of the Lord is the beginning of knowledge, but fools despise wisdom and discipline' (Proverbs 1:7). Wisdom is what saves one 'from the adulteress, from the wayward wife with her seductive words' (Proverbs 2:16). 'How long will you simple ones love your simple ways? How long will mockers delight in mockery and fools hate knowledge? If you had responded to my rebuke, I would have poured out my heart to you and made my thoughts known to you. But since you rejected me when I called and no-one gave heed when I stretched out my hand, since you ignored all my advice and would not accept my rebuke, I in turn will laugh at your disaster; I will mock when calamity overtakes you – when calamity overtakes you like a storm, when disaster sweeps over you like a whirlwind, and when distress and trouble overwhelm you' (Proverbs 1:22–27). (See also Proverbs 5:1–14, 20–23; 7:1–27.)

Consider how these proverbs repeat themselves: 'Say to wisdom, "You are my sister," and call understanding your kinsman; they will keep you from the adulteress, from the wayward wife with her seductive words' (Proverbs 7:4–5).

What I have quoted in the previous paragraph can be summed up as this: if a person has rejected the fear of the Lord – which is the beginning of wisdom and understanding – his or her fall as a result of sexual temptation cannot be a surprise. It would have been only a matter of time. Furthermore, falling into sexual sin is not only foolish; it causes one to forfeit the promise of a greater understanding. Speaking personally, I *live* for understanding, wisdom and insight. One of my greatest fears is that I might accept doctrinal error. Falling into sexual sin removes my hope that God will give me insight from his Word.

Second Chance

Jonah obeyed the word of the LORD *and went to Nineveh.*

Jonah 3:3

God said to Jonah, 'Go to the great city of Nineveh and preach against it, because its wickedness has come up before me' (Jonah 1:2). That is what he had to do. He said, 'Oh no! I'm not going to do that!' God said, 'Really?' So while Jonah was on a Mediterranean cruise, God sent the wind. The only choice of the mariners was to throw him overboard. Then God sent the fish. The same Jonah who prayed he wouldn't have to go, now prayed, 'Oh God, please let me go!' It's amazing how God can get your attention. The very thing you said no to, you end up praying for! God said OK: 'Then the word of the LORD came to Jonah for a second time: "Go to the great city of Nineveh and proclaim to it the message I give you"' (Jonah 3:1–2). He was given a message he hadn't wanted to deliver: 'In forty days Nineveh will be overthrown.' God may give you a word you have to preach. It's not what you wanted to preach, but you do it because he tells you to. It hurts when things don't go according to our plans.

There is great potential in an unwanted calling. It refers to what you are capable of becoming. God sees what you are capable of being and saying. If you got to do only what you wanted to do, you wouldn't ever know your capability in another area. Your potential is what God sees, but you can't. God can see potential in you which you can't see, so he leads you in a way which – at first – doesn't seem to make any sense.

The Thorn in the Flesh

For I am already being poured out like a drink offering, and the time has come for my departure. I have fought the good fight, I have finished the race, I have kept the faith. Now there is in store for me the crown of righteousness, which the Lord, the righteous Judge, will award to me on that day – and not only to me, but also to all who have longed for his appearing.

2 Timothy 4:6–8

Everything that has happened to us – whether it be an unwanted calling, living where we have to live, working with the people we have to work with, having to study the thing and having a career doing the opposite – is because God wants us to know his Son. The potential that you have for intimacy with God would never be discovered if you got to do what you wanted to do. If you had the success you wanted, you wouldn't be teachable. You can always tell a successful man, but you can't tell him much. God knows where to keep us. So when we get to the place where we say, 'I just want to know him,' God says, 'Good.'

But there is another purpose, and it is this: that we might have a reward at the Judgment Seat of Christ. It was so important to Paul: 'I beat my body and make it my slave so that after I have preached to others, I myself will not be disqualified for the prize' (1 Corinthians 9:24–27).

In a word, the thorn of an unwanted calling is the best thing that could have happened to any of us. We all need a thorn to save us from ourselves, and Paul could say at the end of the day, 'It's worth it all!' Or, as Joseph put it, 'God meant it for good.'

The Thorn in the Flesh

The man said, 'The woman you put here with me – she gave me some fruit from the tree, and I ate it.'

Genesis 3:12

The first conversation God had with Adam after the Fall in the Garden of Eden finds Adam blaming not himself but his wife Eve for his partaking of the forbidden fruit. But if you look closely at these words you will see that Adam was actually pointing the finger at God himself. 'The woman *you* put here with me.' This was a dead giveaway that depravity had taken hold in Adam's heart. Corruption and vileness of the human heart has been with every man, every woman, every child – of all races, cultures and colours – ever since. Instinctively we do not see our own sin but that of others. We want to blame God, then others – but never ourselves if we can help it.

One of the irrefutable proofs that we are sinners is that we want to defend ourselves, shift the blame to someone else and avoid as long as possible the matter of admitting to our guilt. Essential to our natural depravity is self-righteousness. We were born with it. We did not need to attend Harvard or Oxford to learn how to be self-righteous. It is the most natural inclination in the world! It is intrinsic to our nature.

Adam revealed that sin had set in already when God came looking for him in the Garden of Eden, asking 'Where are you?' (Genesis 3:9). Adam did not want to face God and own his own guilt. Trying to shift the blame when it is our own fault is evidence of our sin of self-righteousness. Pointing the finger also shows we have lost control of the tongue.

Your Words Have Power

'Again, you have heard that it was said to the people long ago, "Do not break your oath, but keep the oaths you have made to the Lord." But I tell you, Do not swear at all: either by heaven, for it is God's throne; or by the earth, for it is his footstool; or by Jerusalem, for it is the city of the Great King. And do not swear by your head, for you cannot make even one hair white or black. Simply let your "Yes" be "Yes", and your "No", "No"; anything beyond this comes from the evil one.'

Matthew 5:33–37

From a letter to Rabbi David Rosen, former Chief Rabbi of Ireland:

I have long suspected that many Christians have not grasped the meaning of Jesus' interpretation of the Third Commandment (Matthew 5:33–37). Many of us can only think of this command as being a prohibition against cursing by using God's name when they are angry. Of course God is against that. But the truth is, Jesus spoke against using God's name for the purpose of promoting one's personal interest – for any reason. Whereas Jesus was not speaking against swearing an oath in a court of law (as some surmise), he warned against misusing God's name by swearing: if I were to say, for example, 'I call heaven and earth to witness that God is on my side,' or 'I swear to you in the name of God that he has told me my eschatology is infallible,' I have abused his name. It is the worst kind of 'name-dropping'. But most Christians have not grasped this; they only think they are free of abusing the Third Commandment as long as they don't say things like 'Oh my God'. That is only a small part of abusing his name. So if I am understanding what you say about some of your people – who supposedly feel they are doing their duty in fulfilling the Third Commandment by the way they spell God [i.e. G-d] – so too are there Christians who have their own way of feeling they are not violating the Third Commandment (when in fact they are).

The Christian and the Pharisee

July

Let us therefore make every effort to do what leads to peace and to mutual edification.

Romans 14:19

A few years ago I came up with an acrostic – P. E.A.C.E. – which has been helpful for me. Generally speaking, this has served me well. It is a *general* way of knowing God's will and whether or not we have truly heard God's voice. I put the following questions:

P – is it providential? If God gives a word, it will cohere with his providence. In other words, does God open the door or do we have to knock it down? If I have to pry a door open it is a fairly good hint I am in the flesh.

E – the enemy: what would he want you to do? When we are given an impression, impulse or feeling that we think could be of God, we should ask, 'What do we suppose the devil would want us to do?' In other words, most of us have a fairly shrewd idea what the devil *hopes* we will do with a certain feeling. *Do the opposite* and you will be right most of the time.

A – authority: the Bible. What does God's word say? The Holy Spirit will never, never, never lead us to do anything contrary to God's revealed will – the Bible.

C – confidence. Does the impression you have received increase or diminish your confidence? Be honest here. Does the thought of obeying this 'word' increase your confidence? If so, that is a good sign. If you lose confidence, it is a bad sign.

E – ease: what you feel in your heart of hearts. It is when you are being true to yourself. Conscience. What you feel deep down inside when you are being true to yourself. God will never lead you to be untrue to yourself. He will never lead you in such a way that you violate your conscience.

If all five fit it is a good sign – not an infallible sign, since it is but a general hint – that you are not being deceived.

The Anointing

Since ancient times no-one has heard, no ear has perceived, no eye has seen any God besides you, who acts on behalf of those who wait for him.

Isaiah 64:4

One of the difficulties we all of us have to overcome concerns the way God appears to bless people who (apparently) don't desire to be blessed and withhold blessing (apparently) from those who deserve it. Perhaps you know someone who is flourishing at the moment. He (or she) is prospering in health, in finances, in job and career, getting all the openings, while you who are struggling to make ends meet are also trying to please the Lord in all your ways. What adds to the pain is that the person who is prospering does not seem to care one whit about doing things God's way.

This is nothing new. The psalmist counselled, 'Do not fret because of evil men nor be envious of those who do wrong; for like the grass they will soon wither, like green plants they will soon die away' (Psalm 37:1–2). The psalmist acknowledged that this sort of problem had almost got the best of him. '. . . my feet had almost slipped; I had nearly lost my foothold. For I envied the arrogant when I saw the prosperity of the wicked' (Psalm 73:2–3). But he went on to say that he entered God's sanctuary; 'then I understood their final destiny' (Psalm 73:17).

My favourite verse in the Bible is Romans 8:28 (AV): 'And we know that all things work together for good to them that love God, to them who are called according to *his* purpose.' This is a promise that does not apply to everybody. It is a promise to those who love God and who are called according to his purpose. Rather than envy the arrogant who prosper we should feel sorry for them. Their end is bleak. Very bleak indeed. For those who are constrained to *wait* on God will be found the promise of blessing.

Does Jesus Care?

But eagerly desire the greater gifts.

1 Corinthians 12:31

A. W. Tozer used to say that we could have as much of God as we want. When I first came across this comment I disagreed. But I know now what he meant. We do not prove how much we want of God merely by the intense desire at the moment. We prove it by how we react to circumstances in life, and the opportunities given to us to do such things dignify the trials he hands to us on our silver platter.

When we are content with the anointing God chose for us, we do what we are called to do without fatigue. 'I can do everything through him who gives me strength' (Philippians 4:13). When I become mentally and emotionally fatigued in what I am doing, it is a fairly strong hint that I have chosen to move outside my anointing and what God specifically asked me to do. As long as I do *what* he called me to do and *no more*, I will not be edging towards burn-out.

And yet I would like to have more anointing than I have! This is a legitimate desire because Paul told us to desire earnestly the greater gifts. God will answer this request so long as it is sought with his glory in mind; he will answer the request if it is his will (1 John 5:14). God will consequently supply the need for this by granting the necessary anointing required for what I am called to do.

Pure Joy

As far as the east is from the west,
  so far has he removed our transgressions from us.

Psalm 103:12

Joseph was the hero of Egypt: the people were in awe of him. By interpreting Pharaoh's dreams he had saved the nation, but he knew that if word leaked out that his brothers had actually kidnapped him and sold him to the Ishmaelites, the people would hate his brothers. But Joseph wanted his brothers to be heroes in Egypt – just as he was. This was the only way to ensure that nobody in Egypt would ever discover their wickedness. He allowed no one present to eavesdrop this historic conversation when he was revealing his identity to those startled, frightened men. And not only did Joseph not let anybody know what they had done: he ensured that they *could* not know. That is one of the proofs that one has totally forgiven.

And that is precisely how you and I are forgiven. Our sins are 'wiped out' (Acts 3:19). It is as though our sins don't exist any more – they are gone, gone, gone, gone! As far as our eternal standing and security with God are concerned, they will never be held against us. Back in the hills of Kentucky we used to sing a chorus that says our sins are buried in the 'sea of God's forgetfulness'. This is based on Micah 7:19: 'You will again have compassion on us; you will tread our sins underfoot and hurl all our iniquities into the depths of the sea.'

This means that God will not reveal what he knows.

Total Forgiveness

Then Joseph said to his brothers, 'Come close to me.' When they had done so, he said, 'I am your brother Joseph, the one you sold into Egypt! And now, do not be distressed and do not be angry with yourselves for selling me here, because it was to save lives that God sent me ahead of you.'

Genesis 45:4–5

Joseph was wise, loving and fair. It made his brothers all the more respectful of him.

When I consider that our Lord Jesus Christ knows all about us but promises to keep what he has forgiven a carefully guarded secret, it makes me all the more indebted and thankful to him. Not that Joseph was doing it for that reason; he only wanted to set his brothers free and give them a wonderful future. But it no doubt endeared them to him all the more. The same brothers (other than Benjamin) had been so nervous and scared up until then. But Joseph convinced and won them over, for it says, 'Afterward his brothers talked with him' (Genesis 45:15).

Many of us have one single greatest fear of a certain thing being revealed. I know I do. I know what I would fear the most – were it to be told. But God has no desire for this; the only possibility of that occurring would be if I became self-righteous and unforgiving. (We will deal below with Matthew 6:14–15 in this respect.) In the meantime, I am indebted to a wonderful Saviour who forgives all and will ensure that my greatest secrets will not become known.

God does not blackmail us, and if a Christian is guilty of this, it gets God's attention. He won't stand for it. To hold another person in perpetual fear because I constantly threaten, 'I'll tell' – when I know what I myself have been forgiven of – would bring down God's wrath on me more quickly than anything. When I ponder for very long what I have been forgiven of, it is enough to shut my mouth for the rest of my life.

Total Forgiveness

When perfection comes, the imperfect disappears.

1 Corinthians 13:10

There is not one shred of biblical evidence that the gifts of the Spirit ceased in the early Church just because we now have the Bible, though this is the view of some godly people. With the deepest respect, I maintain that this is simply a theological cop-out by those who want to explain the absence of supernatural power in the Church today.

Those who hold this view support their argument with 1 Corinthians 13:10. But when Paul talks of 'perfection', he is not referring to the Bible, but to love. He has just said, 'Love never fails. But where there are prophecies, they will cease; where there are tongues, they will be stilled; where there is knowledge, it will pass away' (verse 8). And in verse 10 he is showing that the gifts of the Spirit may subside, but love goes on.

All the spiritual gifts described in 1 Corinthians 12:8–10 are available today should God be pleased to grant them. The attainment of a spiritual gift ought not to be any more unusual than the attainment of love. It is clearly our responsibility today to seek the gift of love – and it is equally our responsibility to seek the gifts of the Spirit. As we pray for revival which continues to tarry, so ought we to pray for the gifts of the Spirit. That we may not have them does not mean that we cannot have them, any more than the absence of revival proves that revival will never come.

Worshipping God

Since you are eager to have spiritual gifts, try to excel in gifts that build up the church.

1 Corinthians 14:12

When God gives a gift of the Spirit it is for two reasons. The first is for his glory. We must ask ourselves what our motive is for wanting a gift of the Spirit. What is our motive for wanting to see healings? It may be that we want to get a bit of glory for ourselves. In that case, God knows that we couldn't be trusted with these gifts. How dare we want to compete with God's glory! May we be brought to the place where we are so totally dedicated to his honour and glory that God can trust us with the unusual. The withholding of God's gifts suggests that our motives are wrong.

The second reason he gives a gift is for the edification of others: 'to build up the church.' God gives gifts so that we may be givers.

Worshipping God

And in the church God has appointed first of all apostles, second prophets, third teachers, then workers of miracles, also those having gifts of healing, those able to help others, those with gifts of administration, and those speaking in different kinds of tongues.

1 Corinthians 12:28

Do you know what may well be the greatest gift of the Spirit? It is described in 1 Corinthians 12. Most of us have heard of the gifts of knowledge, of faith, of miracles, of tongues. We have heard of the gift of the interpretation of tongues. But how many know about the gift of *helps*?

Someone may say, 'Help! I've only got the gift of helps!' Maybe your church needs cleaning and you are the one gifted to do it. Or somebody is needed to help in the kitchen. Stewards, musicians, typists, Sunday school helpers, people who go out witnessing, or help run meetings and organisations, consistent tithers – these people should be doing this work with the God-given gift of help. Some can only do one thing. Some can do three or four things without fatigue. The body will never be tired and no one will ever be overworked when we all do our part. If someone is the little toe and works well, that person will see that the body goes on without any pain.

A man may be praying for the gift of healing and be blind to the fact that he has a gift – to help make coffee. How sad for him that he doesn't see it. Maybe by ignoring this gift he is blocking the way for the gift of healing.

Worshipping God

If I speak in the tongues of men and of angels, but have not love, I am only a resounding gong or a clanging cymbal.

1 Corinthians 13:1

Do we want the gifts of the Spirit or have we changed our minds? Today there is an absence of the gifts of the Spirit in the Church, not because they ceased with the early Church, but because we all want short cuts. Paul says, 'Covet earnestly the best gifts,' and here is how to get them. We have forgotten 1 Corinthians 13, and that is why revival tarries, and there is so much that is phoney.

If a man or a woman came to know this kind of love which keeps no record of wrong, knows no bitterness, doesn't want to make another person envious, isn't proud, tolerates others, is gracious and kind and doesn't envy, it may be that he or she will wake up one day and find that God has entrusted him or her with a valuable gift that is more precious than the knowledge of a brain surgeon or the skill of the cleverest barrister in the city. Such a person may say, 'I can't believe it would happen to me.'

But God has done this because love bridges the gap between the sovereignty of God and the obtaining of the gifts. How dare we talk about the gifts and treat love with contempt! If this love were to flow among us, who knows what God might do?

Worshipping God

Then she called, 'Samson, the Philistines are upon you!' He awoke from his sleep and thought, 'I'll go out as before and shake myself free.' But he did not know that the LORD had left him.

Judges 16:20

Samson felt nothing when Delilah first shaved his head. He only discovered the loss of his strength when it was too late. 'Then the Philistines seized him, gouged out his eyes and took him down to Gaza. Binding him with bronze shackles, they set him to grinding in the prison' (Judges 16:21).

For all I know there may have been an unconscious diminishing of Samson's anointing during the time he foolishly allowed Delilah to keep probing him for his secret. 'With such nagging she prodded him day after day until he was tired to death' (Judges 16:16). What we do know is that when his head was shaved his strength utterly left him. The main thing, however, was that he lost the anointing and didn't know it. At first.

There have been servants of Christ – some with high profile – who apparently felt no loss of anointing at the time when they compromised themselves. Since they were used so powerfully – which they often took as proof of God's approval and of the anointing – they sometimes felt nothing when they gave in to sexual temptation. Billy Graham also says that it seems the devil gets 75 per cent of God's best servants through sexual temptation.

The account of Samson is an Old Testament example of what the Apostle Paul calls grieving the Spirit: 'And do not grieve the Holy Spirit of God, with whom you were sealed for the day of redemption' (Ephesians 4:30). When the Holy Spirit is grieved the anointing lifts. We usually feel nothing at the time. It is some time later we notice that we carried on by habit or the momentum of a natural gift. It means we can lose the special presence of God – what we should want most – and that is what happened to Samson. The lifting of the anointing was thus unconscious and painless.

The Sensitivity of the Spirit

Guard the good deposit that was entrusted to you – guard it with the help of the Holy Spirit who lives in us.

2 Timothy 1:14

I believe the Bible categorically affirms the sovereign grace of God in salvation. This means that we are chosen apart from works (2 Timothy 1:9), saved apart from works (Ephesians 2:8–9) and kept apart from works (Romans 8:28–39). We are loved with an everlasting love (Jeremiah 31:3). This means that there is nothing we can do to make God love us more and nothing we can do to cause him to love us less. In a word: we are secure and kept by the sheer grace of God.

But that is not all we need to know when it comes to living the Christian life and pleasing God. God puts us on our honour to guard the 'good deposit that was entrusted' to us. This is done 'with the help of the Holy Spirit who lives in us'. That deposit is the anointing, the special presence of God. This we can lose without forfeiting being saved. God takes the responsibility for our making it to heaven but warns us that the anointing is a trust here below that must be carefully guarded by us with the help of the Spirit.

The Sensitivity of the Spirit

If we claim to be without sin, we deceive ourselves and the truth is not in us.

1 John 1:8

I do not hold with the view that we can reach the place this side of heaven that we will never again move ahead of the Holy Spirit. We all need the rebuke of Ecclesiastes 7:16 from time to time, 'Do not be over-righteous, neither be overwise – why destroy yourself?' As Solomon put it, 'There is no one who does not sin' (2 Chronicles 6:36).

Some people may be so fearful of grieving the Spirit that they are afraid to do *anything* without a minute-by-minute sense of clear guidance. They worry about which pair of shoes to wear, which tie to put on or whether to read a newspaper. They cannot turn on the television without 'guidance'. They are fearful of any entertainment, fearful of laughing at a joke or spending money in a good restaurant. The irony is, such a bondage equally grieves the Spirit! For where the Spirit of the Lord is, there is liberty (2 Corinthians 3:17). One legacy of the Reformation is the doctrine of Christian liberty. 'It is for freedom that Christ has set us free. Stand firm, then, and do not let yourselves be burdened again by a yoke of slavery' (Galatians 5:1).

A healthy fear of grieving the Spirit should not lead you to be afraid to enjoy life to the full, to laugh uproariously with friends or to make common-sense decisions day and night. God is not unreasonable. His commands are never 'burdensome' (1 John 5:3).

On the other hand, I must eagerly desire all of God I can possibly have. I would love it if God would increase my anointing each day I live. I therefore want to learn ways by which I can adjust to the special presence of God.

The Sensitivity of the Spirit

Do not put out the Spirit's fire.

1 Thessalonians 5:19

Paul's words come from the Greek *abennumi* which basically means 'to quench'. In the ancient Greek world it referred mostly to fire or burning objects: that is, to extinguish fire.

It is hard to know the difference between the Holy Spirit being grieved and being quenched. But part of the difference is that his being grieved refers to the Spirit not being allowed to be himself – what he could be *in us*. His being quenched refers to his not being allowed to *do* what he could do through us. When he is *ungrieved* in us we will manifest his personality, called 'fruits of the Spirit': namely, love, joy, peace, patience, kindness, goodness, faithfulness, gentleness and self-control (Galatians 5:22ff.). This means we will be like Jesus. When he is *unquenched* in us we may well manifest his power, perhaps also as in the gifts of the Spirit (1 Corinthians 12:10–12). There is no doubt that the capabilities of being grieved and being quenched overlap and that this distinction too should not be pressed too far. For they are similar in some ways. I suspect there has been a tendency for some, however, to be more concerned with quenching the Spirit, when there is a desire to see his power – like signs and wonders – than grieving the Spirit, which in some ways focuses more on Christ-likeness. Sadly, there has been a disproportionate interest in the gifts of the Spirit among some Christians. For some of us seem to want power more than purity, signs and wonders more than gentleness and graciousness: the forgotten anointing.

The Sensitivity of the Spirit

So, as the Holy Spirit says: 'Today, if you hear his voice, do not harden your hearts as you did in the rebellion, during the time of testing in the desert, where your fathers tested and tried me and for forty years saw what I did. That is why I was angry with that generation, and I said, "Their hearts are always going astray, and they have not known my ways."'

Hebrews 3:7–10

What is needed is a sensitivity to the Spirit. This means a sensitivity to his ways and – may it please God – to an immediate awareness of his *absence*, should he withdraw to any degree. How quickly we recognise his absence is probably a fairly good test as to how well acquainted we are with him. 'They have not known my ways,' said an offended Holy Spirit.

But does not this teaching make the Holy Spirit vulnerable to the charge of being capricious? Under no circumstances. He may appear that way from our point of view. But God always has a reason for what he does. He promised Moses, 'I will have mercy on whom I will have mercy, and I will have compassion on whom I will have compassion' (Exodus 33:19). The Holy Spirit always mirrors the unity of the Godhead. Even though 'the wind blows wherever it pleases', Jesus' reference to the Spirit (John 3:8), the Spirit never does anything 'on his own' (John 16:13). He therefore reflects the will of the Father. The psalmist spoke of the *second* person of the Trinity, 'Kiss the Son, lest he be angry and you be destroyed in your way, for *his wrath can flare up in a moment*. Blessed are all who take refuge in him' (Psalm 2:12). The Holy Spirit likewise can be grieved suddenly – but never without reason. We therefore must lower our voices and adjust to him if it is the anointing we want. This is partly what is meant by knowing his 'ways'.

The Sensitivity of the Spirit

By faith Noah, being warned of God of things not seen as yet, moved with fear, prepared an ark to the saving of his house; by the which he condemned the world, and became heir of the righteousness which is by faith.

Hebrews 11:7 (AV)

God isn't safe. But he's good. We must never forget this when outside our comfort zone but in God's will. God wants only what is best for us. When we are directed by the Holy Spirit to be outside our comfort zone, it is always for our good.

For example, Noah 'walked with God', following in the steps of Enoch who 'walked with God' (Genesis 5:22; 6:9). So far, so good. They both did the same thing. For all I know Noah may have thought that what happened to Enoch would happen to him if he followed Enoch's example in walking with God. As for Enoch, he was taken to heaven one day (Genesis 5:24; Hebrews 11:5). As for Noah, he might have wondered each day if he was doing something wrong because he was still around! But God had different plans for Noah. He was told one day to build an ark and with it came specific instructions (Genesis 6:14ff.). He might have thought, 'I'd far prefer to be taken to heaven since I am walking with God as Enoch did.' But no. Furthermore, he obeyed and 'moved with fear' in doing so, thus being outside his comfort zone. Can you imagine the stigma Noah and his family must have experienced as they erected that ark – a thing unprecedented in history and which must have made them the laughing-stock of the people?

Out of the Comfort Zone

'For your sake I am glad I was not there, so that you may believe.'
John 11:15

The nearest we ever get to the problem of evil is the truth inherent in John 11:15. The eternal problem of evil – why does God allow evil and suffering? – is unanswerable and unknowable in this life. It is the hardest of all. If people think they are clever because they suddenly come up with this heavy question, 'If God is all-powerful but all-merciful, why does he allow suffering?' they should realise it is for their sakes that they don't get the answer. God does us a favour – an infinite favour – by not answering this ancient theological–philosophical question.

In a word: God doesn't answer our questions for our sake. It is a mercy. It means we still have an opportunity to believe – to demonstrate true faith. For God chose to decree that people will be saved by faith alone or be eternally lost. In his wisdom he determined that if he would have a people to himself it would be a people of *faith*. 'For since in the wisdom of God the world through its wisdom did not know him, God was pleased through the foolishness of what was preached to save those who believe' (1 Corinthians 1:21). He wants a people who trust him on the basis of his word, not the outward evidence. He desires a people who rely on him without getting all their questions answered, even a people who believe him when he doesn't seem to make sense.

One day God will clear his name. He will do it so brilliantly and totally and conclusively that our mouths will be forever stopped. It will be the total vindication of God himself. But it will also mean everlasting destruction for those who wait until then to get their questions answered. For seeing is not believing.

Thanking God

*The LORD said to Samuel, 'How long will you mourn for Saul,
since I have rejected him as king over Israel? Fill your horn with oil
and be on your way; I am sending you to Jesse of Bethlehem. I
have chosen one of his sons to be king.' But Samuel said, 'How can
I go? Saul will hear about it and kill me.'*

1 Samuel 16:1–2

Only Samuel knew that Saul was yesterday's man. He had to make
a decision: should he stick to his guns by supporting Saul right or
wrong, or listen to that voice which had never failed him yet? He
listened to God.

This serves to show how all relationships must ever be subservient
to God's greater glory. No matter how close people get to each other
they must be closer to God. The irony is, the closer people are to God,
the more they will love each other. The more they put the voice of
God prior to their commitment to each other, the more they really
respect each other.

I think of some of my close friends. The dynamic that holds us
together is that we love God more than we do each other. If I stopped
listening to God and turned away from him I would expect my friends
to warn me – then lovingly rebuke me if I did not come to my senses.
It works both ways. If my closest friend broke with the principles that
spawned our relationship, however much he has been like a brother, I
would warn him and rebuke him – but I would keep loving him. No
friendship or relationship is worth its salt if it does not have an inflexible commitment to God's glory first and to one another second. It
would break my heart if I had to break with any of my friends – for
any reason. But I would do it if I had to because of my greater love
for God's honour.

The Anointing

But God chose the foolish things of the world to shame the wise;
God chose the weak things of the world to shame the strong.

1 Corinthians 1:27

Some want God only to look nice. Some people are embarrassed that a number of our forebears, some educated, some uneducated, stressed things today that would not appeal to non-Christians. They gave Christianity, it is believed, a 'bad name', and we have inherited this. Some want to shed this image once and for all. Some theology departments and seminaries have consequently sought to turn out ministers and clergymen who will give God a 'better press'. Some are also sensitive to the criticism some non-Christians make of the Church and want to be there – right on the spot – so say, 'Hang on, that is not what I believe', as if this will cause everybody to say, 'Oh good, I will now be a Christian.' Has our apologising for the way God is perceived by many worked? Has it brought tens of thousands into our churches?

No. You know it and I know it.

I would like to think that if we stopped apologising for God – or gave up trying to make him look appealing – we would have greater success. And yet maybe not. But I know we would have his approval. I believe that if we thoughtfully hold up the God of the Bible as he himself chose to describe himself in his Word, he will honour this. I would predict that to the degree we do that will be the degree to which the Holy Spirit will work more than ever, convert more people than ever and bring more awareness of the true God than anything that has been seen.

Out of the Comfort Zone

'How can you believe if you accept praise from one another, yet make no effort to obtain the praise that comes from the only God?'
John 5:44

One of my predecessors at Westminster Chapel, Dr Martyn Lloyd-Jones, used to make me laugh when he would often say, 'The trouble with the Church today is that it has too many nice men in the ministry.' I think he felt that the Church needed men who were not always so pleasant but more rugged and unafraid to step on people's toes. Is he right? Do you think that many in the ministry are nice? Look around. Would you say that most of the ministers, pastors, church leaders and clergymen you know are 'nice people'? If so, was Dr Lloyd-Jones right that this is not a good thing? But I must ask, would people who know me call me a 'nice man'? I suspect that many would. And yet it does not matter what people would call you or me. I once heard Paul Cain say, 'I am too old now to disobey God.' I know exactly what he meant by that. He did not mean that he could not disobey God; we never outgrow the potential for disobedience. What he meant was that, knowing he has a limited number of days and years left to live, he cannot afford to come short of what honours the true God. That's me. I do not want to waste the time I have left to be a pleaser of people, to cater to the majority, to avoid the truth – to be a fraud.

Out of the Comfort Zone

The men of Israel sampled their provisions but did not enquire of the LORD.

Joshua 9:14

Listen to these words from Martin Luther's Journal: 'I have a very busy day today, must spend not my usual two hours – but three – in prayer.' John Wesley was up every morning at four o'clock to spend two hours on his knees before starting his day.

I don't mean to sound unkind, but where are the Martin Luthers today? Where are the John Wesleys?

According to a recent poll, the average church leader – on both sides of the Atlantic – spends between four and five minutes a day in quiet time with the Lord. And we wonder why the Church is powerless!

Children spell 'love' T-I-M-E. What if God spells 'love' T-I-M-E?

When you and I stand before God at the Judgment Seat of Christ, we may have many regrets concerning how we spent our time. But I think I can safely promise that you will not regret any amount of time you spent in prayer – alone with God.

In the time of Joshua, the people of Israel were not prepared for the way they had been deceived by the Gibeonites. The Gibeonites became a thorn in Israel's side for many generations. But it need not have happened. The cause was put simply: they had not enquired of the Lord. A huge mistake could have been avoided – if only they had prayed first.

Did You Think to Pray?

You shall not bow down to them or worship them; for I, the LORD your God, am a jealous God, punishing the children for the sin of the fathers to the third and fourth generation of those who hate me.

Exodus 20:5

God is a jealous God. Jealousy is a quality we detest in others (and seldom admit to in ourselves), but, like it or not, this is the way God is. He is 'up front' about it and makes no attempt to hide his jealousy. And if that weren't enough, he adds that his very 'name is Jealous' (Exodus 34:14)! But the crucial differences between the jealousy that is in us and God's jealousy is: (1) our jealousy is a symptom of insecurity, but God is never insecure; and (2) our jealousy is almost always counter-productive, yet God's jealousy leads to joy. God loves us so much that he wants us to have joy, and that is one of the great reasons that his jealousy is so good for us. Never resent the fact that he is jealous! It is for our good.

The funny thing is (you may want to call it another irony) that what God uses to get our attention may be the very thing that puts us off him! You would think he would use a method or technique that makes him more loveable – or at least more likeable; but often he seems to do the very thing that he must know is making him look pretty awful in our eyes at that moment. It is when he appears to betray us. It is when he seems to turn his back on us. He makes us feel rejected – as though he has dropped us from his good list entirely. It is when he seems disloyal and comes through to us (as best we can tell at the time) as an enemy, not a friend. But Martin Luther used to say that we must know God as an enemy before we can know him as a friend.

Pure Joy

Truly you are a God who hides himself, O God and Saviour of Israel.

Isaiah 45:15

I have been fascinated for years that these words are inserted in a context that makes no sense for that statement of Isaiah. There is nothing in the preceding lines that prepares one for those words. They just come abruptly, as if out of the blue – and there they are. But why? Why these words at this place? They are true words; they are important and needed. But why here? I have come up with my own theory: that is precisely the way the hiding of God's face is – it comes unexpectedly and without any warning or apparent reason. *God just does it.* The Westminster Confession calls it the withdrawing of the light of his countenance. There is no warning. We find ourselves enjoying his sweet presence when – without any notice – he seems saliently absent. If only God were to say to us when we are enjoying his power and presence, 'Oh, by the way, next Tuesday afternoon about a quarter-past three you will notice that I am withdrawing the smile of my face from you.' No. Never. The hiding of his face never – ever (to my knowledge) – comes with advance warning. God just does it.

All disciplining that comes from our heavenly Father has at bottom the hiding of his face. If you haven't experienced it, I may have to tell you that you are probably not a Christian at all. If indeed you are a child of God, but haven't experienced the hiding of his face, it is only a matter of time. I say that because we are told, '. . . he punishes everyone he accepts' as a son or daughter (Hebrews 12:6).

Pure Joy

'The LORD bless you
 and keep you;
the LORD make his face shine upon you
 and be gracious to you;
the LORD turn his face towards you
 and give you peace.'

Numbers 6:24–26

The opposite of the hiding of God's face is the showing, or smile, of God's face. Moses gave the benediction above to ancient Israel. When God shows his face it is absolutely blissful. It is when the Dove of the Holy Spirit comes down and remains for a while. God seems very near. You feel him, can almost see him! You read the Bible with great understanding and without your mind wandering. Prayers seem to get answered quickly. People smile at you, and if they don't, it doesn't bother you too much. It is the feeling of the wind being at your back, giving you a gentle push to get things done and to walk through open doors.

Pure Joy

To keep me from becoming conceited because of these surpassingly great revelations, there was given me a thorn in my flesh, a messenger of Satan, to torment me.

2 Corinthians 12:7

In over forty years of ministry I have met some unusual people. I have probably learned as much from conversations with them as I have from reading books and hearing sermons. One of the most stunning comments I ever heard, almost a throwaway remark, came from one of the most famous ministers in the world. He said to me, 'R.T., the more God uses me, the less I am able to enjoy it.'

This is the last thing we want to hear, and maybe it is incomprehensible to some, but I'm sorry to have to tell you that I know exactly what he meant by that. God has many ways of ensuring that while we enjoy his blessing, we do not become conceited. But in my view, his most powerful way of guaranteeing that blessing is what Paul calls the 'thorn in the flesh'.

I admit that the Apostle Paul is a hero for many of us, but I have to face the fact that he too was open to pride and to taking himself too seriously. But God had a plan; Paul was too precious to be allowed to fall into that kind of folly. And so God acted.

Think hard before you pray for a greater anointing. You too may well end up saying: 'The more God uses me, the less I am able to enjoy it.'

The Thorn in the Flesh

To keep me from becoming conceited because of these surpassingly great revelations, there was given me a thorn in my flesh, a messenger of Satan, to torment me.

2 Corinthians 12:7 (NIV)

And lest I should be exalted above measure through the abundance of the revelations, there was given to me a thorn in the flesh, the messenger of Satan to buffet me, lest I should be exalted above measure.

2 Corinthians 12:7 (AV)

Paul says he was given a thorn in the flesh for two reasons. First, because God had been so gracious to him by giving him great revelations. Paul had an extraordinary experience with God, and whenever this happens we are in danger of allowing people to admire us a bit too much. Paul said, 'I know a man in Christ who fourteen years ago was caught up to the third heaven. Whether it was in the body or out of the body I do not know – God knows. And I know that this man – whether in the body or apart from the body I do not know, but God knows – was caught up in to Paradise. He heard inexpressible things, things that man is not permitted to tell' (2 Corinthians 12:2–4).

Paul is speaking about himself here, and later says so. He thus gives a second reason why God sent the thorn in the flesh: to counteract his tendency to take himself too seriously. He openly admits to this. The way the Authorised Version translates it, this thorn was given to him 'lest I should be exalted above measure'. This implies that God gave it to Paul so that others would not think too highly of him. In other words, the New International Version shows the possibility of Paul taking himself too seriously, and the Authorised Version shows the possibility of others admiring him too much. In my opinion, it is written with an intentional ambiguity; Paul is saying both. He needed this thorn; others needed it too. In any case, for Paul it is a profoundly humbling experience.

The Thorn in the Flesh

If I must boast, I will boast of the things that show my weakness.

2 Corinthians 11:30

Boasting was exactly what Paul's enemies did all the time. And it worked for them, they actually endeared themselves to Paul's opposition in Corinth by this boasting. Naïve Christians in Corinth fell for the bragging that Paul's enemies did continually.

Paul retorts, 'If it's boasting you want, I'll boast!' However, he says, 'I am going to boast of my weaknesses.' That is what he has been doing in the preceding section of 2 Corinthians.

It is one thing to have a marvellous experience with God, and Paul could have referred to dozens of such experiences. We know of eight or ten unusual experiences with God that Luke tells us about in the book of Acts, but Paul doesn't refer to one of them. He refers instead to something that happened to him fourteen years before, and the thorn in the flesh probably came immediately after that. In other words, a great experience came to him fourteen years before, and then – right after – the thorn in the flesh.

What, then, is Paul's point? He is saying very candidly, 'Had I been strong, had I truly been a man of humility, had I complete control of my ego, there would have been no need for God to send me a thorn in the flesh because I could have coped with all my revelations and success.' But he says that the opposite is true: 'God sent the thorn because of what I really am.' He is saying, 'If you only knew how weak, how frail, how fragile my ego is, how I am prone to take myself so seriously', but many of us would say, 'Oh, not you, Paul!' 'Yes me! And the proof of it is that God sent me this thorn in the flesh to keep me from becoming conceited.' And it came, almost certainly, soon after that great experience with God to which he refers in 2 Corinthians 12:2–4.

The Thorn in the Flesh

But for that very reason I was shown mercy so that in me, the worst of sinners, Christ Jesus might display his unlimited patience as an example for those who would believe on him and receive eternal life.

1 Timothy 1:16

It may be argued that Paul having a thorn in the flesh does not mean that we will all have one. That could be true. However, I do think most Christians have one. Furthermore, Paul said that he himself was 'an example for those who would believe on him and receive eternal life'. I am not talking about the general trials and tribulations that beset every Christian. I refer to a crushing blow so definite and lasting that one knows that 'thorn in the flesh' is the best explanation for it.

This 'thorn' may be recognisable to you, but unseen by others. God may afflict you with some sort of impediment – by which you may feel he has stripped you of all your self-esteem – but this could be utterly unrecognisable to anybody else. Why? Because this 'thorn' is for you more than for them. Or it may be for them indirectly. It may be so embarrassing and humbling to you that it will make you a different person, such that others will not have an inflated opinion of you. But it is mainly for you – to keep you humble. Certainly it may end up being for others in the sense that they unwittingly do not extol you as they might otherwise have done. This helps to explain the ambiguous use of the Greek text, which is impossible to translate in a single phrase that captures both meanings. This is why Paul's thorn kept him from being conceited; it kept others from exalting him beyond that which was warranted. But Paul's thorn was mainly for him, and yours is mainly for you.

The Thorn in the Flesh

'Do not judge, and you will not be judged. Do not condemn, and you will not be condemned. Forgive, and you will be forgiven. Give, and it will be given to you. A good measure, pressed down, shaken together and running over, will be poured into your lap. For with the measure you use, it will be measured to you.'

Luke 6:37–38

A few years ago I began reading Luke 6:37–38 every day. I started reading it because God was dealing with me severely over my judgmental spirit. Reading this passage from Luke is a life sentence for me, because I do not trust myself to go a whole day without being judgmental if I am not careful, so I just read it every day. In the same way, the thorn in the flesh is God inflicting the pain to keep us in continuous reminder lest we lapse. It keeps us from competing with his glory. It ensures that we will not take any personal credit and it gives him all the glory.

In a word: the thorn hurts. It is a constant trial, it's ever obtrusive. It's always there, it's a reminder. It's a nuisance. Paul even says, '. . . to torment me . . .' You may say, 'God, that's not very nice.' But to quote F. F. Bruce again, it is to give Paul's pride a knock-out blow. It keeps one's feet on the ground. It keeps me from thinking that I have arrived, that I am good enough, that I am worthy. It hurts so that I might be driven to love more. It is obtrusive so that I might develop empathy and won't be judgmental. Are you, like me, one of those who can hardly keep from pointing the finger? God has a way of sending a thorn in the flesh. It's obtrusive, just to make you aware of it all the time. It's a reminder of your sin. It's a nuisance that produces humility.

The Thorn in the Flesh

Three times I pleaded with the Lord to take it away from me. But he said to me, 'My grace is sufficient for you, for my power is made perfect in weakness.'

2 Corinthians 12:8–9

I am glad that Paul added these words. Except for this: he prayed only three times that his thorn would be removed; I myself have prayed hundreds of times about mine. I have sought the best counsel, been prayed for by the godliest people I could find. But when it finally dawned on me that my problem is best understood as a thorn in the flesh, I felt much, much better. Until then I blamed myself, thought there was something wrong with me, and that I wasn't spiritual enough (or otherwise it would have gone away).

And yet it is because I'm not spiritual enough that I have this thorn. Whether it will go away before I die, I don't know. But I now accept – and I really do believe this – that it is unquestionably the best thing that could have happened to me. I have become convinced that it has saved me from far more serious problems than I have already had. God knew exactly what it would take to keep me from being even more conceited than I am. '. . . for he knows how we are formed, he remembers that we are dust' (Psalm 130:14).

The Thorn in the Flesh

For whom the Lord loveth he chasteneth, and scourgeth every son whom he receiveth.

Hebrews 12:6 (AV)

I will never forget my first introduction to the idea of being chastened. It came at an extremely difficult time in my life. My father and grandmother had turned against me, even though they loved me. It was August 1956. Eighteen months before, when I became a student pastor of a church of the Nazarene in Palmer, Tennessee, my grandmother bought a brand new 1955 Chevrolet for me. I was the first Kendall in the family to become a preacher, and they were so proud of me. But in April 1956 events took place that made me realise that my theological and ecclesiastical direction would go against the wishes of my family. The upshot of this was that my grandmother took the car back. I remember her words, 'Son, give me the keys.' I did, but I then fell across the bed in her room and cried out, 'Why? Lord, you told me you were going to use me.' Nothing was going according to plan. In that moment I felt an impulse to turn to Hebrews 12:6. So I turned to it in my little pocket-version New Testament, having no idea what I would read.

This verse gave me some comfort, but the pain did not go away. I knew God himself was behind everything that was happening. I could live with that. Can you? Just to know that the whole thing is of God.

The Thorn in the Flesh

Elijah went before the people and said, 'How long will you waver between two opinions? If the LORD is God, follow him; but if Baal is God, follow him.' But the people said nothing.

1 Kings 18:21

One of the grandest displays of courage to be found in all Holy Writ is the above statement of Elijah before the priests of Baal. The matter of putting oneself on the line before a godless generation characterised not only Elijah but every single one of the great men of faith in Hebrews 11. Every man that God has ever used has been one who responded to the call to come out of hiding and stand up and be counted.

Coming out of hiding takes courage. Standing up to be counted takes courage. The Christian faith is designed in part to receive cowards and make them into people of courage. Someone has defined the coward as 'a man in whom the instinct of self-preservation acts normally'.

A proof that one is really saved is that one has the courage to confess with one's mouth what one believes in one's heart. Courage is linked to saving faith in a very definite sense. Saving faith is trusting Jesus Christ alone. The proof that saving faith has emerged in the heart is that it will issue in an open, audible and visible confession.

Stand Up and Be Counted

August

For no-one can lay any foundation other than the one already laid, which is Jesus Christ.

1 Corinthians 3:11

I must ask you: do *you* know for sure that, if you were to die today, you would go to heaven? If you do not know for sure, read on. If the answer is yes, then I must ask you another question: if you were to stand before God (and you will) and he were to ask you (which he might do), 'Why should I let you into heaven?', what exactly would you say?

There is basically only *one* answer that shows you are resting solidly on the true foundation: that your reliance for salvation is on Jesus Christ alone – his blood and righteousness. If you know in your heart of hearts that your only hope of getting into heaven is because Jesus Christ *paid your debt on the cross*, you are in good shape! This is because the blood of Jesus shed on the cross cried out for justice – and got it! Jesus Christ who is the God-man *satisfied God's justice* on your behalf by his shed blood on the cross. Never forget that Jesus was and is God. He was and is God as though he were not man, and yet man as though he were not God. He is fully God, fully man. When *you transfer the trust* you had in your good works *to* what Jesus the God-man did for you on the cross, God declares you righteous in his sight (Romans 4:5). God declares you *saved*. That is the foundation – the only secure foundation. 'For no-one can lay any foundation other than the one already laid, which is Jesus Christ' (1 Corinthians 3:11).

Are you on that foundation?

Second Chance

'The one who received the seed that fell on rocky places is the man who hears the word and at once receives it with joy. But since he has no root, he lasts only a short time. When trouble or persecution comes because of the word, he quickly falls away. The one who received the seed that fell among the thorns is the man who hears the word, but the worries of this life and the deceitfulness of wealth choke it, making it unfruitful.'

Matthew 3:20–22

Even the non-Christian often has a fairly shrewd idea of what the Christian is supposed to be like. But do you sometimes find yourself embarrassingly *unlike* what you should be? I have to admit that I do. For example, 'If anyone is in Christ, he is a new creation; the old has gone, the new has come!' (2 Corinthians 5:17). The old has *gone*? What am I to believe when the 'old' seems to return? Furthermore, 'God raised us up with Christ and seated us with him in the heavenly realms in Christ Jesus' (Ephesians 2:6). That being true, how can earthly things possibly matter to me again? I'm sorry, but they sometimes do! Not only that, but 'he who began a good work in you will carry it on to completion until the day of Christ Jesus' (Philippians 1:6) suggests an inevitably good outcome. And yet some fall after their conversion.

What went wrong? Some people dismiss all the examples above by saying that 'they were never converted in the first place'. Would we have said this about King David immediately after he committed adultery and then ordered Uriah's execution? Or about Simon Peter at the time he denied knowing the Lord? It is a fact that, sadly, truly saved people can, and sometimes do, fall.

Not all who make a profession of faith are saved, as the Parable of the Sower makes clear. But the writers of Scripture lead us to assume that the people I mentioned above believed the gospel as much as anybody else who is said to believe. I also know that 'the best of men are men at best' and therefore that the *best* of God's servants – men or women – can fall.

I also know that God can take the fallen and restore them.

Second Chance

For we are God's fellow-workers; you are God's field, God's building.

1 Corinthians 3:9

Paul used two metaphors – one referring to natural vegetation, the other to that of erecting a material structure. He had just said, 'I planted the seed, Apollos watered it, but God made it grow' (1 Corinthians 3:6). That is why he said we are 'God's field' or 'garden' (Living Bible).

When Paul switched the metaphor from a garden to that of a building he used the word *oikodome*, which in this place means two things simultaneously: (1) the *act* of building, and (2) the superstructure – what is *above* a foundation. The act of building is what God does through us – not what he does by himself without us, or what we do without him. 'In this work, we work with God' in order to erect the house he has planned (1 Corinthians 3:9 – Phillips Modern English). God's 'building' therefore refers both to the act of building and to our erecting the superstructure he has in mind for us.

This is what we are – his building, the result of his grace in our lives.

One might therefore hastily assume that if God does the building, we need not worry – he will do it all! After all, if *God* builds anything it is inevitably going to be flawless and magnificent. But that is not necessarily the case. Even with vegetation there was the co-operative effort between Paul's planting and Apollos' watering; but it was God who made it grow, or 'gave the increase' (AV).

This would be the same with God's building – the superstructure. It is therefore both what God does and what we do. Having stated that he laid the foundation, knowing that he had presented sound doctrine to his followers on a silver platter, Paul added these words: 'Each one should be careful how he builds' (1 Corinthians 3:10).

Paul laid the foundation, but he could not build the superstructure for each of his hearers, or readers. It is up to us to build the superstructure over the foundation.

Second Chance

Unless the LORD *builds the house,*
its builders labour in vain.
Unless the LORD *watches over the city,*
the watchmen stand guard in vain.

Psalm 127:1

This is one of my favourite Bible verses. It means that if God is not behind what you are trying to do – or build – it will fail, no matter how hard you try and how long you work at it.

But the Lord still does not build the house without builders. *He* builds it, yes, but he uses builders. Us!

Here is what you and I have going for us in building a brilliant and solid superstructure (as described in 1 Corinthians 3): *God is behind what we are wanting to do* – if that means a desire to glorify God. In other words, we are not called to embark upon a project that is speculative or doubtful. A superstructure based on godly character and transparent honesty is inherent in God's blueprint for us. It is what God *wants* for you and me.

God's blueprint is designed to show what is best for us. For that reason we must take care *how* we build. The reason Christians fall is that they do not take care to build the kind of superstructure that follows his blueprint.

Second Chance

For we do not have a high priest who is unable to sympathise with our weaknesses, but we have one who has been tempted in every way, just as we are – yet was without sin.

Hebrews 4:15

I think the hardest question I get in the vestry is, 'Why does God allow evil?' – to which I just say, 'I don't know!' The next hardest question I get in the vestry is, 'R.T., why can't I find a wife? Why can't I have a husband? Why can't I find a girlfriend or boyfriend?' My heart goes out to such people.

Even before the fall of Adam and Eve in Eden, 'The Lord God said, "It is not good for the man to be alone. I will make a helper suitable for him"' (Genesis 2:18). How much more so after the Fall? I grant that there are a lot of people who are single and very happy; they don't want it any other way. But many would like to be married – they are so lonely. But there is something worse than being single, and that is being married – but *unhappily*. Part of the loneliness of singleness is sexual frustration. Sex is a God-given desire. Sex was not born in Hollywood, but at the Throne of Grace. There is a physical need for sexual fulfilment. Loneliness only adds to this, and my heart goes out to the many who suffer in this way.

Jesus is at the right hand of God. When he was on earth he was tempted at all points, just as we are, but I have to say that he *resisted*. He resisted. But it is comforting to know that Jesus has never forgotten what it was like then. He therefore sympathises now. The difference between Jesus and some of us is that once we come out of something, we forget what it was like. Jesus has never forgotten what it was like. And yet I feel it is fair to say that, as you resist the opportunity for sexual fulfilment outside of marriage, your reward in heaven will be perhaps as great as any missionary leaving home and going to a foreign field. Do not underestimate what it will mean at the Judgment Seat of Christ when it will show that you refused to give in! In the words of the famous sermon of the late Dr R. G. Lee: 'pay day, some day'!

The Thorn in the Flesh

'But I tell you: Love your enemies and pray for those who persecute you.'

Matthew 5:44

To pray for the one who has hurt you means to pray that they will be blessed. That God will bless them and show favour to them rather than punish them. You pray that they will prosper. In a word: you pray that they will be dealt with as you want God to deal with you. You apply the Golden Rule as you pray (Matthew 7:12). You don't pray, 'God, deal with them.' You don't pray, 'Get them for what they did.' And neither is it enough to say, 'Father, I commend them to you.' That's a cop-out. You pray that they will be totally forgiven just as you want to be yourself.

And yet praying like this, to quote John Calvin, 'is exceedingly difficult'. Chrysostom (*c.* 344–407) called it the very highest summit of self-control. And yet Job's suffering did not begin to turn around until he prayed for those 'friends' who had become his thorn in the flesh (Job 42:10). But when we do this we are becoming like our heavenly Father (Matthew 5:44ff.). That is true godliness, the quintessence of Christ-likeness.

To me the greatest motivation to live like this is Stephen. He is one of my heroes. When I think of the Spirit on him – his enemies being unable to withstand his wisdom, the miracles he did, and his radiant countenance (Acts 6:8–15) – I say to myself: 'I'd give anything in the world for that kind of anointing.' His secret, however, emerged at the end of his life. When they were stoning him he prayed – seconds before his death – 'Lord, do not hold this sin against them' (Acts 7:60). There lies the secret to his unusual anointing.

Total Forgiveness

If we claim to have fellowship with him yet walk in the darkness, we lie and do not live by the truth.

1 John 1:6

What is the darkness? The darkness is bitterness, as well as that confusion of mind and oppression in our hearts because we haven't really forgiven others. You may say, 'Oh, but I *am* having fellowship with God.' No. You just *claim* you are having fellowship with God if there is bitterness. If we claim to have fellowship with God but walk in darkness, then we lie. Walking in darkness is the consequence of not forgiving. When I don't forgive, I may still spend many hours a day in prayer, but I am not having genuine fellowship with God. If I can't forgive that person who has hurt somebody near to me, or if I can't forgive that person for whatever they did, then I am in darkness. I can preach and people may even say, 'Oh what a wonderful sermon; you must be having intimacy with God!' I can come and sing with my hands in the air and you may say, 'Oh look how R.T. is worshipping the Lord!' I could possibly put on such an act that you might think that I am the holiest person ever. In reality, if I have bitterness inside or am holding a grudge, I am just *claiming* to have fellowship with God, for really I am in darkness.

Total Forgiveness

'For if you forgive men when they sin against you, your heavenly Father will also forgive you.'

Matthew 6:14

What sin is it that we must forgive? Any sin. We must begin by not judging. That's not easy, but it is not for us to judge another's motives. Not judging is already the beginnings of forgiveness. We must leave it to God to judge how guilty they are. Whether what they did was deliberate or not, we only know that we are hurt. It may be they are like they are because of bad parenting. I am sure that all our children sooner of later will realise where we as parents have failed and will need to forgive us. I have had to forgive my father for his imperfections. Perhaps you have to forgive that unfair school teacher, your incompetent boss who has been promoted to a level beyond his or her competence. Moreover, you must forgive a fellow Christian who is insensitive.

Jesus is talking about a chosen privilege. 'If you forgive men' – that is, 'people' – that means you *choose* to do it, or you can choose not to. 'A man's wisdom gives him patience; it is to his glory to overlook an offence' (Proverbs 19:11). Can you think of many things that can bring glory? Having a funeral at Westminster Abbey? Being given a knighthood? Winning a gold medal in the Olympics? Winning the Nobel Peace Prize? That's glory, but Proverbs 19:11 says, 'It is to a man's glory to overlook an offence.' That is doing something far more spectacular than winning an Olympic medal or being made a member of the House of Lords. It is glory *to overlook an offence*. It is crossing over into the supernatural.

Total Forgiveness

*When Mary reached the place where Jesus was and saw him, she
fell at his feet and said, 'Lord, if you had been here, my brother
would not have died.'*

John 11:32

Obedience is doing what one is told to do. We get our instructions
from the Bible – God's revealed will. We cannot bypass the Bible and
opt for a special 'word of knowledge' (often a 'quick-fix' solution) if
we truly want to know God. The more we read the Bible the more we
discover what God wants of us. God wants us to know him by knowing
his word. Can you say you love God when you don't read his word
and seek his face daily in it? The word of God doesn't adjust to us;
we must adjust to it. When you are on a road with a map and get lost,
the place you are heading for doesn't come to you; you have to look
at the map again more carefully and adjust to it before you reach your
destination. The Bible is like a map; it shows the way to go every day.

We are often angry with God at first for what he allows to happen
– whether evil in the world generally or some misfortune he incredibly allows to happen in our own lives. But if we can learn to lower
our voices we will eventually see that there *was* a good reason.

It made no sense that Jesus didn't turn up to heal Mary and Martha's
brother Lazarus before he died. But at the end of the day it turned
out that there was a good reason for it after all. For Jesus thought
that raising Lazarus from the dead was a better idea than keeping him
from dying. This simply shows how things that we don't understand
at first can be understood later – if we will wait. This is true with
everything that has ever happened that we didn't understand at the
time.

The Sensitivity of the Spirit

*'Woe to me!' I cried. 'I am ruined! For I am a man of unclean lips,
and I live among a people of unclean lips, and my eyes have seen
the King, the LORD Almighty.'*

Isaiah 6:5

One of the reasons we are expected to adjust to God's rules, rather
than vice versa, is to develop a sense of sin. There was a time in my
life when this thought was alien to me. That is, until I was baptised
by the Holy Spirit. The words of 1 John 1:8 then became real to me:
'If we claim to be without sin, we deceive ourselves and the truth is
not in us.' Sadly, there was a time when I thought, 'I have no sin.' But
that was largely because of a faulty theology plus excusing any sin as
a mistake, error or 'shortcoming'. I dared not use the word 'sin'. But
that changed. Not that I began sinning to prove I was a sinner, but
because the greater sense of *God* resulted in a greater sense of sin.

When we discover what grieves the Holy Spirit we learn more deeply
what sin is. It has far more to do with what we are like in ourselves
than doing things some Christians have called 'sin': kinds of entertainment, dress and what is commonly called 'worldliness' in some
circles. Not that one always approves of such; it is only that not doing
some things can give a self-righteous feeling and also masquerade as
godliness. I've known of people who condemn the cinema and trendy
dress, but who could have an out-and-out fight in the church's car park
– and feel no conviction of sin for it at all! Adjusting to the Holy
Spirit is to develop a sensitivity *to* him by coming to terms with what
hurts his feelings.

The Sensitivity of the Spirit

For the kingdom of God is not a matter of eating and drinking, but of righteousness, peace and joy in the Holy Spirit.

Romans 14:17

I recall the story of the returning missionary who had spent forty years in Africa; he was going home to America. The big ship sailed into New York harbour, and as it was being moored the old missionary heard a band playing. He said to himself, 'Ah, they shouldn't have done that for me!' He could envisage his friends getting a band to welcome him home, but when he tried to get off the ship, they said, 'Stop right here, please!' It turned out that President Theodore Roosevelt was on the ship – he was also returning from Africa. He had been there for three weeks, big game hunting. The band of course was playing for the President of the United States. Roosevelt got off the ship first, was welcomed, and away he went. The old missionary was the last person to get off the ship. He walked down the gangplank and looked around, holding his suitcases. There was nobody there, nobody. He made his way to an old, third-rate hotel in Manhattan and fell down on his knees. He said, 'Lord, why? The President of the United States goes to Africa for three weeks and a band is playing for him when he comes home, and I come home after forty years and there's nobody!' Then he heard God whisper to him, 'But you're not home yet!'

We must understand the message of Abraham, Isaac, Jacob and Moses: that this life is not all there is. The more we set our sight on that city that has foundations whose builder and maker is God, then the little bit of heaven that God will give us on the way to heaven will be the greatest compensation.

The Thorn in the Flesh

'For I have come to turn "a man against his father, a daughter against her mother, a daughter-in-law against her mother-in-law – a man's enemies will be the members of his own household."'

Matthew 10:36

I wonder how it made David feel that his own father would never have sent for him had not Samuel kept pressing, 'Are these all the sons you have?' (1 Samuel 16:11). His father naturally hoped Samuel would anoint Eliab, the first-born. David was the 'runt of the litter', the youngest and most underestimated. Sometimes our parents, who tried the hardest on the oldest, take the younger ones for granted. In any case, it is painful when your own parent – mother or father – underestimates you. 'But the Lord looks at the heart' (1 Samuel 16:7). God saw in David what Jesse underestimated – a young man with a heart after God.

Do you know what it is like to live beneath your parents' expectation or approval? Do you feel pain as you wait for your time to come that is aggravated partly by a frustrated relationship with your father or mother? We all grow up wanting to please our parents. I'm not sure we ever outgrow that.

The Anointing

Truly you are a God who hides himself, O God and Saviour of Israel.

Isaiah 45:15

Do you feel that Jesus is your friend, but that he has let you down? Did you feel him near, only to feel suddenly deserted? If so, you will know how Isaiah felt.

What makes the hiding of God's face so painful is that it never comes with advance warning. God doesn't give warning. He just *does* it.

But to be treated in this manner is a singular kindness. It is an invitation to 'move up higher', to join the ranks of the great saints of old. That is the way they 'made it'. That is what made them successful. The writer of Hebrews says they did it 'by faith'. 'Some faced jeers and flogging, while still others were chained and put in prison. They were stoned; they were sawn in two; they were put to death by the sword' (Hebrews 11:36–37). Such people were graced with enormous faith, all because they dignified the trial God gave them. 'Blessed is the man who perseveres under trial, because when he has stood the test, he will receive the crown of life that God has promised to those who love him' (James 1:12).

Does Jesus Care?

*Therefore, I urge you, brothers, in view of God's mercy, to offer
your bodies as living sacrifices, holy and pleasing to God –this is
your spiritual act of worship.*

Romans 12:1

The ancient sacrificial system in the Old Testament was designed to
show the seriousness of sin and the cost it would be to God to forgive
sin. This is because the sacrifice of animals in the Old Testament
pointed to the ultimate sacrifice – when God gave his one and only
Son to die on a cross (John 3:16).

But sometimes the word 'sacrifice' is used with regard to what *we*
give up. Although the primary meaning of 'sacrifice' refers to the
slaughter of animals to appease God's justice, it also means to give
up something for the sake of something more important. Peter said
we offer 'spiritual sacrifices acceptable to God through Jesus Christ'
(1 Peter 2:5). Paul deemed his gifts from the Philippians as a 'fragrant
offering, an acceptable sacrifice, pleasing to God' (Philippians 4:18).
David said, 'I will sacrifice a thank-offering to you and call on the
name of the LORD' (Psalm 116:17).

When we take the time to praise God we sacrifice time. We all can
think of things we ought to be doing. It is easier to watch television
than it is to take the equal amount of time to praise God. Which is
easier – to watch *Frazier* for thirty minutes or to praise God for thirty
minutes? To praise God for thirty minutes is a sacrifice, of time, of
pleasure, of our basic wishes, and possibly, our temperament. It isn't
easy!

But when we are *low* and the outlook bleak and we are anxious,
it is doubly hard to praise God. But God likes it. I believe it pleases
him more than ever – he sees what we feel, what we are giving up and
struggling to do.

Thanking God

'God is spirit, and his worshippers must worship in spirit and in truth.'

John 4:24

Worship is the response to, and/or preparation for, the preached word. I say this, not because I am trying to defend the Reformed tradition, or because I want to perpetuate any church's tradition as a preaching centre, but because I happen to be convinced that worship as described in the New Testament makes preaching central.

I think everyone would agree that the greatest service that has ever been held took place on the Day of Pentecost. Acts 2:42 gives us a description of the pattern of the earliest known Christian worship. This was obviously in response to the preached word.

What, then, is the role of the Spirit in worship? The Spirit always comes first. In worship, the Spirit prepares our minds and hearts to receive God's word, and, as we see at Pentecost, it is the Spirit who brings about a change of heart and enables us to continue in the apostles' doctrine.

But if the first thing is the Spirit, what is the role of the truth? Truth – Christian doctrine as revealed in the word of God – is the proof and guarantee that one is in the Spirit; it also serves as a yardstick for testing actions which are allegedly in the Spirit but which in fact are not. The truth keeps worship from going off the rails. The Bible was not given to replace the Holy Spirit. The Bible is there to correct abuse, and to help us make sure that our worship and our Christian walk are genuinely in the Spirit.

Worshipping God

The Spirit himself testifies with our spirit that we are God's children.

Romans 8:16

A. W. Tozer, in his book *Whatever Happened to Worship?*, quotes Dr George Watson, who said there are two levels in the worship of God: gratitude and excellence. He went on to say that most people never get beyond the level of gratitude; few worship God for his excellence, for all that he is, for his transcendent and immanent glory.

When we think of God's transcendence, we usually think of the glory of God. Many of our hymns praise God for his majesty, glory and the awefulness of his throne. And to some people, this aspect of God is all that matters. But there is another side to the worship of God. Paul said, 'Because you are sons, God sent the Spirit of his Son into our hearts, the Spirit who calls out, "*Abba*, Father"' (Galatians 4:6). This is most intimate language. '*Abba*, Father' literally means (I almost blush to use it) – 'Daddy'.

Many of us are so sophisticated that the only kind of worship we can envisage is that which deals with the transcendence of God, and we are offended by some of the more intimate choruses. But we need to realise that it is just as honouring to God to praise him for his immanence as it is to praise him for his transcendence. By God's immanence, I mean the wonderful way he works within nature, within our world and daily events, and deep within our lives. I mean his closeness to us.

Worshipping God

But Abel brought fat portions from some of the firstborn of his flock. The LORD looked with favour on Abel and his offering, but on Cain and his offering he did not look with favour. So Cain was very angry, and his face was downcast.

Genesis 4:4–5

There is a crucial difference between giving presents to our friends, and offering worship to God: it is not for us to try to decide what will please God. God has already decided what kind of worship he wants. Worship that pleases him must be 'by the Spirit of God'.

'Well,' someone may say, 'if I'm going to worship God by his Spirit, then I'm really not doing anything. It's just God doing it for himself. But I want to please him by showing him what I can do.' But anyone who talks like this does not know God, because God doesn't want what we can do. He has already decided what he wants, and we must decide whether we are going to worship in his way. As the writer to the Hebrews says, 'Through Jesus, therefore, let us continually offer to God a sacrifice of praise' (Hebrews 13:15). The word 'sacrifice' is used here because to worship by the Spirit of God involves self-denial. It is a *sacrifice* of praise.

One of the earliest worship services in the history of mankind is described in Genesis 4. And in it Cain decided that he would worship God by bringing an offering of the works of his own hands, while his brother Abel sacrificed some of his best lambs. God wanted sacrifice, and so looked with favour on Abel, but without favour on Cain.

Worshipping God

'Then the master called the servant in. "You wicked servant," he said, "I cancelled all that debt of yours because you begged me to. Shouldn't you have had mercy on your fellow-servant just as I had on you?" In anger his master turned him over to the jailers to be tortured, until he should pay back all he owed.'

Matthew 18:32–34

God loves gratitude. He knows what he has forgiven us of; he is fully aware of it. Read the account in Matthew 18 where the servant fell on his knees and went to his master and said, 'Be patient and I will pay you back everything', and the servant's master took pity on him and cancelled the debt and let him go. The master knew what he had forgiven the servant of. But then that particular servant went out and found one of his own servants who owed him one hundred denarii; he grabbed him and began to choke him and said, 'Pay back what you owe!' Then that servant did exactly what his master had done: fell on his knees and said, 'Please forgive me, I will pay you back.' The one who had been forgiven refused and threw his servant into prison. Word got back to the one who originally forgave, who of course knew exactly what he had forgiven that person of. To think there could be such ingratitude and anger!

Jesus then added, 'This is how my heavenly Father will treat each of you unless you forgive your brother from your heart' (Matthew 18:35). God knows what we have done. He knows what he has forgiven you of. There are things you have done, possibly that no one else will ever know about. You say, 'Well, they will never know', but God knows. If you turn right around and say, 'I can't forgive a person for this', he doesn't like it at all. He hates ingratitude. It shows we aren't very excited about having our sins forgiven; we are not very grateful. Therefore God judges us when we don't pass this forgiveness on.

Total Forgiveness

For it is God's will that by doing good you should silence the ignorant talk of foolish men.

1 Peter 2:15

If you are tomorrow's man or woman, it is only a matter of time before people will be jealous of you. Perhaps you were underestimated by a perfectionist parent, perhaps a brother or sister has been jealous of you; such is the stuff of life that gets you ready for a battle ahead.

People can't help it. And, by the way, *you're* no different!

How we respond to another's jealousy will determine whether we will truly come through as tomorrow's man or woman. It is what saved David and eventually made him great, although it could have been his undoing. I love the way the Authorised Version puts it: 'David behaved himself wisely in all his ways' (1 Samuel 18:14). When you know someone is jealous of you, you know you will have to be extremely shrewd. You never let them know you know what their problem is. You simply put it into your 'computer' and act accordingly – running for cover and, if possible, giving them no cause to speak against you. 'Who is going to harm you if you are eager to do good? But even if you should suffer for what is right, you are blessed. "Do not fear what they fear; do not be frightened"' (1 Peter 3:13–14).

The Anointing

'Lord,' Martha said to Jesus, 'if you had been here, my brother would not have died.'

John 11:21

I know this about my Lord Jesus Christ: I can say anything to him. I can talk to him about anything and express any feeling that I have. If I were to say what I feel to you, it might hurt you. It may not be good for you to know I had a particular feeling. But Jesus allows me to express my feelings to him.

There are times when we need to express what we feel – to someone. Earlier I talked about repression, denying what we truly feel. This is almost always a bad thing to do. The worst thing in the world is not to be able to express a feeling. It may be a bizarre feeling, yes. It may be misguided. It may be ill-conceived. It may be quite unjustified. But if you feel it, it does you no good to repress it – to push it down into the cellar of unconsciousness. It is not healthy, either physically or emotionally. Repression can be the cause of any number of physical or psychological illnesses. Many times people have illnesses that are traceable to repressed feelings.

If there is no one on this earth we can turn to (lest they make us feel even worse), we can always turn to Jesus. We can say *anything* to him. Martha did just that: 'Lord, if you had been here, our brother would not have died.' A few moments later Mary came with the same comment. It was as though they rehearsed it together. You can be sure they discussed it and agreed on it. If anything in the world was obvious to them it was this. It was a statement of fact but also of feeling.

And yet it was also a statement of familiarity. It shows that they already had a relationship with Jesus. We might think that this was impertinent language. But they were not being impertinent because they knew him very well. They knew they could talk like this to him.

Does Jesus Care?

'You may ask me for anything in my name, and I will do it.'

John 14:14

Unanswered prayer is an enigma – that is, puzzling in the light of Jesus' words above.

James said, 'You do not have, because you do not receive, because you ask with the wrong motives, that you may spend what you get on your pleasures' (James 4:2–3). It follows from this that God does not answer prayers that are not in his will. After all, John said, 'This is the assurance we have in approaching God: that if we ask anything according to his will, he hears us. And if we know that he hears us – whatever we ask – we know that we have what we asked of him' (1 John 5:14–15).

I can only conclude that asking in Jesus' name must in some direct sense relate to God's will. There is a verse that haunts me, 'So he gave them what they asked for, but sent a wasting disease upon them' (Psalm 106:15). This may refer to the murmuring of the Children of Israel in the desert (Exodus 16) or it may refer to Israel's ill-posed request for a king (1 Samuel 8:6–7). I do know that God later said, 'So in my anger I gave you a king, and in my wrath I took him away' (Hosea 13:11).

The enigma of unanswered prayer lies in the apparent incongruity between what seems good to us at the time and what God knows is good for us.

The Thorn in the Flesh

So Peter was kept in prison, but the church was earnestly praying to God for him.

Acts 12:5

Because of the situation at the time, I would not be surprised if the early Church prayed for Peter as if he were a member of each person's own family. They were utterly gutted. They had not dreamed God would allow the wicked King Herod to arrest someone like James the brother of John – and put him to death. But he did. They could not imagine that Herod would arrest Simon Peter. But he did. Peter was now on Herod's hit list (Acts 12:1–4). This got the Church's attention and they prayed 'earnestly' for Peter ('without ceasing' – AV – Acts 12:5). The Greek word is *ektenes*. It means that deep and fervent prayer was offered for Peter in order that he be spared martyrdom. The Jerusalem Bible says that the Church prayed to God for him 'unremittingly'. The New English Bible uses the word 'fervently'.

I therefore ask: did this intensity of praying make a difference? Yes.

Did their strong feelings somewhat make up for their lack of faith? I believe so.

What we do know is that Peter was suddenly and miraculously delivered from prison and went straight to the place where the people were praying. When he turned up, they didn't believe it was Peter! And when they eventually did accept that it was him, they were still 'astonished' (Acts 12:6–16). This suggests to me that they had more *feeling* in their praying than they had faith! If so, God responded to their feeling more than he responded to their faith – which they seemed to have so little of.

It is my view that when our faith is minimal, God in his mercy sometimes honours our anxious feelings. He may take notice of our emotional involvement, our fears, our heart-felt burden – even if we do not have much faith.

This encourages me no end. I sometimes feel a little bit guilty that I do not have more faith. But when I get a glimpse of our compassionate *God* and how Jesus told us never, never, never to give up, I am given a burst of hope that keeps me asking God to answer my prayers.

Did You Think to Pray?

For this very reason, Christ died and returned to life so that he might be the Lord of both the dead and the living.

Romans 14:9

Do not think that merely being outside your comfort zone is always good. It could be harmful and very bad for you indeed. The devil might even make an overly conscientious person move outside their comfort zone and cause them to end up in bewilderment, disillusionment, depression or unbelief. For example, I have known some sincere Christians to do foolish things – such as taking all their savings and giving the money away to an unscrupulous preacher; or spending all their time in the work of their church, neglecting their children and letting their marriages break down; or even giving too much time in fasting and prayer – and get weak and tired – when they needed to be physically on top and conscientious about their secular jobs.

My favourite line in Shakespeare is: 'To thine own self be true.' These words are not in the Bible as far as I know but the gist of them is – throughout Proverbs and particularly what Paul is saying in Romans 14, especially verse 9. And I have learned that the Holy Spirit will not lead you to go against Scripture or make you do what gives you an uneasy, unsettled feeling within. Remember this principle that you can hang on to: the Holy Spirit will never lead you to be untrue to yourself or to violate your conscience.

Out of the Comfort Zone

'They are a people whose hearts go astray,
and they have not known my ways.'

Psalm 95:10

The greatest thing one's husband or wife wants to hear from the other is: I love you just the way you are. It is so affirming to be fully accepted as we are. God wants that from us. He wants us to know him, see exactly what he is like and the way he is – he calls it 'my ways'. The thing is, you might not like his ways. You may dislike his ways – intensely, for all I know. But the point is, God wants us to know his ways and love him just as he is. The problem with Israel was, they did not even know his ways. This made him sad. But also angry.

God therefore wants us to know him so well that what he does, does not take us by surprise. For those who do not know his ways there will be a reaction – 'This cannot be God' – when he chooses to manifest himself in a manner that finds us outside our comfort zone.

Is your mind made up as to what God is like? For if our minds are made up we will never know what it would have been like had we the courage to overcome fear and thus explore the awesome things about God that he wants to show us.

Out of the Comfort Zone

Do not cast me from your presence
  or take your Holy Spirit from me.
Restore to me the joy of your salvation
  and grant me a willing spirit, to sustain me.

Psalm 51:11–12

The secret of David's success and usefulness is the Holy Spirit. He experienced the Holy Spirit in power from the moment Samuel discovered him as tomorrow's man (1 Samuel 16:13). Psalm 51 is a reminder that tomorrow's man or woman will not be perfect, although it must be our prayer day and night that you and I will be kept from the sin that lay behind that psalm. But what strikes me is David's consciousness of having grieved the Spirit by his sin; hence the prayer of Psalm 51.

I am also gripped by his plea, 'Grant me a willing spirit', a clear indication of his openness to the Spirit. David did not want to miss anything that could be of God. A willing spirit, what he went on to call 'a broken spirit' (Psalm 51:17), is required of tomorrow's servant of the Lord if our anointing will be useful to God.

I need to spell out one of the differences between being open to the word and being open to the Spirit. Openness to the word is but to be open to the Spirit *indirectly*. This is because the word – to which we must remain open – is powerful to us only when it is applied by the Spirit.

The Anointing

But when he saw many of the Pharisees and Sadducees coming to where he was baptising, he said to them: 'You brood of vipers! Who warned you to flee from the coming wrath?'

Matthew 3:7

We live in what Dr O. S. Hawkins calls 'the No Fear culture'. O.S. suggests it is because 'our generation knows little of the nature of God'. People in and out of the Church have no fear of God. He defines the fear of God as being 'a reverential awe, a sense of being afraid of offending a holy God in any way'. I am glad he is not afraid to use the word 'afraid'. So many water down the fear of God by quickly saying, 'Now it doesn't mean to be afraid of God.' Really? It certainly does mean that; otherwise nobody will begin to feel real respect and awe for the God of the Bible. I have no doubt that at times when the Bible refers to people walking in the fear of the Lord in fact they were scared to death.

The fear of God is a no-nonsense and a no-joke thing. It is very real when described in the Bible and is often intended to strike fear in us. It should shake us to our fingertips. It did in the early Church. This is what generally characterised the atmosphere when Jesus performed miracles and when the apostles preached the gospel.

The first message of the New Testament was to 'flee from the coming wrath'. Why would a person flee – which means 'run'? Because to grasp the meaning of John the Baptist's message meant they were to be afraid of the coming wrath. Not just politely to tip the hat toward God or show a bit of respectful deference but to be truly in fear of what was coming. It is my view that the revival that is coming will usher in simultaneous fear and joy to the people. It will send terror to the lost and to the backslidden and bring both fear and joy to those found walking in the light.

Out of the Comfort Zone

Let us have grace, whereby we may serve God acceptably with reverence and godly fear.

Hebrews 12:28 (AV)

A deep and true fear of God will keep you from committing adultery – because of what it does to God, to the Church, to the one you would be involved with, to your spouse and family, and to you. A fear of God will mean that we are afraid to kill anybody for the same reasons. But when we develop a sensitivity to the Holy Spirit, we are equally afraid to commit adultery in our *heart*, to hurt another person's *reputation*, to hold a *grudge* or to do anything to bring vengeance. The Sermon on the Mount was given to develop a true fear of the Lord, shown by the way we live.

The Holy Spirit mirrors the God of the Bible and is as sensitive to what displeases the Father as the Father himself. Therefore when we develop a care not to grieve the Holy Spirit we will do nothing knowingly that would bring him displeasure. It is a healthy Christian who fears God's chastening, or his disciplining us. Said the psalmist, 'O LORD, do not rebuke me in your anger or discipline me in your wrath' (Psalm 6:1; 'hot displeasure', AV). The reason God disciplines us is because of his jealous love.

Out of the Comfort Zone

'How can you believe if you accept praise from one another, yet make no effort to obtain the praise that comes from the only God?'

John 5:44

This verse assumes that God is jealous. He doesn't like it when we opt for human approval rather than his alone. This is exactly what the ancient Jews did and the precise reason they missed their own Messiah when he came. When Jesus stood before the Jews and they rejected him he told them why they were blind: it is because they seek honour from one another and that they did not seek the honour that comes from the only true God. Had they been seeking his honour instead of each other's they would have recognised the One God sent to them. Hence Jesus asked, 'How can you believe [in other words, 'You are not able to believe'] when you do not make any real attempt to receive the honour that comes from God alone?'

In a word: when we seek his honour over the approval of people, God rewards us – whether with vindication, other good things or with insight; when we seek the approval of people instead, God's jealousy sets in and he withholds such blessings, including insight. That is what happened to ancient Israel in Jesus' day. They knew that he was a jealous God. But they let pride rule – wanting approval of each other, not what God wanted to give them.

This principle still applies. John 5:44 is one of those verses that grips me to such depths that I am often overcome with godly fear.

Out of the Comfort Zone

'For my thoughts are not your thoughts, neither are your ways my ways,' declares the LORD. 'As the heavens are higher than the earth, so are my ways higher than your ways and my thoughts than your thoughts.'

Isaiah 55:8–9

One of the most surprising aspects of God's personality is that he is jealous by nature. He is very 'up front' about it. He even says that his very name is Jealous! 'Do not worship any other god, for the LORD, whose name is Jealous, is a jealous God' (Exodus 34:14). Not a very flattering thing to have said about us. I don't want to admit it when I am jealous. I don't want to be that vulnerable before you. But he admits it.

Strange as it may seem, the jealousy that is seen as a product of our sinful nature (see Galatians 5:19–21) is the very word used to describe the God of the Bible. He can be like that. But we can't! But is this unfair? I can only reply with the words God spoke through Isaiah above.

To put it plainly, when God does not get his way he becomes angry. He may not show it at first. Sometimes *the angrier he is the longer he waits* to bring vengeance. But when he does not have his way with us – his covenant people – his jealousy kicks in and it is only a matter of time before it is openly manifested. He does not appear to be very nice when he does not get his way.

It is this very thing that often, perhaps more than anything else, puts people off the God of the Bible.

Out of the Comfort Zone

*If any man builds on this foundation using . . . wood, hay or
straw . . .*

1 Corinthians 3:12

The 'wood, hay and straw' here refer mainly to building a super-structure without the honour of God in mind. Sadly, there are those Christians who are saved because they are on a solid foundation, but their lives sometimes do not show their love for God. They consequently build a superstructure that will not stand the test of fire.

Why does Paul use these metaphors of wood, hay and straw?

They are corruptible. In other words, they are unable to be permanent. Wood, hay and straw are capable of decay, rot and becoming useless – unlike gold, silver and gems. It is not a good Christian who can be so easily lured away from the things of God and become so easily corrupted.

They are colourless. Unlike gold, silver and costly stones, wood, hay and straw are colourless and do not make a very attractive superstructure. As Christians we should have something about us that attracts the world, making them want what we have.

They are common. You can find wood, hay and straw without looking very hard, whereas precious metals and gems are uncommon. The Christian should radiate an aura that is exceedingly rare in the world. It is a sad day when we are so much like the world.

They are cheap. Wood, hay and straw are relatively worthless when compared to gold, silver and precious stones. The 'world was not worthy' of those people described in Hebrews 11 (verse 38) because they were anything but cheap and ordinary. Christians who are like this discredit the faith of Christ and his name.

They are combustible. Wood, hay and straw are easily consumed when set on fire, but the superstructure we are invited to erect, that of gold, silver and costly gems, can never burn up.

Second Chance

His work will be shown for what it is, because the Day will bring it to light. It will be revealed with fire, and the fire will test the quality of each man's work. If what he has built survives, he will receive his reward. If it is burned up, he will suffer loss; he himself will be saved, but only as one escaping through the flames.

1 Corinthians 3:13–15

There are two kinds of trials that you and I can anticipate: (1) the fiery trials on earth – they are bound to come; we are 'destined' for them (1 Thessalonians 3:3); (2) the fiery trial above, when our superstructure will be shown for 'what it is, because the Day will bring it to light' by fire.

The trial on the Final Day will be the very last test that will ever come to us; it is when the superstructure of wood, hay and straw will be burned up. After the trial on earth we can continue to repent and improve, having seen perhaps that we did not do too well. But there will be no chance to improve after the fiery trial above; it will be too late for further repentance.

The trial below *can* take its shape by God bringing judgment on us. This means being exposed – caught, found out. However awful it must be to be judged in the here and now, it will be far, far worse in the trial above. This is partly why we have this word: 'Why should any *living* man complain when punished for his sins?' (Lamentations 3:39). In other words, be thankful for it. It is far easier to receive God's fierce judgment now than on that Day. At the Judgment Seat of Christ, if our superstructure is comprised of wood, hay and straw, at least we will be saved. Our works will be burned up, but we will be saved by fire (1 Corinthians 3:15). But it will still be a terrible time for those who have no reward. I don't want that to be me.

Therefore the person whose superstructure is burned up will receive no reward. The reward comes to the one who built his house with gold, silver and precious stones. 'If what he has built survives, he will receive his reward' (1 Corinthians 3:14).

Second Chance

September

'Do not judge, or you too will be judged. For in the same way as you judge others, you will be judged, and with the measure you use, it will be measured to you.'

Matthew 7:1–2

When Jesus said, 'Be perfect, therefore, as your heavenly Father is perfect' (Matthew 5:48), he was setting the stage for a higher level of perfection than many Christians have looked at. Therefore what we see in Jesus' words, 'Do not judge, or you too will be judged', is an example of this perfection. We cannot expect sinless perfection, but a very high level of maturity is required of us if we want intimacy with God and a greater anointing. To come to the place where you stop pointing the finger is a very high achievement indeed. Matthew 7:1 restates Matthew 5:7, one of the Beatitudes, 'Blessed are the merciful, for they will be shown mercy', because being merciful is showing graciousness. Paul said, 'Let your *gentleness* [my italics] be evident to all' (Philippians 4:5); this derives from a Greek word which literally means being gracious: when you know you could throw the book at somebody but instead choose to be gracious.

Judging is the opposite of graciousness. Graciousness is the consequence of a choice. So remember, at any moment when you are choosing to judge, you are not being gracious. For we *can* stop ourselves and choose to be gracious.

Total Forgiveness

'Why do you look at the speck of sawdust in your brother's eye and pay no attention to the plank in your own eye?'

Matthew 7:3

Since Jesus addressed this to the Church, it should not surprise us that so many of our quarrels come from within the family of God. This is why the reference is to 'your brother's eye', meaning one's spiritual brother or sister – not one's natural kin. This verse shows so candidly how we tend to let small things in the other person upset us – the 'speck of dust' – and so easily overlook the big, negative things in our own lives: the 'plank'. This lack of objectivity about ourselves disqualifies us from being helpful. It is a vital ingredient in the matter of being qualified to judge. When we lose objectivity about ourselves, seeing only the speck of dust in others but not the plank in our own eyes, we must render ourselves out of order to sort out another person.

Fault-finding, then, is out of order. Jesus' rhetorical question, 'Why do you look at the speck of sawdust in your brother's eye and pay no attention to the plank in your own eye?' is about meddling over what 'gets our goat'. The fault we see is what Jesus calls a speck. That annoys us, but the whole time we don't see our own very serious problem. This shows no objectivity about oneself whatsoever. For the cause of fault-finding, or meddling, is the plank in our own eye which we cannot see. 'Plank' is Jesus' word for what is wrong with us; it is sin in us, evidence of our fallen nature. It is what makes us so eager to point the finger rather than to forgive.

Total Forgiveness

A gentle answer turns away wrath, but a harsh word stirs up anger.

Proverbs 15:1

What should be your response when someone criticizes you or meddles in your life? First, maintain a sweet spirit. Secondly, agree with them. It never hurts to do this. Usually there is a little bit of truth in what a critic will say to us or about us. You can always say, 'I see what you mean.' Thirdly, thank them. This will not only defuse them if they are annoyed, but will also enable them to save face should they be up to no good. That way, we haven't made an enemy unnecessarily in the process. What we must never do when being confronted like this is to defend ourselves or try to impress on others how good or right we are; and never punish. Never get even. Never make them look bad. Ask them to pray for you! But say it in a non-combatant manner. Never say it sarcastically. Say it sincerely, 'I need all the help I can get.' In the meantime you can always pray for them. But don't tell them this; it will annoy them. The principles of total forgiveness should enable us to make friends, not lose them.

Jesus will not allow us to play God. He is the ultimate judge and we must be extremely careful not to trespass into his territory. It may be recalled also that the judging that Jesus prohibits is *unfair criticism.* Jesus now says we are hypocrites if we engage in this kind of judging: 'You hypocrite, first take the plank out of your own eye, and then you will see clearly to remove the speck from your brother's eye' (Matthew 7:5).

Total Forgiveness

'You hypocrite, first take the plank out of your own eye, and then you will see clearly to remove the speck from your brother's eye.'

Matthew 7:5

According to this we can apparently judge another if we have no plank. But who is bold enough to say that he or she has no plank? I am certainly not!

Matthew 7:5 is surely saying at least one of three things: (1) no one ever gets rid of the plank, therefore no one can judge; (2) one can get rid of the plank and then – and then only – can you help another; or (3) there is a way forward when one focuses on his or her *own* plank, and self-effacingly offers correction to another in a way that will be welcomed.

What is our Lord's purpose in these words? He wants to help us in different and difficult situations. We could carry out the principle of total forgiveness to such an extent that we let all rapists, child-abusers and murderers out of prison so that they could roam the streets and do more damage. We could allow carnal Christians (yes, they do exist – 1 Corinthians 3:1ff.) to take over a church and destroy it if we take the principle of total forgiveness without understanding Jesus in Matthew 7:5.

Perhaps the most relevant verse in the New Testament is when Paul says, 'Brothers, if someone is caught in a sin, you who are spiritual should restore him gently. But watch yourself, or you also may be tempted' (Galatians 6:1).

I conclude that in Matthew 7:5 our Lord is promoting honesty and humility, but is none the less offering help in situations where things go wrong. There are situations every day where something needs to happen, such as somebody speaking out. In the light of the New Testament verse quoted above we must surely conclude that Jesus is saying that sometimes there needs to be someone who must step in and offer help; it would be irresponsible not to do so. There is there-fore a way forward and a way whereby we can truly help to remove, delicately, the speck from our brother's or sister's eye without meddling.

Total Forgiveness

'I say to you that many will come from the east and the west, and will take their places at the feast with Abraham, Isaac and Jacob in the kingdom of heaven. But the subjects of the kingdom will be thrown outside, into the darkness, where there will be weeping and gnashing of teeth.'

Matthew 8:11–12

I believe hell exists. It was entirely God's idea. 'Shall not the Judge of all the earth do right?' (Genesis 18:25). When John the Baptist warned people to 'flee from the coming wrath' (Matthew 3:7) – arguably the first message of the New Testament, and eternal punishment was exactly what he meant – his warning made sense. I doubt people would *run* from coming wrath with much concern if they knew in advance it meant only annihilation. Annihilation becomes the same kind of non-existence the unbeliever is counting on when they die. What perhaps worries me most about the promotion of the idea of annihilation is that it hands on a silver platter a *theological* rationale to unbelievers – precisely what they were hoping in the first place was true. They say, 'Why should I believe? Why should I give up my way of life? I will eventually end up as though I never lived – no unending hell to fear.'

The teaching of Jesus regarding hell was not meant to make us comfortable. He had more to say about hell than he did about heaven. People sometimes say, 'I believe in heaven but I don't believe in hell.' I answer: if there is no hell, there is no heaven. The two rise or fall together. As for Jesus' teaching on hell, it blasts us out of our comfort zone. For the God who conceived of the teaching of hell and who created hell is not very nice. It's not my idea, I can assure you. No human being would have thought this up.

But what if it is true? It makes all the difference in our outlook, our evangelism, our view of God and our sense of gratitude that we ourselves will not spend eternity in hell.

Out of the Comfort Zone

Everyone must submit himself to the governing authorities, for there is no authority except that which God has established. The authorities that exist have been established by God. Consequently, he who rebels against the authority is rebelling against what God has instituted, and those who do so will bring judgment on themselves. For rulers hold no terror for those who do right, but for those who do wrong. Do you want to be free from fear of the one in authority? Then do what is right and he will commend you. For he is God's servant to do you good. But if you do wrong, be afraid, for he does not bear the sword for nothing. He is God's servant, an agent of wrath to bring punishment on the wrongdoer. Therefore, it is necessary to submit to the authorities, not only because of possible punishment but also because of conscience.

Romans 5:1–5

There is a difference between saving grace and common grace. Saving grace is given to some, common grace is given to all. We call it 'common' not because it is ordinary, but because it is commonly granted to all men and women. It is the endowment of creation. It is God's goodness to all people. John Calvin called it 'special grace within nature'. It is what gives order in the world. It does not refer to conversion, regeneration (being born again) or sanctification, but to one's natural abilities. It is why we have certain talents and a particular level of intelligence. It explains your having a job and having income. Non-Christians have common grace as well as Christians.

We should be thankful for common grace. It is the reason we have firemen, police, doctors, nurses, medicine, music, literature. When is the last time you thanked God for firemen? I know that many in New York suddenly became grateful for heroic firemen after 11 September 2001. When is the last time you thanked God for your doctor? For farmers that grow vegetables? Food is by God's common grace. God gives us food, water, rain, sun, schools, transportation and sleep. It has nothing to do with being saved, but saved people ought to be the first to be grateful for these things.

Thanking God

*In the presence of God and of Christ Jesus, who will judge the
living and the dead, and in view of his appearing and his kingdom,
I give you this charge: Preach the Word; be prepared in season and
out of season; correct, rebuke and encourage – with great patience
and careful instruction.*

2 Timothy 4:1–2

Oswald Chambers once asked a provoking question: 'Am I close
enough to God to feel secure when he is silent?' In other words, must
I have a constant two-way communication with God to feel approved
and loved by him? One of the reasons Paul exhorted Timothy to 'be
instant in season, out of season' (2 Timothy 4:2, AV) is because we
must develop a maturity that does not panic 'between the times', to
use Richard Bewes's helpful phrase. 'In season' is a time of refreshing,
when God clearly manifests himself; 'out of season' is when he seems
to hide his face from us. He is silent.

God wants us to learn from his silence as much as he does from
his absence. For one thing, we perhaps learn more about ourselves
when God hides himself than in times of conscious blessing. His silence
is like sitting an examination in which we demonstrate how much we
have learned about his 'ways'.

The Sensitivity of the Spirit

After the Feast was over, while his parents were returning home, the boy Jesus stayed behind in Jerusalem, but they were unaware of it. Thinking he was in their company, they travelled on for a day. Then they began looking for him among their relatives and friends.

Luke 2:43–44

Presumption. It is an easy thing to take on board. But in many cases it can be costly. It is so hard not to presume. It is a word that means 'to take for granted', or 'to suppose to be true'. I believe that we should pray every day to beware of presumption. It is assuming something to be true without the evidence. False assumptions have led many people into difficulty and some to destruction. One of the scariest of the proverbs is this: 'There is a way that seems right to a man, but in the end it leads to death' (Proverbs 14:12).

What did Joseph and Mary presume when they headed home after the Feast of the Passover in Jerusalem? In a word: that Jesus moved with them just because they moved. That was reasonable to presume at the time. There was no reason to think otherwise. But it was a lesson they never forgot. It could have been the most traumatic moment for Mary, that is, between Jesus' birth and his public ministry. I only know that it was the only event of that era she apparently chose to share with Luke. She could have told hundreds of stories. But she gave only this one. It was admirable and vulnerable of her to reveal how she spoke to Jesus – 'Why have you treated us like this?'

The chief lesson here is that we should not presume upon God merely because we have had a close relationship with him. Nobody was closer to Jesus than his parents. That is about as close to the Lord as one could ever get! And if they made the mistake of presuming that Jesus moved because they moved, how much more should you and I be cautious in this area.

The Sensitivity of the Spirit

But Martha was distracted by all the preparations that had to be made. She came to him and asked, 'Lord, don't you care that my sister has left me to do the work by myself? Tell her to help me!' 'Martha, Martha,' the Lord answered, 'you are worried and upset about many things, but only one thing is needed. Mary has chosen what is better, and it will not be taken away from her.'

Luke 10:40–42

Alexi Bischkov, the former General Secretary of Baptists of the Soviet Union, made a very interesting observation about Christianity in Russia, *vis-à-vis* his observations in Britain and America. He thought that Christianity in the West was largely patterned after Martha, whereas in Russia Christianity was more like that of Mary.

On one occasion Jesus went to the home of Mary and Martha to be given hospitality by them. As soon as Jesus arrived Mary sat at his feet 'listening to what he said'. But Martha was 'distracted by all the preparations that had to be made'. She no doubt was annoyed with Mary for spending her time with Jesus rather than getting things ready, but it was Jesus to whom she made her feelings known.

Mr Bischkov's observations of Christians in the West was that they are 'careful and troubled about many things', as the Authorised Version translates the passage above. He thought that we in the West are bogged down by organisations and preparation for spiritual things while Christians in Russia merely want to spend time in the presence of the Lord. Having spent two weeks in the Soviet Union in 1985, visiting a number of their churches and getting to know many Christians, I would concur with his statement. I detected a level of genuine piety and devotion to the person of Jesus there that I have seldom found anywhere else. The Christians there had a simple dependence on the Lord Jesus and an experiential knowledge of him that moved my wife and me very deeply indeed.

Does Jesus Care?

'Lord,' Martha said to Jesus, 'if you had been here, my brother would not have died. But I know that even now God will give you whatever you ask.'

John 11:21–22

It is a wonderful thing to be able to say 'But I know' in a time of distress. Martha had an abiding faith that kept her in touch with the living God in her time of sorrow. This is because she knew something before sorrow came. This comes by hearing the words of Jesus and putting them into practice. Whoever does this, said Jesus, is like 'a wise man who built his house on the rock. The rain came down, the streams rose, and the winds blew and beat against that house; yet it did not fall, because it had its foundation on the rock' (Matthew 7:24–25).

We never know when trouble will come. When it does come it tests us by causing what we are to come to light. If we hear the teachings of Jesus but do not put them into practice in our experience, we shall be like what our Lord called the 'foolish man who built his house on sand. The rain came down, the streams rose, and the winds blew and beat against that house, and it fell with a great crash' (Matthew 7:26–27).

Can you say, 'But I know', when trouble comes to you? The Bible says we can *know* certain things. For example, do you *know* that you are saved? Do you *know* that, were you to die today, you would go to heaven? One of the reasons for the Bible being written was that you might know this. 'I write these things to you who believe in the name of the Son of God so that you may know that you have eternal life' (1 John 5:13).

Does Jesus Care?

And we know that in all things God works for the good of those who love him, who have been called according to his purpose.

Romans 8:28

I believe everything that happens in the world is with a purpose, that God allows things to happen and there is a reason for it. But only the Christian has the assurance that 'all things work together for good'. You may say, 'It will all turn out well.' Only to the saved is there such hope. All things work together for good for them that *love God.* To them who are the called according to his purpose. And so if you don't love God – surprise, surprise – this verse will never make sense. It cannot. This is a promise for members of the family only. It is the family secret. Those outside the family can never make sense of a verse like Romans 8:28; they cannot claim that promise.

One day, however, God will clear his name – openly. But those who clear his name now can say with Job, 'Though he slay me, yet will I hope in him' (Job 13:15). They are the ones who will stand proud in that day when everybody sees that the God of the Bible is a God of faithfulness, that he is just and righteous.

The Day the World Changed

'"Though seeing, they do not see; though hearing, they do not hear or understand . . . Otherwise they might see with their eyes, hear with their ears, understand with their hearts and turn, and I would heal them."'

Matthew 13:13–15

Have you thought about the way Jesus introduced his parables? The way to understand the parables is to grasp the sovereignty of God. In introducing the parables he told why he spoke in parables.

The purpose of the parables, said Jesus, is to keep those who will not be saved from being saved – or healed. Parables were to keep those for whom they *are* intended to wait until the right time for them to have them unveiled. Parables were actually designed to keep certain people in the dark! This aspect of the teachings of Jesus has been largely neglected by the Church. We all know that Jesus spoke in parables but seem to sweep under the carpet his own rationale for using them. His reason for using them was his own belief in the sovereignty of God.

Out of the Comfort Zone

It is not rude, it is not self-seeking, it is not easily angered, it keeps no record of wrongs.

1 Corinthians 13:5

'You are responsible for the wrong I am suffering' (Genesis 16:5). But it was Sarah's own suggestion that Abraham sleep with Hagar, her maidservant, in order that Sarah could 'build a family through her' (Genesis 16:2). The result of this union was that Hagar gave birth to Ishmael. This caused immense problems in the household.

Once we realise we have made a wrong decision our self-righteous nature often lures us into thinking it was not our fault – but someone else's. So we blame others. We do this because we feel so guilty ourselves. Those who carry the greatest sense of guilt are brilliant in giving guilt trips. Or, to put it the other way around, those who give the greatest guilt trips usually have the deepest sense of guilt themselves. We foolishly think that pointing the finger is going to shift the blame and make us feel better.

Many marriages could be healed overnight if both the husband and the wife would *stop pointing the finger*. It is our words that make the other person feel bad. If we could stop keeping a record of wrongs in our marriage we would be miles ahead. Why do we keep records? To prove that we paid, to prove we said this, promised that. But love will tear the records up – so they cannot be referred to again. But when we keep the record of the wrong it is because in that moment we have already decided to refer to it one day. 'I will remember that – I won't forget that,' the husband says to the wife. And he keeps his word. The marriage could be on the rocks.

Abraham and Sarah survived. But her pointing the finger put a severe strain on their marriage. It shows that the best of God's servants have marriage and family problems. But so many of them could be avoided if we stopped playing the blame game.

Your Words Have Power

Do not put out the Spirit's fire; do not treat prophecies with contempt. Test everything. Hold on to the good. Avoid every kind of evil.

1 Thessalonians 5:19–22

God wants to communicate with us not just at an intellectual level. I'm touching now on a problem many of us have. It's easy to think that the only stimulation that matters is cerebral brilliance or depth. But God wants to communicate with our whole being – our emotions and senses as well as our minds.

If we suppress genuine Spirit-led feelings we put out the Spirit's fire. Why does Paul tell us not to put out the Spirit's fire? He's talking about rejoicing evermore, praying without ceasing, giving thanks in everything, then tells us not to quench the spirit, nor to treat prophecies with contempt. It is because we all have a fear of things getting out of hand. Just as there are those who are afraid to believe in justification by faith because of the fear of lawlessness, so also there are those who want things to be done in rigid order because of the danger of fanaticism. These people are in danger of quenching the Spirit.

However, in the next verse Paul says to test all things and hold fast to what is good. We are to use our minds. God wants us to have our heads screwed on. We are to be harmonious, whole and balanced people.

Worshipping God

When he came near the place where the road goes down the Mount of Olives, the whole crowd of disciples began joyfully to praise God in loud voices for all the miracles they had seen.

Luke 19:37

Real worship takes place when we are unafraid to express what we feel. There's nothing that leads to greater pain than repressed feelings. Repression is a defence mechanism. We can't face up to what we feel, so we deny it, sometimes unconsciously, involuntarily. But we don't get rid of something by repressing it. It goes down into our subconscious and comes out later as high blood pressure or mental illness or something else.

We need to learn to express our feelings, at least to ourselves and to God. We need to admit to ourselves what we really think and feel. For example, perhaps we weren't honest about our feelings a year ago, but now we can say, 'This is the way I really felt. I see it now. I wish I had seen it then, and been true to myself at that time.'

Worship ought to bring us to the point where we can be honest right now. We never need to repress what we feel when we are around Jesus. He will never scold us for our honesty. It doesn't mean we are right, but if we are being honest, he can help us and bring us to see where we are wrong, and to face the truth.

We may envy the people's exuberance on Palm Sunday. We may say, 'I wish I could do that. I just can't get excited like this. They shouted out aloud, but that's not my nature. How could they do it?'

There's only one answer. Jesus was right there. When Jesus is there you forget everybody else and let yourself go. Possibly the highest goal in worship is simply not to be self-conscious but only conscious of Jesus. *Then* we will express our feelings!

Worshipping God

How precious to me are your thoughts, O God!
  How vast is the sum of them!
Were I to count them,
  they would outnumber the grains of sand.
When I awake,
  I am still with you.

Psalm 139:17–18

When God speaks to us face to face, as he did with Moses, it is impossible to say who enjoys it most – God or us. I am moved to know that God spoke to Moses face to face, 'as a man speaks with his friend' (Exodus 33:11). God loved Moses' company; he loved Abraham's company, also calling him his friend (Isaiah 41:8; James 2:23). What a compliment to the disciples that Jesus said to them, 'I have called you friends' (John 15:15). Friendship is developed by spending time with a person.

The thought that God likes my company thrills me more than I can explain to you. And if he likes my company, he likes yours too – he is no respecter of persons (Acts 10:34; 1 Peter 1:17). The same blood that purchased Peter's and Paul's salvation bought yours and mine. Moreover, it is that blood which gives all of us equal access into God's presence (Hebrews 10:19). I therefore can put out of my mind the thought that some people are more acceptable to God than others. One's profile in the Church has nothing to do with our being accepted by him – or loved, or enjoyed. We are all on level ground.

Did You Think to Pray?

'I have made you known to them, and will continue to make you known in order that the love you have for me may be in them and that I myself may be in them.'

John 17:26

As St Augustine put it, God loves every person as if there were no one else to love. I hate the thought of being a bore; I hate wasting people's time. I can sometimes tell by the look on their faces if they are not happy to see me. I fear rejection. And if I'm not careful, I can carry this fear of rejection right into the presence of God, assuming I am boring him too. Why should God care about me? Why should he listen to what I have to say? And why would he like my company?

It is such a dazzling thought, that the same God who has countless billions of angels worshipping him sixty seconds a minute day and night, to whom the nations are but a drop in the bucket and who knows all about every leaf on every tree in the world, also welcomes my company – because I am very important to him.

Indeed, I can think of no more amazing thought than this, that God loves me as much as he loves Jesus. That's right! You and I are co-heirs with Jesus (Romans 8:17). Jesus even prayed that we would grasp that the Father loves us just as much as he loves Jesus.

If there is anything that will make us blush in heaven it will be the realisation of how much we were loved on this earth – but didn't appreciate it. And if we knew how much God welcomes us when we turn to him, we would almost certainly pray more than we do. God likes our company.

What does prayer do for God? It blesses him.

Did You Think to Pray?

What is man that you are mindful of him?

Psalm 8:4

Have you ever wondered why God cares so much for us? David asked the same question. Why does God have a *special* concern for *human beings* as opposed to plants, animals, fish – and the rest of creation? There are at least three reasons for God's jealous care over us: (1) we – not *any other creature* – are made in God's own image (Genesis 1:26); (2) God's eternal Son (before the eternal Word was made flesh) chose to take on *not* the nature of angels but the seed of Abraham (Hebrews 2:16, AV); and (3) Jesus died indiscriminately *not* for animals or angels but for every human being (Hebrews 2:9).

Whether you are a believer or not, you are bought with a price (1 Corinthians 6:20; 2 Corinthians 5:15). Yes, even those who do not submit to his lordship are none the less *bought* with the blood of Jesus. Peter referred to those who actually denied the Lord who 'bought' them (2 Peter 2:1), referring to people who never were truly converted. This means that God has sovereign rights over each of us – saved or lost.

Did You Think to Pray?

But some of them said, 'Could not he who opened the eyes of the blind man have kept this man from dying?'

John 11:37

Jesus refused to respond to the question of these critical Jews. He mirrored God's silence when it comes to answering this kind of question. But it does not mean he does not care.

The next sentence says, 'Jesus, once more deeply moved, came to the tomb' (John 11:38). The Authorised Version says, groaning in himself! This tells me that Jesus *felt* what they said but ignored it. He heard it. He knew what they meant by it. He was not unaffected by it. But he ignored it.

When God hears people utter contemptible things about himself, what does he do about it? He hears his name taken in vain. He hears disgraceful things said about his beloved Son. He hears awful things said about his beloved Church – the apple of his eye. Why doesn't he step down from heaven and strike people dead who speak about him like this? Doesn't he care? If God cared about this, surely he would show it (we may think).

He ignores it; but he cares. He groans within himself. He hears it and feels it. But he goes on with his purpose in the world. He has a plan. In a little while all will see what he was up to. The same God who weeps when we weep equally groans when scoffers utter ridicule towards his Son, but he ignores it and gets on with his perfect plan.

Does Jesus Care?

Likewise the tongue is a small part of the body, but it makes great boasts. Consider what a great forest is set on fire by a small spark. The tongue also is a fire, a world of evil among the parts of the body. It corrupts the whole person, sets the whole course of his life on fire, and is itself set on fire by hell.

James 3:5–6

One evening at about eleven o'clock, as I was going to bed, I found myself having an imaginary conversation about someone. I imagined I had an opportunity to spill the beans about this person. I pictured the scenario in which I made myself look good and the other person look bad. But the Holy Spirit – miraculously – got into the matter. I felt I heard him say, 'You can get a victory right now if you refuse to think anything in order to clear your name.' Even though it was but a conversation that existed only in my own mind, I realised that I had an opportunity to triumph – in my spirit! It was a wonderful moment. It was pivotal. Because it was as if it was *real* – and I refused to say anything at all about the person. A peace entered my heart, and I knew then and there that I must never again enter into imaginary conversations – unless it meant refusing to vindicate myself. I would not recommend you to engage in an imaginary conversation. But for those who find the practice therapeutic, I would only say let your thoughts be positive and wholesome; keep no records of wrongs in your *thoughts* and you will be less likely to expose such records by your *words*.

When I am tempted to say something negative but refuse to speak, I can often feel the release of the Holy Spirit within. It is as if God says, 'Well done.' It is a very good feeling. After all, Jesus is touched with our weaknesses (Hebrews 4:15), and equally he lets us feel his joy when we overcome them! He rewards us with an incredible peace; he sends the Spirit to witness.

Total Forgiveness

For his anger lasts only a moment,
  but his favour lasts a lifetime;
weeping may remain for a night,
  but rejoicing comes in the morning.

Psalm 30:5

The ability to forgive ourselves comes partly from understanding guilt. Guilt means feeling that one is to blame. For example, when you blame others, you have kept a record of their wrongs. When you blame yourself, you have kept a record of your wrongs. True guilt is where sin is involved. The Holy Spirit shows us our sin. The initial work of the Spirit according to John 16:8 is that he convicts of sin. When Isaiah saw the glory of the Lord he was convicted of sin (Isaiah 6:1–5). When we walk in the light we know the blood cleanses of sin; but walking in the light also reveals sin in us that we may not have seen before (1 John 1:7–8).

But the sense of guilt that God instigates is temporary; it is momentary. God only uses guilt to get our attention. When we say, 'I'm sorry' (because we mean it), that's enough for God. He doesn't beat us black and blue and require us to go on a thirty-day fast to supplement Christ's atonement. He convicts us of sin to get our attention; but having done that, he wants us to go forward.

Total Forgiveness

Love . . . keeps no record of wrongs.

1 Corinthians 13:5

The sweet consequence of not keeping a record of wrongs (theirs and ours) is that we let go of the past and its effect on the present. In this way, we cast our care on God and rely on him to restore the wasted years and to make everything turn out for good. We find ourselves, almost miraculously, accepting ourselves as we are – which God does. With all our failures – as God does. And even accepting ourselves, while still knowing we have the potential to make more mistakes. God never gets disillusioned with us; he loves us and knows us inside out already. That's why he can still use us.

Moses had a past; he was a murderer. Years later he would proclaim the eighth commandment: you shall not murder (Exodus 20:13). David had a past, and a future after his shame: 'Then I will teach transgressors your ways, and sinners will turn back to you' (Psalm 51:13). Jonah deliberately ran from God, but was still used in an astonishing revival (Jonah 3). Peter's disgrace – denying Jesus – did not abort God's plans for him. All these men had to forgive themselves.

Can you do that? Having forgiven others, it is time to forgive yourself. Even if that sin takes so long to forgive. But once you have done it, forgive yourself as well. That is exactly what God wants of you and me. It is long overdue: let the past be past . . . at last.

Total Forgiveness

'"Love your neighbour as yourself."'

Matthew 22:39

I must now define what I mean by totally forgiving ourselves: it is accepting God's forgiveness of all my past sins and failures so completely that I equally let myself off the hook for my past as God himself has done. It also means that since I must forgive others totally, I must equally forgive myself totally. This is an example of what it means to love my neighbour as I love myself.

To put it another way, Jesus commanded us not to judge others: 'Do not judge, and you will not be judged. Do not condemn, and you will not be condemned. Forgive, and you will be forgiven' (Luke 6:37).

If I am not to judge or condemn others, it follows I should not judge or condemn myself (since God promised not to condemn me). If I am to forgive others, I must also forgive myself (since God has forgiven me). If I do judge or condemn others I will be judged and condemned (Matthew 7:1–2). And if I don't forgive others I forfeit the blessing of being forgiven (Matthew 6:14–15). So if I condemn myself for my past and refuse to forgive myself, I likewise forfeit the wonderful benefit that is promised to those who enjoy God's forgiveness.

Why should God require me to accept *his* forgiveness and command me to forgive *others* but close his eyes as to whether I have forgiven *myself*? He doesn't.

I'm sorry, but this matter of forgiving ourselves is not an optional extra in God's plan for us; it is something we are required to do as obedient children of our heavenly Father.

Totally Forgiving Ourselves

*I care very little if I am judged by you or by any human court;
indeed, I do not even judge myself. My conscience is clear, but that
does not make me innocent. It is the Lord who judges me.*

1 Corinthians 4:3–4

What Paul means is this. He is not going to let people who judge
him also govern how he feels about himself. Indeed, he is not going
to let their opinions bother him! He even adds, 'I do not even judge
myself.' Think about that! He is so free from any guilt over his past
that he refuses to go where God himself has declared, as it were, 'No
Trespassing Allowed' – to quote Corrie ten Boom. She used to say that
this very sign is posted over our sins that have been washed by Christ's
blood – to keep us from trying to go into forbidden territory. So if
God has forgiven Saul of Tarsus, why should Paul now question that
fact by judging himself? The answer is: he won't!

Totally Forgiving Ourselves

Do not be anxious about anything, but in everything, by prayer and petition, with thanksgiving, present your requests to God.

Philippians 4:6

Philippians 4:6 mentions two words: translated as 'prayer' (Greek: *proseuche*) and 'petition' (Greek: *deesei*). These two words can be used interchangeably and are often both translated as 'prayer'. But *deesei*, translated 'petition' ('supplication' – AV), is on occasions used with the more earnest kind of praying and is sometimes used to mean 'intercession'. For example, 'Brothers, my heart's desire and prayer [Greek: *deesis*] to God for the Israelites is that they may be saved.' This is a reference to Paul interceding on behalf of Israel. Nothing mattered more to Paul than the salvation of Israel, so he used *deesei* in this instance, which shows a deeper yearning and wish. This word is found in Luke 2:37 where it is used alongside fasting. It referred to Anna, a prophetess, who at the age of eighty-four worshipped night and day with 'fasting and praying' (Greek: *deesein*).

However, the slight difference in the two Greek words for prayer must not be pushed too far. They both can be translated as 'prayer' – that is, 'asking' or 'requesting'.

But when *asking God to act* is carried out on behalf of *others* we are lifted into the Big Leagues – we enter into intercession not unlike that of our Lord Jesus and of the Holy Spirit. It is an unselfish enterprise that brings great glory to God and does incalculable good for others.

Did You Think to Pray?

God, whom I serve with my whole heart in preaching the gospel of his Son, is my witness how constantly I remember you in my prayers at all times.

Romans 1:9–10

When people tell us they pray for us it affirms us. It makes us think that we must matter to others, and makes us feel good. So, yes, when you pray for others, tell them – so long as you don't do it to 'score points'! Our self-righteousness can nullify any good we hoped to accomplish within seconds.

The Pharisees prayed only to be seen doing so (Matthew 6:5–6), and Jesus remarked that all that they did was 'done for men to see' (Matthew 23:5). If this is our motive, then it is clearly wrong to tell people we pray for them. But we can push the fear of being like the Pharisees a little bit too far; therefore, to reiterate, I think on balance it is good to tell people that you pray for them.

Paul is my biblical example for believing it is OK to tell people we are praying for them. To the church at Rome he stated that he remembered them in his 'prayers at all times' (Romans 1:9–10); to the Ephesians, 'I keep asking that the God of our Lord Jesus Christ, the glorious Father, may give you the Spirit of wisdom and revelation, so that you may know him better' (Ephesians 1:17); to the Philippians, 'In all my prayers for all of you, I always pray with joy' (Philippians 1:4); to the Colossians, 'Since the day we heard about you, we have not stopped praying for you' (Colossians 1:9); to the church of the Thessalonians, 'We always thank God for all of you, mentioning you in our prayers' (1 Thessalonians 1:2). What an encouragement it must have been for Timothy to receive these words, 'Night and day I constantly remember you in my prayers. Recalling your tears' (2 Timothy 1:3–4). The same would be true of Philemon, 'I remember you in my prayers' (Philemon 4).

Did You Think to Pray?

Now to each one the manifestation of the Spirit is given for the common good . . . to another gifts of . . . distinguishing between spirits.

1 Corinthians 12:7–10

One of the gifts of the Spirit is called 'the ability to distinguish between spirits' (1 Corinthians 12:10). It seems that some people assume that this means only the ability to recognise the demonic. This is a lop-sided emphasis. For it also, if not primarily, means the ability to recognise the genuine Holy Spirit. It is one thing to be an 'expert' in the area of the demonic, quite another to be able to discern the genuine presence of God. If anything, it takes a higher level of spirituality to recognise the *real* than it does to detect the counterfeit. But sadly there are people who mainly think in terms of recognising the devil and seeing a demon behind every bush! It is just as important to discern when God is present as when Satan is active.

We cannot really discern God's absence until we have experienced his presence. Could it be that some Christians have not really experienced the special presence of God and would therefore not have a clue what is meant by his absence? I don't mean to be unfair, but I suspect either would feel the same to some of us.

The Sensitivity of the Spirit

When Jacob awoke from his sleep, he thought, 'Surely the LORD is in this place, and I was not aware of it.' He was afraid and said, 'How awesome is this place! This is none other than the house of God; this is the gate of heaven.'

Genesis 28:16–17

The manifestation of God's presence can be unveiled in more than one way. Jacob felt the presence of God at Bethel and he was *afraid*. That feeling of awe was what people experienced as a result of a healing presence in Galilee (Luke 5:17, 26). They felt this immediately after Pentecost (Acts 2:43) and following Ananias and Sapphira being struck dead by the Spirit (Acts 5:11). And yet in Ezra's day when the builders laid the foundations of the temple of the Lord many 'shouted for joy' (Ezra 3:12). And when Ezra gave an exposition of the Law, 'Nehemiah said, "Go and enjoy choice food and sweet drinks, and send some to those who have nothing prepared. This day is sacred to our Lord. Do not grieve, for the joy of the Lord is your strength"' (Nehemiah 8:10). David said, 'You will fill me with joy in your presence' (Psalm 16:11). The angel of the Lord said to the shepherds, 'I bring you good news of great joy' (Luke 2:10). As a result of Philip preaching in Samaria, 'So there was great joy in that city' (Acts 8:8).

We must try to remain open to the manner in which God chooses to manifest his glory. For some there is a bias in the direction of the fear of God. That to them proves that God is present. Some would even be uneasy with joy. *Fear* is their comfort zone. They also have a ready-made theological rationale for not smiling and looking sad. When we don't have much joy we can hide behind the convenient view that God's glory always produces a sense of fear. And yet for some there is a bias in the direction of joy and happy worship. I recall a man at my old college in Nashville who stood up – right after singing 'When I survey the wondrous cross' – and shouted, 'Let's stop singing these dead songs and get some life in this place.' How sad, but that is exactly what he said. We don't seem to realise sometimes that a comfort zone so easily masquerades as what we deem to be the presence of God.

The Sensitivity of the Spirit

When his parents saw him, they were astonished. His mother said to him, 'Son, why have you treated us like this? Your father and I have been anxiously searching for you.'

Luke 2:48

Mary revealed her anxiety to Jesus when she and Joseph found him after three days in Jerusalem's temple courts. We have all been like that, even in the presence of God; but not in his special presence – when the Spirit is *at home* in us. Ungrieved.

That is truly the way it is in his special presence. It is a peace that 'transcends all understanding' (Philippians 4:7). It is God's own peace. This is different from peace *with* God (Romans 5:1) which assures us that we are his and are accepted. And that, of course, brings peace. And yet there is even more than that which is promised: the peace *of* God. It is that alone which transcends all understanding: 'You will keep in perfect peace him whose mind is steadfast, because he trusts in you' (Isaiah 26:3). This is why Paul counselled, 'Do not be anxious about anything' (Philippians 4:6), which seems ridiculous – until one has experienced it.

God has not given us a 'spirit of fear' (2 Timothy 1:7, AV), which best describes anxiety. One possible difference between fear and anxiety is that you probably know what you fear, but anxiety – a spirit of fear – is a general state of mind when you can't put your finger on what you are afraid of. It is what almost certainly emerges in our hearts when God's special presence subsides. It is precisely because Christ's special presence is available to us that Paul could say, 'Do not be anxious about anything' (Philippians 4:6), or 'Let nothing move you' (1 Corinthians 15:58). For when that sweet anointing settles on us, our problems disappear.

The Sensitivity of the Spirit

'If anyone chooses to do God's will, he will find out whether my teaching comes from God or whether I speak on my own.'

John 7:17

God never panics. The degree to which we have the mind of the Spirit will be the degree to which we reflect his calm and gentleness. Clear thinking will demonstrate sound judgment, wisdom and also truth in doctrine. The ungrieved Spirit in us is the greatest preservative against theological error. Panic throws our thinking about biblical truth into disarray and, sadly, we sometimes foolishly defend propositions that have no warrant in Scripture as a result. There is therefore a close connection between our personal relationship with the Holy Spirit and what we believe. If we come to the calm that characterises God himself, we will be led to truth.

It is an awful feeling to be left to ourselves without the aid of the Spirit. It has happened to me – publicly. In our church's greatest crisis many years ago I was conducting a church meeting in which my leadership was under question. I was not prepared for what was being said. I allowed the meeting to get out of hand and those who opposed my ministry got the upper hand. Nothing that came out of my mouth was inspired. I never felt so deserted. As people left the meeting – some with a look of glee on their countenances – I knew I had failed to demonstrate presence of the mind of the Spirit.

I was all right the next day. Clear thinking returned and I was able to anticipate even greater challenges soon coming. Why did the Lord 'stay behind' the night before? I do not know. But I learned not to pretend that I had the mind of Christ when I didn't. It taught me to know that the absence of clear thinking is the absence of God's special presence.

The Sensitivity of the Spirit

October

There is no fear in love. But perfect love drives out fear, because fear has to do with punishment. The one who fears is not made perfect in love.

1 John 4:18

John said that perfect love casts out fear and that 'fear has to do with punishment'. The Authorised Version says 'fear hath torment'. This is true of course, but that is not exactly what John actually said in 1 John 4:18. Fear *kolasiv echei* – 'has, or possesses, punishment'. The person living in fear is obsessed with the idea of punishment. This means at least four things: (1) that the person who lives in fear is already punished by this fear, truly living in torment; (2) the person is in fear of being punished by God; (3) the person in fear is always punishing himself or herself; and (4) the person who lives in fear always wants to punish others.

Various translations bring out some of these meanings. 'If we are afraid, it is for fear of what he [God] might do to us' (Living Bible). 'Fully developed love expels every particle of fear, for fear always contains some of the torture of feeling guilty' (Phillips Modern English). 'To fear is to expect punishment' (Jerusalem Bible).

Fear is in a sense its own punishment. In much the same way that love is its own reward, which means it is fulfilling in itself, so too fear is tormenting. When one lives in fear, we often feel that we are being punished by God all the time. If that is not enough, we do it to ourselves – we beat ourselves black and blue for our past sins. If that too is not enough, we almost always take it out on others. In other words, we fear that justice isn't going to be carried out on those who have been unjust to us. We move in on God's territory because we are fearful that they won't get what's coming to them. Never mind that God said, 'It is mine to avenge' (Hebrews 10:30); we get impatient with the way he seems not to avenge them. So we try to do it for him.

Totally Forgiving Ourselves

And what I have forgiven – if there was anything to forgive – I have forgiven in the sight of Christ for your sake, in order that Satan might not outwit us. For we are not unaware of his schemes.

2 Corinthians 2:10–11

I love the Living Bible's translation: 'A further reason for forgiveness is to keep from being outsmarted by Satan; for we know what he is trying to do.'

Why would Paul refer to forgiveness in connection with the devil's schemes? The answer is very sobering: because our lack of total forgiveness is an open invitation for the devil to move in. In other words, when I do not totally forgive those who have hurt me, I have said to the devil, 'Come and get me, do what you want with me.' This is scary. I certainly don't want to do that. But Satan is crafty and is lurking around us day and night, looking for an entry. When he finds us holding a grudge he exploits it to the full. He knows that as long as I do not totally forgive, the Holy Spirit – the heavenly dove – will fly away for a season. God cannot use me to the full when I am carrying a grudge.

So too, then, with forgiving ourselves. Satan does not want you to forgive yourself. He loves your misery. Your bondage makes him happy. You are no threat to him or his interests when you are punishing yourself, fearing God's wrath, living in torment over what happened yesterday – or years ago. By the way, the devil knows what happened in your past too. He has been around thousands of years and got on your case the moment you sided with his arch-enemy Jesus Christ. He will exploit your past to the hilt. His design: to keep you paralysed and living in a pit of near despair over what is in the past.

Would you not agree, then, that a good reason to forgive yourself is because it is the opposite of what the devil wants for you? Since you know that what he wants is for you not to forgive yourself, then do the opposite. I pray that in this moment you will begin to forgive yourself – totally.

Totally Forgiving Ourselves

No man can tame the tongue. It is a restless evil, full of deadly poison.

James 3:8

The tongue is not a neutral thing. It is a vile part of our being and is – in and of itself – intrinsically evil, wicked and poisonous. It is not our words that make the tongue deadly poisonous; the tongue is already poisonous before we utter a single word. This is because the tongue mirrors the heart. Jesus said, 'Out of the heart come evil thoughts, murder, adultery, sexual immorality, theft, false testimony, slander.' This is Jesus' diagnosis of the heart of all men and women. These startling words to the self-righteous Pharisees followed his statement that 'the things that come out of the mouth come from the heart' (Matthew 15:18–19).

Now you know where James got his teaching.

James contrasts the tongue with nature: 'All kinds of animals, birds, reptiles, and creatures of the sea are being tamed and have been tamed by man, but no man can tame the tongue' (James 3:7–8). Such living creatures are not guilty of deadly poisonous tongues.

Does this surprise you? Did you think that the tongue of a human being was a neutral member of our personality? Natural, yes, but not neutral.

Your Words Have Power

Truly you are a God who hides himself, O God and Saviour of Israel.

Isaiah 45:15

The thing about the hiding of the face of God is that it never comes with advance warning. If only I could say to my church members, 'I need to make an announcement. This week it is going to be on Wednesday. At about a quarter past eleven you will notice the withdrawal of the light of God's countenance, and you will feel desperate. You are going to be on the brink of despair. You are going to call upon the name of God and receive no reply. Things are going to go wrong. You will feel utterly deserted. It will happen, as I said, on Wednesday morning.'

If I could do that, everyone would brace themselves for it. It would be like getting a hurricane or a storm warning. But the thing about the hiding of God's face is that we don't expect it.

And it can happen when we are not aware that we have done anything wrong. God does, of course, hide his face when we are disobeying him – but when that happens, we understand it. What is particularly painful is when we are doing our best to walk in the light, and God hides his face.

We don't understand why it is, but sometimes when we obey God, he seems to desert us. Martin Luther said that you must know God as an enemy before you can know him as a friend. Until you have experienced the hiding of his face and come out on the other side, you won't really come to know God as a friend.

Worshipping God

The righteous will live by his faith.

Habakkuk 2:4

This is a famous verse which is quoted three times in the New Testament. In the Hebrew, it reads: 'The just shall live by his faithfulness.'

There is an intentional ambiguity here. The faithfulness can be God's faithfulness to us, or our faithfulness to God: the verse can be read either way, and it means both. In the Dead Sea Scrolls, discovered in 1947, there is a commentary on Habakkuk 2:4, and it reads, 'The just shall live by God's faithfulness.' This refers to living by the fact that God is faithful to his promises. It is the way Hebrews 10:38 interprets this verse.

But it can equally describe the faithfulness of the individual himself, who doesn't give up hope. The person who trusts God, and lives by his promise to bless, is declared righteous in the sight of God. That became one of the main verses Paul used for the doctrine of justification by faith. It applies to the future – to the fact that God will accept us in heaven – but it also applies to the present. God is saying that we are declared righteous now. There is an existential element here. The word 'existential' means existence – the here and now. What needs to be seen from this verse in Habakkuk is that as we live by God's faithfulness we are in each moment being declared righteous.

If we could only see this today, it would set us afire. If, in the moment when we don't see answered prayer, we could just look up to heaven and say, 'God, I love you anyway,' God would declare us righteous just because our faith pleases him. That kind of faith has a cleansing result. We feel clean. We don't understand why God lets things happen, but we trust him anyway.

Worshipping God

For the revelation awaits an appointed time; it speaks of the end and will not prove false. Though it linger, wait for it; it will certainly come and will not delay.

Habakkuk 2:3

The key phrase here is, 'though it linger, wait for it'. This principle applies to the Second Coming of Christ. Jesus said, 'Suppose that servant is wicked and says to himself, "My master is staying away a long time," and he then begins to beat his fellow-servants and to eat and drink with drunkards. The master of that servant will come on a day when he does not expect him and at an hour he is not aware of. He will cut him to pieces and assign him a place with the hypocrites, where there will be weeping and gnashing of teeth' (Matthew 24:48–51).

When Jesus comes again, or when God comes to fulfil any promise he has made to us, will he find us patiently waiting for him?

After Jesus was raised from the dead, he addressed 500 at once (1 Corinthians 15:6). And on the Day of Pentecost there were 120 praying in the Upper Room. I believe more than 120 people could have been there. I believe that on the first day when Jesus went to heaven they all went to Jerusalem to wait for the promised Spirit. There were probably 500 people, all very excited. Then after a couple of days they began to drift away, so that when the Day of Pentecost arrived there were only 120. How do you suppose the others felt when they found out what had happened and realised that they had missed out?

Many people make a commitment in a moment of inspiration and get a good feeling, but months later that dwindles away. There is an appalling lack of commitment in so many. People start out saying, 'Yes, Lord,' then six months later, where are they? It's true with church attendance, with witness on the streets, with tithing, with prayer.

Worshipping God

How long, O LORD, must I call for help, but you do not listen? Or cry out to you, 'Violence!' but you do not save?

Habakkuk 1:2

Habakkuk's complaint makes me think of that verse in Revelation 6:10 which says, 'They called out in a loud voice, "How long, Sovereign Lord, holy and true, until you judge the inhabitants of the earth and avenge our blood?"' In Psalm 13 we read 'How long, O LORD? Will you forget me for ever? How long will you hide your face from me?'

The question, 'How long?' is a familiar question among us all. For most of us God never acts quickly enough. Have you ever asked the question: why is God slow? One reason is that he sees the end from the beginning. Knowing how it's going to end up, he is in no hurry. Another reason is that time is on his side. Also, as the Bible says, 'With the Lord a day is like a thousand years, and a thousand years are like a day' (2 Peter 3:8). God is in no hurry. He is patient.

And very often we are glad that God is patient. Aren't there times when we thank him for being slow to anger and rich in mercy? How would we like it if God stepped in the moment we sinned? The time comes later when we blush and say, 'God, I'm sorry. I was wrong.'

And God says, 'I knew you were wrong, but I knew you would eventually see it.'

Then we say, 'Thank you, Lord, for being so patient with me.'

Worshipping God

Why do you make me look at injustice? Why do you tolerate wrong? Destruction and violence are before me; there is strife, and conflict abounds.

Habakkuk 1:3

The atheist says 'I'll tell you why I don't believe in God . . .' And he is proud of himself for coming up with such a devastating question: why does God allow suffering? But Habakkuk, a godly man, said, 'Lord, why do you tolerate wrong?' and for a long time God didn't answer. He was silent.

But then, at last, God stepped in. He told Habakkuk that he would send an evil nation, the Chaldeans, to destroy his people. There does come a time when God acts. One after another the prophets all hoped to see the coming of the Messiah, and eventually, after hundreds of years the Messiah came. As Paul put it: 'When the time had fully come, God sent his Son, born of a woman, born under law' (Galatians 4:4).

Worshipping God

Though the fig-tree does not bud and there are no grapes on the vines, though the olive crop fails and the fields produce no food, though there are no sheep in the pen and no cattle in the stalls, yet I will rejoice in the LORD, I will be joyful in God my Saviour. The Sovereign LORD is my strength; he makes my feet like the feet of a deer, he enables me to go on the heights.

Habakkuk 3:17–19

Are you looking for the vine to blossom before you can rejoice? Are you looking for the fig tree to give figs before you can praise the Lord? Are you waiting for the rise in pay? Or for that answered prayer? Are you waiting for everything to fit in before you start praising the Lord? If that is so, then turn in your badge now and give up. As Proverbs 24:10 says, 'If you falter in times of trouble, how small is your strength!' Here was Habakkuk who still had all these complaints but yet said, 'I will rejoice.'

Nothing changed outwardly. The basis for Habakkuk's complaints was still there, the injustices were still there. Nothing had happened to them, but a lot happened to him. Habakkuk was given grace to trace the rainbow through the rain.

Habakkuk saw something that we all need to see: that grace will always be there to keep us one step ahead of the enemy. At the beginning when he talked about the Babylonians, he said, 'Their horses are swifter than leopards' (1:8), but now he says, 'God makes my feet like the feet of a deer'. Whereas a horse can run fast, a deer can climb to places a horse cannot reach. Grace will always be given to us so that we can be one step ahead of the enemy. As Moses said, 'Your strength will equal your days' (Deuteronomy 33:25).

Worshipping God

I am not saying this because I am in need, for I have learned to be content whatever the circumstances. I know what it is to be in need, and I know what it is to have plenty. I have learned the secret of being content in any and every situation, whether well fed or hungry, whether living in plenty or in want.

Philippians 4:11–12

But the main point I want to make is this. There is no categorical promise in the New Testament that God wants you to prosper and that not to prosper is due to your own lack of faith. I do believe that in the long run we cannot outgive the Lord (see 2 Corinthians 9:6–9). But to say that 'God wants you to be well off financially or to prosper materially on the condition you will send us your money' is to cross over a line that shows contempt for the sovereignty of God. The most one should promise is that God may prosper you. But God is sovereign. He cannot be controlled. To use his name to get people to give to one's ministry with the promise 'You will be prosperous' is to manipulate people and offer them hope that is beyond what God's Word guarantees.

Preaching that godliness with contentment is great gain (1 Timothy 6:6) honours God and enables people to build up a reward in heaven. He promises prosperity in this life . . . to some – those who can be trusted with great riches. But not all. The promise is, 'I will have mercy on whom I will have mercy.' Let the prosperity gospel ministers be gripped by God's sovereignty, and see what their preaching would be like after that.

Out of the Comfort Zone

For the message of the cross is foolishness to those who are perishing, but to us who are being saved it is the power of God.

1 Corinthians 1:18

Paul believed in healing. He was an instrument of the Holy Spirit in seeing people healed many times. But he did not claim that the blood shed on the cross *guaranteed* that those who trust Jesus would not only be saved but also healed.

But God has become very nice in recent times, according to some. Nice indeed. We are now told by some – often the same preachers who promise prosperity – that when Jesus died on the cross it was for our being healed of all diseases. That if we are not healed it is because of our lack of faith.

I long to hear one of these preachers uphold the real reason Jesus died: to save us from our sins, to ensure that we will get to heaven, not hell, when we die; to clothe us with the righteousness of Jesus, to free us from the demands of the Mosaic Law, to bring us into intimacy with God the Father and to enable us to have communion with the Holy Spirit. This is Paul's gospel.

Out of the Comfort Zone

12 October

The Lord disciplines those he loves, and he punishes everyone he accepts as a son.

Hebrews 12:6

To be granted repentance is a gracious mercy of God. It is being changed from glory to glory (2 Corinthians 3:18, AV). It is when you discover new ways to please God, when a renewed measure of his presence shows our sin and forgiveness, and greater help in doing God's will; it is insight. The worst thing that can happen to a man or woman is to become stone deaf to the Holy Spirit, losing all sensitivity and thus being unable to be renewed any more to repentance (Hebrews 6:6).

Therefore one should be exceedingly grateful that God succeeds in getting our attention in order to show our need to make a 180-degree turn in our lives. We should take any rebuke, discipline or chastening with both hands! The word 'discipline' or 'chasten' (AV) in Hebrews 12:6 comes from a Greek word that means 'enforced learning'. It is when we virtually have no choice but to take God's will on board. It shows not only that we are loved but that God isn't finished with us yet. Never forget this: whenever God chastens it means we have a future and that the best is yet to come!

The Sensitivity of the Spirit

Then David said to Nathan, 'I have sinned against the LORD.*'*
Nathan replied, 'The LORD *has taken away your sin. You are not*
going to die.'

2 Samuel 12:13

Sexual immorality brings disgrace upon the honour of God's name probably like no other kind of sin. A greater measure of discipline may be necessary. How one reacts to the need of discipline may also be a factor. There are two possible reactions to 'getting caught'. One is to be sorry at once and not be defensive. This was David's reaction when Nathan the prophet confronted him. David immediately sought the Lord, wrote Psalm 51 and was given assurance that he would be used again. 'Then I will teach transgressors your ways, and sinners will turn back to you' (Psalm 51:13).

The other reaction is not responding so graciously. Some dig in their heels and resent those who 'blow the whistle', and stay defensive. People like that are probably going to have to wait a long, long time before they can be restored. They should not blame God if this takes time.

There are therefore degrees to which we can move along without Jesus. If you have done this in a big way, (1) admit it, (2) don't be defensive, (3) turn the matter over to God, and (4) seek his face with all your heart. God will pick up things from where you are, this being true no matter how old you are or how deeply you grieved the Lord! God is a gracious God and will begin at once to cause all things to work together for good (Romans 8:28). This is his promise!

The Sensitivity of the Spirit

Therefore confess your sins to each other and pray for each other so that you may be healed.

James 5:16

Is there a connection between illness and sin? How many of us ask, when we do get ill in some way, 'What have I done?' We all fear that we've done something wrong and God has 'got it in for us'.

Sometimes sin and suffering *are* related. Sometimes they are so related that James actually said, if one has sinned (meaning that if the illness they are praying for is traceable to sin), when the prayer of faith is offered, then the one who is healed will also have this sin forgiven. So James is showing the *possibility* of the connection with sin. This is why he says 'if' he has sinned, one will be forgiven. And that's a big 'if' because it is implying that sin may not be the cause of illness at all. Do not let the devil accuse you or make you believe that your illness is because of sin. However, if you have a valid suspicion that it is, then, before God, ask for the elders of your church to pray for you. I would even suggest that you confess your sin to them. It might be embarrassing to do so, but that will show that you really want to get well. If you say, 'I have reason to believe that I am in this condition because I haven't really forgiven so-and-so or I have been in a relationship that's not right, or whatever, and God is dealing with me', tell people you trust. If you think there is a connection between your illness and sin, share it with those who will tell no one. That is part of the meaning of James 5:16.

The Thorn in the Flesh

Because our gospel came to you not simply with words, but also with power, with the Holy Spirit and with deep conviction. You know how we lived among you for your sake.

1 Thessalonians 1:5

I don't know who expressed the following for the first time, but the reasoning behind it goes something like this: if you do nothing but read your Bible you will *dry up*, if you only pray you will *blow up*, but if you read your Bible *and* pray you will *grow up*. There is a lot of truth to this, but I also think more is needed than this. One needs to *experience* God.

I have cherished a prophetic word given to me many years ago by Alex Buchanan. He said, 'R.T., you must not only convey the Word when you preach, but you must convey God *himself*.' I knew exactly what he meant and that he was right. I needed that. It was not enough that I was sound in my teaching. The question was whether my people were experiencing *God* when I preached. I sought from that moment to make that my goal, not theological soundness.

This should happen when we pray; we should experience God. This is why both Bible reading and prayer go together.

This combination will bring us right into the presence of God. But by 'presence of God' I really mean his *manifest* presence – God himself is always present of course, being omnipresent. But it is the conscious, experienced presence that you and I need to feel when we are alone with God. Yes, *feel*. Don't be afraid of that word. We are all emotional beings and we love feeling happy and joyful. That is what we should experience in God's presence.

Did You Think to Pray?

'But the Counsellor, the Holy Spirit, whom the Father will send in my name, will teach you all things and will remind you of everything I have said to you.'

John 14:26

Let me give you what I regard as one of the best reasons to read the Bible. Jesus promised that when the Holy Spirit came he would remind us of what we had been taught. Think about it. The disciples heard Jesus teach so much. They heard the Sermon on the Mount, they heard the parables, they heard his applications, they heard his replies to the Pharisees. 'How can I remember these things?' they must have thought. Jesus said in so many words: 'Not to worry. The Holy Spirit will bring to your remembrance what I have taught.' And he did!

So with you. Perhaps reading the Bible is not always inspirational. There are times ('in season') when the Bible comes alive, and there are times ('out of season') when it seems boring. This is why Paul said to be prepared 'in season and out of season' (2 Timothy 4:2). Why? Because the Holy Spirit will suddenly remind you of what you have read! You felt nothing at the time, but later on the Holy Spirit comes alongside and reminds you of what you thought you had forgotten!

Let me put it another way. If the Spirit of God comes down on the Church (as I pray for and believe), who will he use? What servants of Christ will be his sovereign instruments in a time of genuine revival? I answer: those who took the time to read, listen to teaching, and learn when it seemed so uninteresting. That's who! I don't mean to be unfair, but if you are empty-headed before the Spirit comes down, you will be empty-headed afterwards!

So why should you read the Bible? So there will be something in your head for the Spirit to remind you of!

Did You Think to Pray?

Rejoice in the Lord always. I will say it again: Rejoice!

Philippians 4:4

When Paul tells us to rejoice it is almost certainly because we don't feel like rejoicing. Otherwise, there was no need for him to say it. The Philippians were not rejoicing because at that time there was a split in the church between two powerful women (Philippians 4:2ff.). Paul's initial counsel to them was: 'Rejoice in the Lord always. I will say it again: Rejoice!' You don't do it because you feel like it, you do it in faith. Faith is trusting in God without empirical evidence, only his word. God likes that. If we have the empirical, objective evidence (as we often do have once the trial is over) and *then* rejoice, our response does not qualify as *faith*. Faith is believing without seeing. To the worldly person, seeing is believing. 'Let this Christ, this King of Israel, come down now from the cross, that we may see and believe' (Mark 15:32). That is always the order for the unregenerate person, seeing first – then believing. But it is *not* true faith when that order is followed. Faith is when you believe without the evidence and can say, with Job, 'Though he slay me, yet will I hope in him' (Job 13:15).

Pure Joy

18 October

Their father Jacob said to them, 'You have deprived me of my chil-dren. Joseph is no more and Simeon is no more, and now you want to take Benjamin. Everything is against me!'

Genesis 42:36

President John F. Kennedy used to say that 'life's not fair'. I do not know what made him say that. He had far more advantages than most, but perhaps he was thinking of people less fortunate than himself. However, what he said is true. It is a wicked world.

Some think that being a Christian will eliminate all that is not good. But bad things happen to God's best, and often good things happen to the vile and venal. A Christian soon discovers that God allows injus-tice to happen to him or her, and such a person is then challenged over whether to complain or accept adversity with dignity.

Self-pity is not acceptable for the Christian, although we have all been guilty of this. If anything, I feel I have at times been the world's worst. Self-pity always feels right at the time, but it is almost always counter-productive when you vocalise it. Feel it if you must, but verbal-ising those feelings does not move the heart of God to come to your rescue. He is more likely to wait a while, and lead you step by step to grow up so that one day you can help others who have the same problem.

Your Words Have Power

'"Love your neighbour as yourself."'

Matthew 19:19

Totally forgiving yourself will help you love people more. The reason you do not forgive yourself totally is very possibly because you do not like yourself. Some people think it is an admirable thing to say, 'I hate myself'. I must lovingly tell you, that it is an abominable thing to say. Do you honestly think that God wants you to hate yourself? It is normal to love yourself. You were created that way. It is sin that brings about self-hatred.

People who do not totally forgive those who hurt them often do not like themselves. It is not surprising, then, that they struggle with liking people. So too with forgiving yourself. When you totally forgive yourself, your perception not only of yourself but others changes. They aren't so bad after all! What is more, you begin more and more to care for others – and to love them.

The fringe benefits that come from forgiving yourself are vast. And one of them is: you find it easier to love people. I do not say that forgiving yourself will make you a Mother Teresa, but you may well be surprised how much easier it is to get involved in other people's problems and worries. But when you and I are so preoccupied with ourselves, we somehow never get around to caring for others, much less loving them. Forgiving ourselves is emancipating. You begin to love yourself as God intends, and you find it easier to care for others.

Jesus did not hate himself. He was sinless, of course, and we are not expected to become entirely like him in this life (that awaits our glorification, 1 John 3:3). But I am saying that totally forgiving ourselves will help us to love people 'more' than before. For when we have not forgiven ourselves we are not in a position even to think about loving others because we are consumed with ourselves.

Totally Forgiving Ourselves

Then Peter remembered the word Jesus had spoken: 'Before the cock crows, you will disown me three times.' And he went outside and wept bitterly.

Matthew 26:75

Then Peter stood up with the Eleven, raised his voice and addressed the crowd: 'Fellow Jews and all of you who live in Jerusalem, let me explain this to you; listen carefully to what I say.'

Acts 2:14

When you have totally forgiven yourself, it brings considerable confidence. Consider Simon Peter. He denied that he even knew Jesus to a Galilean servant girl. This is because the authorities were watching. Peter was in utter fear before them. But when the rooster crowed and Jesus looked at him, Peter knew he was found out and wept bitterly (Matthew 26:69–75). Some seven weeks later Peter addressed thousands on the Day of Pentecost with a fearlessness and confidence that baffled everyone (Acts 2). How was this possible? Peter was totally forgiven and totally forgave himself.

When we cannot forgive ourselves it is hard to look at people in the eyes. It is hard not to look down. We feel guilty, look guilty.

God wants to use those who are free of guilt – totally forgiven. But that forgiveness is of little value on our psychological frame when we do not truly believe we have been forgiven. When we truly believe we have been forgiven, it shows. When we have totally forgiven ourselves, it shows. God can use us. People will want what we have.

Totally Forgiving Ourselves

Do you not know that your body is a temple of the Holy Spirit, who is in you, whom you have received from God?

1 Corinthians 6:19

It has been proved by medical research that holding a grudge can injure your health. Studies have revealed that un-forgiveness can lead to high blood pressure, heart disease, kidney disease, arthritis and other ailments. I don't want you to think that, if you have any of these problems, this is the reason. But with some people this is the case.

It is reasonable to assume, then, that if anger and bitterness are injurious to your physical health, not forgiving yourself is bad for your health too. This is because you are holding a grudge against yourself!

In the Lord's Prayer Jesus put our physical needs before the spiritual. First came 'give us this day our daily bread'; then came 'forgive us our trespasses as we forgive those who trespassed against us' (see Matthew 6:9–13; Luke 11:2–4). Why did Jesus put the physical before the spiritual? It is because we have to eat in order to live. God gave us bodies. He is looking after us in the Lord's Prayer. Furthermore, our daily bread does not only mean food; it means the essentials of life – shelter and clothing as well.

This means God cares about our health. We must take care of our bodies. They are temples of the Holy Spirit. When forgiving ourselves is related to one's health, that is a fairly substantial reason to take this matter seriously!

Totally Forgiving Ourselves

'For everyone who exalts himself will be humbled, and he who humbles himself will be exalted.'

Luke 14:11

One of my favourite parables of Jesus is when he cautioned us not to go to the top table when invited to a banquet. This is because the host might have to say to you, 'Take a lower place' because someone more distinguished than you may have been invited and you will be humiliated! In order to save face, then, take the least prominent seat in the room and then, just maybe, you will be invited to move to a better place and be honoured in the presence of all your fellow guests.

I have had to ask myself many times, do I want to be exalted if it is not God's time – or do I want to be exalted if he does not want me to be exalted at all? My answer is 'No'. What use is it to be exalted before people and have everybody notice when I know in my heart that God the Father is not behind this and is not pleased? It is only a matter of time and the truth will be out! The humiliation later won't be worth it. God wants only what is best for us and our trying to make things happen to make ourselves look good will backfire on us if we do not let him do the exalting.

Out of the Comfort Zone

He said to them, 'You are the ones who justify yourselves in the eyes of men, but God knows your hearts. What is highly valued among men is detestable in God's sight.'

Luke 16:15

My old friend Pete Cantrell often says, 'The greatest freedom is having nothing to prove.' I think this is one of the profoundest words I have ever heard. The person who needs to prove how right or how strong he or she is, is one who is not free. There is a struggle inside to make others think they are right and strong. The truth is, if we really are right and strong, we don't have to say anything! Freedom is being experienced, therefore, when one has nothing to prove. He or she does not need to justify themselves or make themselves look good. It is enough for people like that that *God knows* (see John 5:44).

Your Words Have Power

Then Jesus answered, 'Will you really lay down your life for me? I tell you the truth, before the cock crows, you will disown me three times!'

John 13:38

There are five lessons we can learn from Peter's fall and subsequent restoration:

1 *All who fall can be forgiven.* Never forget that good old promise, 'If we confess our sins, he is faithful and just and will forgive us our sins and purify us from all unrighteousness' (1 John 1:9). It cannot be stressed enough that *all* manner of sin and blasphemy (except the blasphemy of the Holy Spirit) is pardonable.

2 *We are all loved with an everlasting love.* What was true of ancient Israel is true of every born-again child of God: 'I have loved you with an everlasting love' (Jeremiah 31:3). Jesus never stopped loving Peter in all he did. There was nothing Peter could have done to make Jesus love him more, and nothing he could have done to make Jesus love him less.

3 *God is still married to the backslider.* When God rebuked Israel for her waywardness and backsliding, he still said, 'I am your husband' (Jeremiah 3:14). That has not changed; we are the bride of Christ. God hates divorce (Malachi 2:16) and practises what he preaches! Since we are the bride of Christ, God is determined to present us faultless in the end (Ephesians 5:27; Jude 24).

4 *God can use anybody.* If there is any message I would be pleased to convey, and be remembered for most of all, it is this: God can use anybody. If he could use Peter, Moses, Jonah, David, Judah or Gideon, he can use me. And, believe me, dear reader, if God can use me, he can use anybody.

5 *All who anticipate being used again must repent as sorrowfully as Peter did.* Peter's sense of shame was private and personal, and knew no bounds (Mark 14:72). What he felt in those moments – and for days (perhaps, for all we know, for the rest of his life) – could never have been adequately described.

Second Chance

The apostles left the Sanhedrin, rejoicing because they had been counted worthy of suffering disgrace for the Name. Day after day, in the temple courts and from house to house, they never stopped teaching and proclaiming the good news that Jesus is the Christ.

Acts 5:41-42

God did a wonderfully gracious thing for Peter, despite his public disowning of Jesus. He gave him a second chance. It came when Peter and John were summoned before the Sanhedrin. They were flogged and then ordered not to speak in the name of Jesus (Acts 5:40). I can imagine how some in the Sanhedrin must have been thinking. 'We showed them, this will teach them a lesson, they have been punished and humiliated. We won't have to be bothered with them again. They are now sorry for what they have done' – or words along these lines.

The truth is, Peter and John were so excited and thrilled to be blessed in this way that they had to pinch themselves to believe it. Whereas most people I know dread any kind of shame or humiliation, all I know is that Peter and John left the Sanhedrin, 'rejoicing because they had been counted worthy of suffering disgrace for the Name'. Think about that phrase: 'counted worthy'. Who counted them 'worthy'? Answer: God. What a privilege it was to be 'counted worthy' to suffer shame for Jesus! That is exactly the way they felt. It was Peter's second chance. He was so grateful that he had been given a second chance to stand up for the name – and that he hadn't blown it this time. God is so gracious.

If God can use Peter – with all his weaknesses and biases – he can use you and me.

Second Chance

26 October

*But godliness with contentment is great gain. For we brought
nothing into the world, and we can take nothing out of it. But if
we have food and clothing, we will be content with that. People
who want to get rich fall into temptation and a trap and into many
foolish and harmful desires that plunge men into ruin and destruction. For the love of money is a root of all kinds of evil. Some
people, eager for money, have wandered from the faith and pierced
themselves with many griefs.*

1 Timothy 6:6–10

Are you that? Do you want to get rich? God in heaven may be folding
his arms and saying, 'Really?' Some Christians cannot get ahead financially. I am going to tell you why. God won't let them. He's doing some
an enormous favour. It could destroy them. They already have trouble
handling money and they think, 'Well, if I had a little more . . .' Almost
certainly, if they had a little more they would be deeper in debt. This
is the way most of us are. We are by nature greedy. Very few people,
truly, can handle money.

There is a difference between needs and wants. 'And my God will
meet all your needs according to his glorious riches in Christ Jesus'
(Philippians 4:19). The psalmist said, 'I was young and now I am old,
yet I have never seen the righteous forsaken or their children begging
bread' (Psalm 37:25). It is not always easy to know the difference
between our wants and needs.

The Thorn in the Flesh

'Though he slay me, yet will I hope in him.'

Job 13:15

It is my experience that sooner or later nearly every Christian – virtually ten out of ten – will find some occasion when he or she feels God has betrayed them. But it is also my pastoral experience that roughly only one in ten will break through the betrayal barrier. This is, of course, very sad. Most people, when God is smiling on them, can worship with jubilation, give cheerfully to his work, sacrifice time and pleasure for him, and be expected to volunteer for any help needed at one's church. But let God appear to betray them, and these same people, I am ashamed to say, indicate a rather different story. Roughly nine out of ten say – not in a sweet or submissive voice, but cynically if not sarcastically – 'Thanks a lot, God.' They feel God has let them down at the most crucial moment. It always seems like that. Such people never discover the joy awaiting them on the other side were they to break through that barrier.

Are you wanting more of God? He invites you to break the betrayal barrier. A. W. Tozer used to say that we can have as much of God as we want. I disagreed with that at first. This is because I felt I didn't have as much of God as I wanted! But I have decided that Tozer was right: we *can* have as much of God as we want; but that wanting more of him gets tested – by the betrayal barrier. It comes unexpectedly and at the 'worst' time. It is not my *feeling* of wanting more of God – as when I worship or respond to an inspiring message – that proves I really want more of him; it is how I respond to things that happen to me later on that proves I really want more of him.

Pure Joy

These were all commended for their faith, yet none of them received what had been promised.

Hebrews 11:39

The great men and women of the Old Testament had in common not only their achievements by faith (as in Hebrews 11), but also their breaking of the betrayal barrier (staying with God in faith when it seems he has abandoned or betrayed us). It is what Job did. It is what the three Hebrew men did when they refused to bow down to the king's image of gold (Daniel 3) and what Daniel did when he kept praying three times a day despite the threat of being thrown into the lions' den (Daniel 6). A close look at the lives of all those described in Hebrews 11 will show that they broke the betrayal barrier. That is the person who God uses. It was said of Hezekiah, 'God *left* [my italics] him to test him and to know everything that was in his heart' (2 Chronicles 32:31). Hezekiah broke the betrayal barrier.

Do you feel that God has left you? Be assured that he has not left you in the absolute sense; it only seems that way. When God hides his face it is not because he has utterly left us; it only feels that way. That is what Hezekiah felt. The writer put it as he did to show that a great man of God, one of Israel's best kings, was tested to the hilt. Are you too being tested? Are you experiencing the hiding of God's face? I say this with all the integrity I have in me: be encouraged. God is calling you to pure joy. You therefore must follow those who went through the equivalent kind of testing before they could be used to the full and for their potential to be realised. They broke the betrayal barrier. You can do it as well. '. . . no-one has heard, no ear has perceived, no eye has seen' what God will do for those who wait for him (Isaiah 64:4; 1 Corinthians 2:9).

Pure Joy

No discipline seems pleasant at the time, but painful. Later on, however, it produces a harvest of righteousness and peace for those who have been trained by it.

Hebrews 12:11

How to break the betrayal barrier (staying with God in faith when it seems he has abandoned or betrayed us):

1 Affirm from your heart that what is happening is God's idea. What is designed to get your attention may put you off, yes, but it is God's idea to do it this way. His ways are higher than our ways and his thoughts are higher than our thoughts (Isaiah 55:8–9). Affirm what he is doing in the heat of the battle. Tell him: 'Lord, I know this is from you, I accept it.'

2 Realise this is possibly the greatest opportunity you will ever have to know him intimately.

3 Pray more than ever. Take every available moment to seek his face. Spend every minute you can in secret with him without the television on, or people around who could intrude. Seek him with all your heart. Get to know him and his ways and see if there is anything in particular he may be trying to show you. 'Search me, O God, and know my heart; test me and know my anxious thoughts. See if there is any offensive way in me, and lead me in the way everlasting' (Psalm 139:23–24).

4 Walk in all the light God gives you. 'But if we walk in the light, as he is in the light, we have fellowship with one another, and the blood of Jesus, his Son, purifies us from all sin' (1 John 1:7). Confess any sin God brings to your attention. Accept any form of new obedience he puts before you.

Just do what he says! Don't look over your shoulder to get approval or to see if others are doing the same thing; just obey the Lord and never look back. This is the path to pure joy.

Pure Joy

But Moses said, 'O Lord, please send someone else to do it.'

Exodus 4:13

It was such an honour to be called to deliver the people of God from Pharaoh's bondage. Moses may well have appreciated this, but all he did was to argue back. God did not like that. 'The Lord's anger burned against Moses', but he offered to let Aaron assist him (Exodus 4:9–17).

The fact that God was displeased with Moses' response indicates that the role of Aaron was Plan B. We will never know what might have occurred in ancient Israel had Moses not given in to fear. What we do know is that Aaron turned out to be a real problem again and again, co-operating with the rebellion that surfaced with the Israelites.

Many people think that it is modest and noble to avoid Christian service due to a feeling of inadequacy. But when it is sheer unbelief, the Holy Spirit is quenched. What God calls us to do he enables us to do. St Augustine prayed, 'Command what Thou wilt, and give what Thou commandest.' When we say 'No' to the calling of God, whatever our reason, our tongue will witness against us.

We may think that our words do not matter if only God hears us. But he is the most important witness of all! We should care most of all what he thinks about our reaction to his word.

Your Words Have Power

You, dear children, are from God and have overcome them, because the one who is in you is greater than the one who is in the world.

1 John 4:4

One of the more disquieting aspects of modern Christianity in some places is the high profile given to the devil and 'spiritual warfare'. One gets the impression sometimes that all things that go against our will are of the devil. He gets more attention than God sometimes! Most of all, I wonder if some people fear the devil more than they do God.

One of my favourite lines from Martin Luther's hymn, quoted at the beginning of this chapter is: 'Lo! his doom is sure. One little word shall fell him.' Luther had many battles with the devil. I suspect the devil was very threatened by him indeed. Luther was not the slightest bit afraid of the devil.

I would not want you to be naïve or unaware of his power, however. My dad used to say to me that the devil is 'very crafty, second only to God in power and wisdom'. Yes. Quite. But don't forget it: he is second to God, a far second and nowhere equal to him. It is God to whom *he* answers and it is God to whom we answer. The buck stops with God.

Totally Forgiving Ourselves

November

One day the evil spirit answered them, 'Jesus I know, and I know about Paul, but who are you?' Then the man who had the evil spirit jumped on them and overpowered them all. He gave them such a beating that they ran out of the house naked and bleeding.

Acts 19:15–16

We need a fearless, rugged commitment to the God of the Bible we are prepared to die for. My friend Joseph Tson says, 'The most dangerous person in the world is a person who is not afraid to die.' We need Christians who are a threat to Satan as much as certain terrorists are to the West. I wish I were that. We are too much like the sons of Sceva who were intrigued with the supernatural underworld but no threat to Satan. Indeed, the devil didn't even know them! When trying to cast out devils in Jesus' name, claiming to know Paul and promoting themselves to the level of their incompetence, they were utterly overcome by demonic powers (Acts 19:16). They tried *using* Jesus' name but the evil spirit answered, 'Jesus I know, and I know about Paul, but who are you?' (Acts 19:15).

Another old friend Rolfe Barnard used to preach a sermon entitled 'The man who was known in hell' (based on the aforementioned verse). In other words, Paul was a real threat to Satan, he was well known in the evil world. 'I want to be known in hell', said Rolfe in that unforgettable sermon. But are we? I don't mean to be unfair, but do you really think that you are a threat to the devil? Is he aware of you? Is he working overtime to keep you from threatening his interests?

Out of the Comfort Zone

Then I heard a loud voice in heaven say: 'Now have come the salvation and the power and the kingdom of our God, and the authority of his Christ. For the accuser of our brothers, who accuses them before our God day and night, has been hurled down. They overcame him by the blood of the Lamb and by the word of their testimony; they did not love their lives so much as to shrink from death.'

Revelation 12:10–11

It is interesting to me that Satan is called the 'accuser of the brothers'. This phrase has been an immense comfort to the people of God over the centuries. Anybody who has had any experience in the wiles of the devil can tell you this is his chief tactic – to accuse. Two other things which are incorporated in the way in which Satan was defeated are: (1) the means by which he was overcome – namely the 'blood of the Lamb'; (2) how they were unashamed to confess faith in the blood of Jesus – 'the word of their testimony'. In other words, it was not only the blood of Jesus that defeated Satan; it was faith in his blood.

When Satan accuses you of your past, remind him that your sins have been forgiven by God – through the shed blood of Jesus.

Put all your eggs in one basket – the blood of Jesus. Don't point Satan to your good works, your best efforts, your resolve to do better or the fact that you may have improved over the years – no, don't do that. Point him to the blood of Jesus. Nothing more. Rest your case there. You know that you are a great sinner, but you have a great God and a great Saviour and all your sins are washed away by Jesus' blood. That is what Revelation 12:11 means by the word of your testimony.

Totally Forgiving Ourselves

Above all, you must understand that no prophecy of Scripture came about by the prophet's own interpretation.

2 Peter 1:20

We can't possibly know everything – it is not all explained to us. Above all, if we know that we are saved – born again and prepared for heaven when we die – all else becomes unimportant by comparison. Take eschatology (the doctrine that deals with 'last things') for example. How things will turn out in the end is of immense interest to us, but nobody knows for sure (that I know of) how the details of the book of Revelation are to be understood. No two books written on the subject agree entirely on the finer points. This tells me that God must not consider this of crucial importance to us.

When I first came to Westminster Chapel someone asked me if I was a pre-millennialist (the belief that Jesus will come *before* the 1000-year reign of Christ as it is described in Revelation 20), a post-millennialist (the belief that Jesus will come *after* the millennium) or an a-millennialist (the belief that the 1000 years mentioned in Revelation 20 are to be interpreted symbolically). I said, 'I've been right *once*.' For I do believe that I have embraced each of these views at some period in my life. If only I knew when I got it right. I then concluded that I am a pan-millennialist, because I believe everything will pan out all right in the end.

And yet God uses men, whatever their millennial views seem to be – even those who make their own particular view or point of orthodoxy! I wonder what God in heaven thinks when he sees us so exercised below on certain matters.

Does Jesus Care?

*When Judas, who had betrayed him, saw that Jesus was condemned,
he was seized with remorse and returned the thirty silver coins to
the chief priests and the elders. 'I have sinned,' he said, 'for I have
betrayed innocent blood.' 'What is that to us?' they replied. 'That's
your responsibility.'*

Matthew 27:3–4

Judas 'repented' of his betrayal of Jesus. The Greek word here is from
metamelomai, which the New International Version translates as 'seized
with remorse'. This indicates that *metanoia* ('change of mind') was
not given to Judas. He was sorry only that he got caught, or found
out. Even if he did have a bit of a change of mind ('I have betrayed
innocent blood', Matthew 27:4), it came too late. Matthew does not
dignify Judas' 'repentance' with the word *metanoia*, the word generally reserved in the New Testament for true repentance. Matthew
apparently wants to make the point that Judas was sorry only that
things did not work out for him, and that the knowledge of his folly
came too late. Remorse is often an essential ingredient in true repentance, but such a feeling can still be short of a true change of mind.

The granting of *metanoia* will not come to those on *earth* if they
do not believe the Scriptures. God works through his word to bestow
repentance. So if people do not repent when they hear God's word,
neither will they be convinced even if one rose from the dead (Luke
16:27–31).

People will experience remorse, as Judas did, in hell.

In a word, Judas Iscariot was never converted in the first place.

Second Chance

'In repentance and rest is your salvation, in quietness and trust is your strength, but you would have none of it.'

Isaiah 30:15

The highest and most intense worship takes place when we can do nothing but be amazed, when we are rendered helpless and speechless with wonder and gratitude, when we just sit back and watch God work.

In worship at this depth we are kept from even saying, 'Thank you.' For, at the risk of being misunderstood, I am prepared to say that our gratitude sometimes gets in the way of praise. Gratitude can be an attempt to get the balance even again. Probably you have experienced on a human level something of what I am getting at. Someone does something for you, and you know very well that he or she wants you to be thankful, and you are, so you express your gratitude. You try to be extremely thankful so that this person will really see how you feel. Or you try to return the favour in some way. This gives you a feeling of satisfaction.

Have you ever been placed in a situation in which there was nothing you could say or do? Someone did something immensely wonderful and you weren't able to do anything but feel grateful? Perhaps this person went away, and you wished you could find him or her to say how much you appreciated what was done. And maybe you felt frustrated, and some of your joy was taken away because it was not possible to express your gratitude. On the natural level, we always feel that we must do something.

But Isaiah says that our salvation lies in the fact that we do nothing: 'In repentance and rest is your salvation.' I did not say that we feel nothing, but that we do nothing. This, says Isaiah, is the best way to live – the way God wants us to live. It constitutes the greatest joy there is. And even though we are rendered helpless – as though we are just standing there with our mouth wide open – God sees how we feel and knows that we are grateful.

Worshipping God

But godliness with contentment is great gain.

1 Timothy 6:6

So much of what drives us to success can be traced to the desire to please one's parents. I waited a long time before I got my own father's approval. I had wandered from my old teaching as well as my old denomination. I tried hard to compensate. In the end, what secured my father's approval more than anything else was that I was occupying G. Campbell Morgan's old pulpit – one of his heroes.

But the wish for parental approval is not the full explanation. I suspect that the greater driving force to succeed is probably traced to peer relationships – old and contemporary. We want to 'show them' what we have done, especially if they were rivals of some sort.

The raw, naked wish to make people envious of us must eventually be changed, above all else, to become an ambition to make God proud of us – not making other people jealous of us. God may use sex to drive a person to marry; and he may use ambition to drive a person to service. But *agape* love and a love for the glory of God must then move in, or you and I will be anything but content with godliness. We will want more. And that is the recipe for downfall.

Second Chance

A fool gives full vent to his anger, but a wise man keeps himself under control.

Proverbs 29:11

Speaking personally, I fear this is where I have sinned the most over the years. I have shouted at my wife and my children more often than I dare think about. I know that the Deacons at Westminster Chapel feared my temper, certainly in earlier days there – some of them bravely told me so. I know what it is to speak sharply to a slow waitress in a restaurant, an incompetent clerk in a store or to people moving too slowly in the queue at a supermarket. I have been impatient with people in the Vestry at Westminster Chapel – right after preaching a good sermon! Instead of demonstrating gentleness I would look at my watch and wonder how long these people were going to keep asking inane questions. Undoubtedly one of my greatest weaknesses has been that I do not 'suffer fools gladly'.

The man who controls his temper is greater than a powerful warrior 'who takes a city' (Proverbs 16:32). 'Wisdom makes one wise man more powerful than ten rulers in a city' (Ecclesiastes 7:19). Remember that wisdom is knowing what to say next – and what not to say. It is no small consolation to know that God does not give up easily on us and he has graciously shown me that he is not finished with me yet.

There is a thin line sometimes between righteous anger and losing your temper. The difference is that when it is righteous anger you do not lose control.

Your Words Have Power

Preach the Word; be prepared in season and out of season; correct, rebuke and encourage – with great patience and careful instruction.

2 Timothy 4:2

My best times are when I pray. Yes, that is absolutely true. But I have to tell you also that some of my worst times are when I pray. My prayer life is more 'between the times' than times of breakthrough, discovery, insight, immediate and direct witness of the Spirit and an acute sense of the presence of God.

It is what Paul means by being faithful, consistent and prepared 'out of season'. I regard that expression as one of Paul's most helpful and practical commands. Keep in mind that 2 Timothy was, almost certainly, Paul's very last epistle before he went to heaven. He wrote that letter to Timothy while he was waiting for his own execution in Rome. He exhorts Timothy to be 'prepared [*instant* – AV] in season *and* out of season'. One must be faithful with or without a sense of accomplishment and help from the Holy Spirit. Paul does not want to depart from this earth by giving Timothy the impression that Christian ministry is always accompanied by a great sense of the presence of God – in other words, when preaching or praying is happy and exciting.

'In season' is when God shows up. 'Out of season' is between the times – when you wait, and wait, and wait. It is when God hides his face. 'Truly you are a God who hides himself, O God and Saviour of Israel' (Isaiah 45:15).

Did You Think to Pray?

And without faith it is impossible to please God, because anyone who comes to him must believe that he exists and that he rewards those who earnestly seek him.

Hebrews 11:6

Jackie Pullinger, the legendary servant of Christ who has worked with drug addicts in Hong Kong, told me how her ministry there 'took off'. She said she began praying in tongues for fifteen minutes a day – 'by the clock', she added. 'I felt nothing,' she went on to say, 'but that is when we began to see conversions.'

This goes to show that when God hides his face he only appears to hide his face. When there is no sense of his presence, it is down to our subjective feelings – not what is objectively true.

God holds back a sense of his presence many times when we pray, to test us – to see how much we persevere without that sense of his presence. It is easy to pray when we feel his presence; it is hard to pray without this. But either way his presence is there – whether we feel him with us or not.

I have a hunch that we please him most when we persevere in faith, pray, work and rely on him without a sense of his presence. When he allows us to feel his presence we may think we are pleasing him more. I rather think it is him pleasing *us* more in such times. I suspect we please *him* most when we continue on and, as Jackie Pullinger put it, we feel 'nothing'.

Did You Think to Pray?

For the love of money is a root of all kinds of evil. Some people, eager for money, have wandered from the faith and pierced themselves with many griefs.

1 Timothy 6:10

Some people can be trusted with a lot of money. I have always assumed I am not one of those people. I know that a long time ago – over forty years ago in fact – God dealt with me firmly that I was not to make a lot of money but that he would take care of me. That is the way it has been across the years. We have come to retirement after living carefully and without a lot of money over the years, and God has blessed us to exceed all expectations.

But there are those who are called to make money. Chances are, certainly if you are a Christian and walking in the Spirit, if you are called to make a lot of money it will be not because of a love for money you have but because you are motivated to accomplish extraordinary things. I have watched Christian businessmen who did have a love of money and watched them crash! Those the Lord loves he disciplines (Hebrews 12:6). If you are governed by the love of money, you will pay dearly for it down the road. 'Godliness with contentment is great gain' (1 Timothy 6:6). If God blesses you financially, fall on your face and thank him and become a great giver to the Lord's work.

Out of the Comfort Zone

The sacrifices of God are a broken spirit;
a broken and contrite heart,
O God, you will not despise.

Psalm 51:17

What David did in committing adultery and trying to cover it up was pretty awful. In many ways, it doesn't get much worse than that. But 'a broken and contrite heart' meant that he could be used again. There was brokenness from the first moment that Nathan showed David his sin. No defensiveness, no excuses, no blaming others.

He was found out, and forgiven, and restored. If God could do that with David, he can do it with you and me too. Let the 'downside of David' be your blueprint and model. Look at what David did in 2 Samuel 15:

1 *He did not resist God's judgment.* 'Come! We must flee, or none of us will escape from Absalom' (2 Samuel 15:14). The king set out, with his entire household following him.
2 *He did not try to amass a greater following.* When Ittai the Gittite showed up to follow David, the king tried to discourage him. 'Go back and stay with King Absalom' (2 Samuel 15:19).
3 *He accepted what was apparently the new regime.* Note: he calls his son *King* Absalom! He had no idea whether he would be back in Jerusalem – ever again.
4 *He refused to take the ark of God with him.* Zadok the priest, who was determined to stay with David, had brought the hallowed ark, symbolising the Presence of God, from Jerusalem. 'Take the ark of God back into the city,' David ordered (2 Samuel 15:25).
5 *He submitted utterly to the total sovereignty of God regarding his future.* 'If I find favour in the Lord's eyes, he will bring me back and let me see it [the ark] and his dwelling-place again. But if he says, "I am not pleased with you," then I am ready; let him do to me whatever seems good to him' (2 Samuel 15:25–26).
6 *He prayed.* Whereas he did not lift his smallest finger to defend his kingship, there was one thing David could engage in that was entirely legitimate: prayer (2 Samuel 15:31). That is something we can all do. We turn to God and put our requests – then wait and watch him work.

Second Chance

Cast all your anxiety on him because he cares for you.

1 Peter 5:7

There is a difference between temptation and sin; it is not a sin to be tempted (James 1:13–15). Jesus was tempted (Hebrews 4:15). It is a sin when you give in to temptation, which Jesus never did (1 Peter 2:22). Some people feel guilty merely because they are tempted. This is pseudo-guilt. The devil will exploit this. Who among us can help it if we are tempted? God does not want you to feel guilty because you are tempted. If however you do succumb to temptation and go against God's revealed will, then sin has been committed and true guilt now exists.

False guilt leads to anxiety. Depression. Arthritis. Irritability. Ill health of all sorts. I am so glad that we are invited to cast all our anxiety on the Lord – he cares for us. Giving him our anxiety enables us to participate in Jesus' own experience, for he said: 'My yoke is easy and my burden is light' (Matthew 11:30). The person who can say that feels no guilt. Not the slightest bit.

Jesus never felt guilty. He never felt guilt of any kind – except when he was bearing our sins on the cross. But until that moment Jesus never felt guilty – ever. He wants that total freedom from guilt for you and me.

Did You Think to Pray?

'Woe to me!' I cried. 'I am ruined! For I am a man of unclean lips, and I live among a people of unclean lips, and my eyes have seen the King, the LORD Almighty.' Then one of the seraphs flew to me with a live coal in his hand, which he had taken with tongs from the altar. With it he touched my mouth and said, 'See, this has touched your lips; your guilt is taken away and your sin atoned for.'

Isaiah 6:5–7

Isaiah apparently had a respectable prophetic ministry without any great sense of sin. But when he saw the glory of the Lord he cried out, 'Woe is me! . . . I am ruined!' That is what the Holy Spirit did. Moreover, Isaiah was not left in that state – God never leaves us like that; he was cleansed and assured that his 'guilt is taken away and your sin atoned for'. It is not that Isaiah had been living in any scandalous sin prior to this moment; he no doubt was an upright, clean servant of God. But the Holy Spirit convicted him of sin he could not otherwise have been aware of.

When, therefore, I refer to a sense of sin, I am certainly not referring to engaging in any sinful act. Some sincere Christians have not been taught along these lines and can only imagine a sense of sin coming from having committed some awful, overt evil act. The funny thing is, as we have seen, some people can commit overt acts of blatant wrongdoing and feel nothing! Others sense a conviction of sin by merely being in the presence of God. For the presence of God can make us see things about ourselves that we are unable to see were it not for the Holy Spirit showing us our wrong. Without the Spirit of God convicting us, we do things that are sinful and never feel the slightest sense of wrong – like the unkind retort, holding a grudge, boasting of yourself to clear your name, running ahead of God, saying something about another that makes them look bad.

Did You Think to Pray?

Jesus said, 'This sickness will not end in death. No, it is for God's glory so that God's Son may be glorified through it.'

John 11:4

The word which Jesus gave to Lazarus and his sisters was that the particular illness was for God's glory. I cannot imagine a more consoling word. Why? Because this tells me (1) that my illness is unrelated to any personal guilt, and (2) God has the matter in hand. Many of us ask God, 'Why did you let this happen to me?' when we are unwell. Not far away is the ominous thought that God is 'getting even' for something we have done which offended him. After all, who among us cannot think of some sin or fault which God could, if he chose, deal with? But to hear that our illness is for God's glory makes us see straightaway that not only is the matter in hand – God knows all about it and has things under control – but also that he is not blaming us.

There is a sense in which all illness is for God's glory. On one occasion Jesus encountered a man who was blind from birth. His disciples asked, 'Rabbi, who sinned, this man or his parents, that he was born blind?' Our Lord replied, 'Neither this man nor his parents sinned, but this happened so that the work of God might be displayed in his life' (John 9:1–3).

Does Jesus Care?

'Is not your wickedness great? Are not your sins endless?'

Job 22:5

In ancient Judaism there was a popular consensus that serious illness was the direct consequence of some heinous sin. This is why many Jews never understood the book of Job. Job was 'blameless and upright; he feared God and shunned evil' (Job 1:1). When catastrophe struck, leaving him financially and physically broken, his 'friends' kept probing Job for some secret sin which they believed lay at the cause.

It is true that sometimes sin is the cause of sickness. This was implied when Jesus said to a paralytic, 'Take heart, son; your sins are forgiven' (Matthew 9:2). For example, sexual sin can lead to venereal disease. The inability to control one's appetite can lead to overweight which in turn can be the cause of any number of diseases – from high blood pressure to heart trouble. Not only that, it can be demonstrated that such things as bitterness or holding a grudge can lead to various illnesses, including arthritis.

But the Bible does not teach that every serious illness can be traced to sin. James told us to anoint with oil on behalf of the sick who ask for such and promised that the prayer of faith would make them well. But he added, 'If he has sinned, he will be forgiven' (James 5:15). This suggests that illness *may* be the consequence of sin. But the word 'if' categorically proves that such a person may *not* have sinned and still be unwell.

Does Jesus Care?

'And I will do whatever you ask in my name, so that the Son may bring glory to the Father.'

John 14:13

Sometimes God shows that he cares by healing the person right on the spot. I have known of dozens of cases in which divine healing took place. 'Jesus Christ is the same yesterday and today and for ever' (Hebrews 13:8). As surely as Jesus lives today and is reigning from the right hand of God the Father we may believe that he will heal. We should never be surprised at the miraculous.

I am sure that one of the reasons we do not see more of the miraculous is merely because we neither ask for it nor expect it. James said, 'You do not have, because you do not ask God' (James 4:2).

Who knows what God might do? The King of Nineveh took Jonah's prophecy seriously that in forty days Nineveh would be destroyed. The king proclaimed a fast and hoped. 'Who knows?' he asked. 'God may yet relent and with compassion turn from his fierce anger so that we will not perish' (Jonah 3:9).

When there is illness we should pray. We should turn to God. We should turn to him who once promised, 'Call to me and I will answer you and tell you great and unsearchable things you do not know' (Jeremiah 33:3). This was the word to Jeremiah to whom God had previously said, 'I am the LORD, the God of all mankind. Is anything too hard for me?' (Jeremiah 32:27).

Does Jesus Care?

'Master,' said John, 'we saw a man driving out demons in your name and we tried to stop him, because he is not one of us.' 'Do not stop him,' Jesus said, 'for whoever is not against you is for you.'

Luke 9:49–50

Nothing is more deadly than a rival spirit in the Church of God. Take the subject of revival, for example. I think we all generally agree that there is a heart-cry for revival nowadays. I doubt there is any evangelical group or church that is not praying for revival – a sovereign outpouring of God's Spirit that will revive the people of God and result in many conversions.

The problem here is, we all want it to come to *us*! We all tend to see ourselves as having 'borne the burden of the work and the heat of the day' (Matthew 20:12). We resent it if God would make others 'equal to us'! We want God to bless *our* efforts, *our* party line, *our* denomination or group. We therefore tend to dismiss out of hand any report of God coming down powerfully on anyone but *us*. We honestly believe it couldn't happen to those who are of a different theological persuasion or ecclesiastical setting.

None of us has a monopoly on the anointing. Jesus' disciples wanted to stop someone praying in Jesus' name 'because he is not one of us'. But Jesus stepped in. It is a reminder that we should rejoice over, not resent, someone praying in Jesus' name who isn't quite in our own group. Even Joshua, when he was young and still had a lot to learn, was unhappy when certain people were prophesying without recognised credentials. 'But Moses replied, "Are you jealous for my sake? I wish that all the LORD'S people were prophets and that the LORD would put his Spirit on them!"' (Numbers 11:29).

The Sensitivity of the Spirit

After three days they found him in the temple courts, sitting among the teachers, listening to them and asking them questions.

Luke 2:46

The Jesus that Mary and Joseph found in the temple courts was a Jesus they hardly knew!

Why? When we are away from the Lord, he moves on. By the time we catch up with him he is not the same – to us. He continues to work. We have not been in on it. We therefore have to make new adjustments to what he is doing at the time we rediscover him.

Many people who have opposed what God is doing – in any generation – were not as close to the Lord at the time as they thought. For if they had been, they would not have been so slow to recognise him. It is when we move on without him – while he continues to manifest his glory elsewhere – that warps our discernment. 'All is yellow to the jaundiced eye.' Our sight of the Lord is often fixed in one direction – the way we knew him when we last felt his presence. But if we move on and he is at work elsewhere we must be prepared to bow to him – wherever he is working and whatever he is doing.

The Sensitivity of the Spirit

'How can ye believe, which receive honour one of another, and seek not the honour that cometh from God only?'

John 5:44 (AV)

It is interesting to note that Jesus did not rebuke the Jews he was addressing because they had not *obtained* the honour of God; he rebuked them because they had *made no attempt* to obtain it. It was not even in their minds to think in this manner. The implication is, they should have done so; they should have known better. Hundreds of years of teaching about the honour and glory of God should have resulted in their seeking it above all else. Indeed, had they been bent on seeking the honour that comes from God, they never would have missed the Messiah in the first place. They missed the Man that God sent to them because it was not a part of their way of thinking or doing things. This is the reason Jesus said, 'How *can* you believe . . . if you make no effort to obtain the praise that comes from the only God?' Not to make an attempt to obtain God's praise is what removes the possibility of true faith. Their seeking the praise of people apparently rendered faith an impossibility in one stroke.

This is a warning and an encouragement to you and me. The warning: if you and I do not make an attempt to receive the praise that comes from God rather than the praise of people, we too will find it impossible to exercise genuine faith. The encouragement: we are not required to have obtained the honour and praise of God, but only to *make an effort* to obtain it. God's commands are not burdensome (1 John 5:3). He is not demanding that we perfectly repudiate the praise of people and absolutely receive his praise; he is only asking us to make an effort to obtain his praise. Nothing can be more reasonable than that.

Pure Joy

And a voice from heaven said, 'This is my Son, whom I love; with him I am well pleased.'

Matthew 3:17

We all grow up wanting parental approval. My desire to excel when I was a small boy in school was motivated almost entirely by the look on my dad's face when he saw my report card. I am not sure I ever outgrew that! During the last seven years of his life he had Alzheimer's disease, but just a year or two before this illness set in, when he was in his eighties, his approval meant the world to me. But how much more do we need our heavenly Father's approval. There is no greater joy to be had on this earth than the conscious awareness of his praise. Nothing compares. It is pure joy.

It was no small thing for Jesus to hear the words, 'This is my Son, whom I love; with him I am well pleased.' That was at Jesus' baptism. Later on, when he was transfigured before Peter, James and John, he used the same words again, 'This is my Son, whom I love; with him I am well pleased. Listen to him!' (Matthew 17:5). These words thrilled Jesus to his fingertips. It is all he wanted to hear; to know he was pleasing his Father. That is all he lived for. '. . . I always do what pleases him' (John 8:29). This is what gave him joy.

It is what will give us joy as well. Pure joy. The best feeling in the world. The most satisfying and fulfilling feeling in the world. It means a good conscience. It means you are walking in the light (1 John 1:7). It means God can use you. It means you won't miss anything he may want to do in your life and that you will be 'in' on it should he be pleased to move in your time. You won't be left out. All he envisages for you will be yours.

Pure Joy

That if you confess with your mouth, Jesus is Lord, and believe in
your heart that God raised him from the dead, you will be saved.
For it is with your heart that you believe and are justified, and it is
with your mouth that you confess and are saved.

Romans 10:9–10

God has given us a solution for dealing with true guilt. He has done
this in basically two ways: objectively and subjectively – and the two
must come together. The objective way God has dealt with true guilt
is by sending his beloved Son Jesus Christ to die on the cross for our
sins. Yes, God sent his Son into the world to *die on a cross for our*
sins. There is no grander knowledge in the universe than this. Never
let yourself get over it. God sent Jesus to die for us. God punished
Jesus for what we did. Why? Because he was our substitute. All our
sins were laid on him as though he were the guilty person (Isaiah 53:6).
This is why the New Testament claims he 'bore our sins' (1 Peter 2:24).
The Bible in a nutshell is this: 'For God so loved the world, that he
gave his one and only Son, that whoever believes in him shall not
perish but have eternal life' (John 3:16).

The subjective way true guilt is dealt with is by acknowledging our
guilt to God. All that Jesus did and suffered for us is of no value until
we believe. The essential work of the Holy Spirit is to convict of sin
(John 16:7). But the Holy Spirit never leaves us to wallow in shame
before God; he also convicts of 'righteousness', said Jesus, 'because I
am going to the Father, where you can see me no longer' (John 16:10).
This means that Jesus would not only die on a cross but rise from the
dead and ascend to the Father's right hand. When we believe in our
hearts that Jesus died and was raised from the dead, God counts us
as righteous in his eyes. He declares us just. This is because our sin
has been paid for and we are affirming God's way of dealing with our
sins.

Did You Think to Pray?

For we do not have a high priest who is unable to sympathise with our weaknesses, but we have one who has been tempted in every way, just as we are — yet was without sin.

Hebrews 4:15

The reason we don't turn to God as we ought is partly owing to the fear of being rejected. The fear of rejection can be a very powerful but always negative force in our lives. I know many young men who are lonely but will not ask a Christian lady on a date for one reason: the fear of rejection. The fear of rejection can be paralysing and so inhibiting that we can become warped in our personalities. With Jesus there is total acceptance, even with our weaknesses (Hebrews 14:5, above). 'For no matter how many promises God has made, they are "Yes" in Christ' (2 Corinthians 1:20). God does not reject us. He will answer. His answer will be in total love and compassion and totally right. Our very turning to him will open the way to his higher purposes for us.

Does Jesus Care?

Yet when he heard that Lazarus was sick, he stayed where he was two more days.

John 11:6

I doubt not that, when Jesus heard Lazarus was unwell, his immediate impulse was to drop what he was doing and make his way to Bethany where Lazarus was. But before he did that, he did something else: he looked to get the green light from his Father. What he got instead was a word which he sent to Lazarus and his sisters. He did what he had to do. 'For I have come down from heaven not to do my will but to do the will of him who sent me' (John 6:38). Paul said, 'For even Christ did not please himself' (Romans 15:3). He pleased his Father.

Perhaps you will say, 'Then Jesus is for me and God is against me.' Wrong! The Father of Jesus is *our* Father who has 'lavished on us' great grace and does so 'with all wisdom and understanding' (Ephesians 1:8). After all, it was the Father's will that Lazarus was not healed because he had a better idea! Never think that Jesus is working for you and God the Father is working against you. Jesus perpetually accepts us as we are but will intercede according to the will of God. The will of God is infallible. At the end of the day not only shall we have no complaints; we shall marvel at God's goodness and wisdom – even thanking him for *not* doing what we initially wanted.

Does Jesus Care?

Finally, my brothers, rejoice in the Lord! It is no trouble for me to write the same things to you again, and it is a safeguard for you . . . Rejoice in the Lord always. I will say it again: Rejoice!

Philippians 3:1; 4:4

Rejoicing is, more often than not, a choice. We all love spontaneous rejoicing. Such comes from answered prayer, the answers to our questions, the manifestation of the miraculous, the success and prosperity we wanted. It takes little faith to rejoice when it is precipitated by happy, external circumstances. But the command to rejoice comes because we don't always feel like rejoicing – and yet Paul said to do it all the time. Not rejoicing *because* of all that has happened but rather '*in* all circumstances' (1 Thessalonians 5:18). The choice we make to rejoice comes because we simply don't feel like rejoicing. *We have to just do it.*

There were apparently two kinds of rejoicing in the Old Testament era: (1) because the Law required it; and (2) out of gratitude. The first time the word 'rejoice' appears in the Bible is in Leviticus 23:40: 'On the first day you are to take choice fruit from the trees, and palm fronds, leafy branches and poplars, and rejoice before the LORD your God for seven days.' This was a requirement – what they had to do under the Law whether they felt like it or not; and this kind of injunction appeared frequently under the Law (Deuteronomy 12:7, 12, 18, etc.).

But the choice to rejoice in the Old Testament era also came out of sheer gratitude and not from a legalistic motive. 'I will be glad and rejoice in you' (Psalm 9:2). In a psalm that indicates the hiding of God's face came also the words: 'But I trust in your unfailing love; my heart rejoices in your salvation' (Psalm 13:5). 'I will rejoice in your promise like one who finds great spoil' (Psalm 119:162). '. . . let the hearts of those who seek the Lord rejoice' (1 Chronicles 16:10). These are not words that come from the overflow of happy circumstances; neither do they indicate that they are motivated by fear of punishment (which is the way the Law produced obedience), but out of a godly sense of thanks to God. This shows how you and I can live if we put our minds to it.

Pure Joy

'However, do not rejoice that the spirits submit to you, but rejoice that your names are written in heaven.'

Luke 10:20

Some of us have ridiculed the popular idea of 'the power of positive thinking', mainly because of the lack of solid orthodoxy that tended to lie behind it. But there is something worthwhile in this that people like me could learn from. Negative thinking not only requires little or no grace; it plays abundantly into the devil's scheme for us. Rejoicing, thinking positively, usually requires great effort and is often a sign of great grace in our lives. It is exactly what we are told to do!

Jesus told us to rejoice in adverse conditions. The climax of the Beatitudes is a command to rejoice under the worst of circumstances. The best translation of *makarios* (usually translated 'blessed') is really 'congratulations'. Jesus thus says 'Congratulations' when people insult us or persecute us. 'Rejoice and be glad' (Matthew 5:11–12).

Jesus also commanded us to rejoice because our names are written in heaven. He implicitly rebuked his disciples because they were so excited over demons being subject to them. There are Christians, I fear, who put a higher priority over the miraculous, the signs, wonders and gifts of the Spirit, and forget the main thing: our names being written in heaven. Believe me, *that* is something to rejoice about! We should rejoice every day of the year that one day we are going to be in heaven. Life at its longest is still short, especially when compared to eternity (which has no end). I thank God I am not going to hell, but to heaven. Whatever is going wrong at this moment – whatever it is – the one thing that nobody can take from you and me is our citizenship in heaven (Philippians 3:20). I will never forget as long as I live the opening words of a prayer offered by Dr W. M. Tidwell when he visited Trevecca Nazarene College years ago: 'Lord, we thank you that we are not in hell.' Not many believe in hell today, but one day they will.

Pure Joy

'Blessed are you when people insult you, persecute you and falsely say all kinds of evil against you because of me. Rejoice and be glad, because great is your reward in heaven, for in the same way they persecuted the prophets who were before you.'

Matthew 5:11–12

How do you rejoice when you don't feel like it? The answer is, you find things for which you certainly should be thankful and then discipline yourself to *voice that gratitude*. Recently, when returning to Key Largo in Florida (where we now live) from the airport, my wife Louise said, 'Let's thank the Lord for twenty-five things that took place over the weekend.' We had a wonderful weekend in Connecticut. We began, taking turns, naming particular things – such as seeing the colour of the leaves at the height of the autumn in New England; standing on the spot where Jonathan Edwards preached his historic sermon 'Sinners in the hands of an angry God' (an event that has affected me profoundly); the good meeting at Groton; the lovely pastor and his wife – Jim and Louise Schnider; the sweet time with John Paul Jackson and his wife Diane in New Hampshire; how we enjoyed noting the English names of cities and towns wherever we went (did you know there is an Acton in Massachusetts?); the way our ministry was received – and many other little things in between. When we finished, Louise said we had mentioned fifty-three things. I think God liked that. It is the sort of thing you can make yourself do whether you feel like it or not. There are *always* things you can thank God for if you look around. In a word: if you don't feel like it, do it anyway.

Pure Joy

In this you greatly rejoice, though now for a little while you may have had to suffer grief in all kinds of trials.

1 Peter 1:6

There is nothing better for overcoming depression or turning a negative mood away than thanking God for things and, simply, praising the Lord. During my era at Westminster Chapel I became convicted over the lack of emphasis on worship. Happily this changed at the Chapel, but also in my own private devotional life. Louise and I try to sing together for fifteen minutes every morning and I sing for ten minutes nearly each evening before retiring to bed. Sometimes the hymns or choruses that we sing have a way of speaking to us as to where we are in our pilgrimage and perspective, and that is of course quite wonderful. But there are other times I have wanted to choose hymns that do nothing other than proclaim the goodness of the Lord without any reference, if possible, to my present situation. Hymns like 'I'll praise my Maker while I've breath' or 'And can it be that I should gain an interest in my Saviour's blood?' or 'O worship the King'. Why? Because there is a place for doing nothing but *praising the Lord* without any reference to myself or present need. The funny thing is, believe it or not, doing this often has the effect of blessing you more than ever! In other words, you don't do it because you feel like it; you do it because it is right to do it. But the good feeling often follows the sheer discipline of showing thankfulness and praise to God.

Pure Joy

God, who has saved us and called us to a holy life – not because of anything we have done but because of his own purpose and grace. This grace was given us in Christ Jesus before the beginning of time, but it has now been revealed through the appearing of our Saviour, Christ Jesus, who has destroyed death and has brought life and immortality to light through the gospel.

2 Timothy 1:8–10

From a letter to Rabbi David Rosen, former Chief Rabbi of Ireland:

I loved what you said about the matter of being chosen, that it has nothing to do with how deserving one is. My favourite verse in this connection is Exodus 33:19: 'I will have mercy on whom I will have mercy, and I will have compassion on whom I will have compassion.' We both apparently have in common a robust doctrine of election, that God makes the choice. No intelligent reader of the Bible can deny that God chose ancient Israel. But some good people disagree on whether God chose individuals, including Gentiles, in his eternal plan. I believe he did. And, again, the choice is not based on our being deserving. Indeed, Paul said that we have been called not because of anything we have done but because of his own purpose and grace, then adding that the choice was made 'before the beginning of time'.

The Christian and the Pharisee

Elijah was a man just like us. He prayed earnestly that it would not rain, and it did not rain on the land for three and a half years.
Again he prayed, and the heavens gave rain, and the earth produced its crops.

James 5:17–18

There is no 'gift of prayer' in the list of the spiritual gifts in 1 Corinthians 12:8–10 or in Romans 12:6–8. The reason is probably because we are all on level ground when it comes to prayer. Not all of us can have the talent or spiritual gifts we may wish for; they are sovereignly given (Romans 12:3; 1 Corinthians 12:11). But all of us can pray, and all of us can excel in prayer. Indeed, 'the prayer of a righteous man is powerful and effective' (James 5:16). But if that adjective 'righteous' is as threatening to you as it is to me, take heart; James followed this with a reference to Elijah as 'a man just like us' (James 5:17 – 'a man subject to like passions as we are' (AV)). Elijah was as human as you get, but through it all had some of the most extraordinary answers to prayer in all the Bible (James 5:17–18; 1 Kings 17–19).

I find this so encouraging. Nobody is given a supernatural ability or private gift to excel in this matter of prayer, and yet anybody can pray and see great answers to prayer. God invites ordinary people to experience the supernatural.

Did You Think to Pray?

Through Jesus, therefore, let us continually offer to God a sacrifice of praise – the fruit of lips that confess his name.

Hebrews 13:15

When you realise that these words 'sacrifice of praise' were given to discouraged, somewhat backslidden Christians, you wonder what their reaction might be to words like that! Discouraged people don't readily respond to the idea of praising God when things aren't so good and when God doesn't make sense. And yet that is exactly what the writer said to them.

Praising God is both a privilege and a duty.

And yet what we give up in our sacrifice of praise is either temporary or compensated for many times over. The truth is, ultimately we do not give up anything. We get much more back.

But that is not the reason to do it. We should not give to get, neither should we praise God to receive more. We praise him because he deserves it. We praise him because he is worthy. We praise him because we are eternally indebted to having a God like he is.

By the way, the best time to do it is when you are at your lowest – that is when you really go against human nature. Don't wait until you feel like doing it. The consummate victory is to those who struggle to do it. When you prevail over the enemy as Jacob did, you find your best friend. There is no better way to begin than by starting to praise God, whatever the circumstances. Do it now.

Did You Think to Pray?

December

Let us not give up meeting together, as some are in the habit of doing, but let us encourage one another – and all the more as you see the Day approaching.

Hebrews 10:25

It is my opinion that a chief reason people get off the rails is because they remain accountable to no one and feel good about it. 'I am accountable to God alone,' some piously say. That sounds good. But it isn't good at all. This is one of the best reasons for being a member of a church and under the authority of its fellowship and leadership. The truth is, we need each other.

We all fancy that we are the exceptions to the rule. We all like to think that our particular temptation or trial is unique, and therefore God lets us off the hook as a special case. This is to believe the devil's lie. 'No temptation has seized you except what is common to man. And God is faithful; he will not let you be tempted beyond what you can bear. But when you are tempted, he will also provide a way out so that you can stand up under it' (1 Corinthians 10:13). God simply does not bend the rules for his people, not even the 'best'. This is why the Bible does not gloss over its heroes. King Saul became yesterday's man because he thought he was not accountable to anybody. King David, the only person in Scripture called a man after God's 'own heart' (1 Samuel 13:14; Acts 13:22), thought he could get away with adultery, but was found out (2 Samuel 12:1–12). Are you accountable? Are you surrounded by people who know what you are up to and will help keep you on the straight and narrow? I would urge you to be accountable to trusted friends and leadership. 'But if you fail to do this, you will be sinning against the Lord; and you may be sure that your sin will find you out' (Numbers 32:23).

The Sensitivity of the Spirit

Now Moses used to take a tent and pitch it outside the camp some distance away, calling it the tent of meeting. Anyone enquiring of the LORD would go to the tent of meeting outside the camp.

Exodus 33:7

I don't know who said it first: 'When the meeting is over, the service begins,' meaning that when the meeting at church ends, Christian service in the world begins. But I think the reverse is sometimes true as well: when the church service is over the meeting begins. The word 'meeting' was special in ancient Israel. The Tent of Meeting was the place where God promised to meet with Moses, and God kept his word, for the Lord would speak to Moses 'face to face, as a man speaks with his friend' (Exodus 33:11).

Sometimes a church service will finish but God isn't finished. The meeting – with God – may suddenly take place even before people leave the building, and then remain for hours. That is how the Hebrides Revival (1948–49) is said to have begun. After a service was over, one man was found kneeling at a pew, praying aloud for revival. He kept saying, 'Your honour is at stake, your honour is at stake.' God stepped in; within an hour hundreds spontaneously turned up at the church. Revival came to the islands and lasted for months. And yet any meeting with God often truly begins – whenever we go home – as we apply what we learned at the church service.

The Sensitivity of the Spirit

'But finally he said to himself, "Even though I don't fear God or care about men, yet because this widow keeps bothering me, I will see that she gets justice, so that she won't eventually wear me out with her coming!"' And the Lord said, 'Listen to what the unjust judge says. And will not God bring about justice for his chosen ones, who cry out to him day and night?'

Luke 18:4–7

Don't rob God of what he does 'best': the enterprise of vindicating those who are wronged. Everything God does is extremely good; you could say there is nothing he does best because nothing he does can be improved upon. But if I may be forgiven for putting it this way, what he does so brilliantly – the ways he does it boggle the mind – is to clear a person's name who has been falsely accused, lied about or hurt in any way. God is for the underdog and if you have been hurt, lied about, put down or mistreated, you got God's attention – then and there. The problem is, we tend to want to 'help him out'. Big mistake. He gets off our case before you can bat an eyelash. But when we will do nothing (yes, you read it correctly) but let him work on our behalf, we will be so glad we did. Don't necessarily expect vindication to come today or tomorrow but, if you have been the object of injustice, he took notice. Remember that the example of not giving up in praying was a widow who kept asking for justice (Luke 18:1–8). Bottom line: don't ever – ever – try to clear your own name. That's God's job.

Out of the Comfort Zone

Now the Lord is the Spirit, and where the Spirit of the Lord is, there is freedom.

2 Corinthians 3:17

My friend Pete Cantrell always says, 'The greatest freedom is having nothing to prove.' I think too of Shakespeare's famous words, 'Methinks the lady doth protest too much.' This principle borders on the one above obviously, but is not always the same thing. Sometimes there is a case of making yourself clearer if you have been unclear or misunderstood. Sometimes I don't say things as clearly as I should, even when I write. I must not be defensive but take the criticism on board and set the person free who needs to know what I meant. On the other hand, we can be too occupied with what people think and lose all sense of liberty.

When we have the Lord's smile and approval we must not trade them in for the approval of people. If it will set the other person free, explain yourself; but if it is only to make yourself look good, opt for the liberty of the Spirit instead.

Out of the Comfort Zone

'Blessed are the meek, for they will inherit the earth.'

Matthew 5:5

Meekness is taking criticism without being angry, retorting or even covering up for yourself. Meekness is agreeing with the person's right to say what they say, understanding why they say it and even turning the other cheek (Matthew 5:39). After all, they may be right! There is usually a grain of truth to all criticism we receive, even when it is unfair. The least we can do is say, 'I see what you mean' and maybe it is time to say, 'You are right.' But never should we make the person feel bad for saying what they do. Being defensive in such a case is a dead giveaway that we are very insecure, so why give them that! Somerset Maugham said that when people ask for criticism, they really want praise. So true. When you accept criticism and compliments in much the same way, you are beginning to get free.

Out of the Comfort Zone

'How can you believe if you accept praise from one another, yet
make no effort to obtain the praise that comes from the only God?'
John 5:44

In this significant verse Jesus reveals the real reason the Jews missed
their Messiah – they were too enamoured with the praise of people.
Note that Jesus said that they make no *effort* to obtain the praise
(Greek, *doxa* – honour, glory, praise) that comes from God alone. We
may not master the matter of not being concerned with the praise of
people but we can certainly make an attempt!

A connected verse is Ecclesiastes 4:4: 'And I saw that all labour and
all achievement spring from man's envy of his neighbour.' This verse
shook me rigid one evening when I saw it clearly for the first time. It
shows that what has been accomplished on our planet throughout the
centuries and to the present time has been motivated by people wanting
to make people jealous; therefore they get things done to get their
admiration and their sense of envy. Surely we should strive to rise
above that! Do you?

Out of the Comfort Zone

But you, dear friends, build yourselves up in your most holy faith and pray in the Holy Spirit.

Jude 20

We are therefore commanded to pray in the Spirit because that is the way to be sure you are praying in the will of God. And we are commanded to pray in the Spirit in at least two places – Ephesians 6:18 and Jude 20 – and Paul refers to praying in the Spirit in Romans 8:26–27, to which I will return below.

Although praying in the Spirit is praying in the will of God, we do not always know we are actually praying in the will of God. The only way we can be heard by God is to pray in his will, but praying in his will and actually knowing we are doing it are sometimes two different things. This is why John says, 'If we ask anything according to his will, he hears us' (emphasis mine, 1 John 5:14). This is a big 'if'. If only we all did it! And yet we are commanded to. It is much the same thing as knowing what the will of the Lord is. Paul says, 'Do not be foolish, but understand what the Lord's will is' (Ephesians 5:17). If only we always did!

When John talks about God 'hearing' us, he speaks as a Hebrew; it is Hebraic-type thinking. It goes back to the Hebrew word *shamar* – to hear. Every ancient Jew knew the 'Shemah': 'Hear, O Israel: The LORD our God, the LORD is one' (Deuteronomy 6:4). And yet the Hebrew word not only means to hear but also 'to obey'. A parent will sometimes say to their child 'Did you hear me?' if he or she is not obeying. In Hebrew, to hear was also to obey. Therefore when God 'hears' us, it means he also obeys our request. That is the meaning of Isaiah's words, 'You cannot fast as you do today and expect your voice to be *heard* on high' (emphasis mine, Isaiah 58:4). In order to be heard by God, we must pray in his will. Praying in the Spirit, then, is praying in God's will.

Did You Think to Pray?

And if we know that he hears us – whatever we ask – we know that we have what we asked of him.

1 John 5:15

And he who searches our hearts knows the mind of the Spirit, because the Spirit intercedes for the saints in accordance with God's will.

Romans 8:27

Do you know what it is to have a clear sense of thinking as you pray, aware that you are praying in the will of God? I have known it on occasions, but it certainly does not happen to me every day. It is a conscious intercession whereby you feel the enabling of the Holy Spirit in what you say to God and put through to the throne of grace. You can sense you are being 'heard'. John stated that answered prayer is only promised if we pray in God's will. He also put the possibility of knowing that you have been heard. This is why John throws in yet another 'if': 'If we know that he hears us – whatever we ask – we know that we have what we asked of him' (emphasis mine, 1 John 5:15). Have you experienced this? How often?

This is praying in the Holy Spirit.

Some rather 'pious' person may say, 'If you were as spiritual as you should be, you would always know that you pray in the will of God.' Really? What about the Apostle Paul? Would you consider him a spiritual person? And yet in Romans 8:26–27 he claims he does not always know how to pray or what to say!

Do you also know what it is to want to pray, but you don't know what to say? Have had times when the burden was so great that you only wanted to groan and could not utter an intelligible phrase in your prayer? Have you sensed the intercession of the Spirit, but you have no idea what the Spirit was actually saying? Have you wished you could know what he is actually putting to God on your behalf? Have you experienced the Spirit's intercession 'with groans that words cannot express' (Romans 8:26)? Have you had occasion to pray, but 'words failed'?

This too is praying in the Holy Spirit.

Did You Think to Pray?

But when they said, 'Give us a king to lead us,' this displeased Samuel; so he prayed to the LORD. And the LORD told him: 'Listen to all that the people are saying to you; it is not you they have rejected, but they have rejected me as their king. As they have done from the day I brought them up out of Egypt until this day, forsaking me and serving other gods, so they are doing to you. Now listen to them; but warn them solemnly and let them know what the king who will reign over them will do.'

1 Samuel 8:6–9

You and I are invited, indeed commanded, to pray 'in the Spirit'. If we truly do this, we can be sure – absolutely sure – that two things will follow: (1) we pray in the will of God, and (2) what the Spirit prays for us will be answered. If we pray in the flesh, thankfully our prayer will not be answered. God politely and lovingly ignores foolish requests unless we persist in what is against God's will for us. Never forget that ominous word: 'He gave them what they asked for, but sent a wasting disease upon them' (Psalm 106:15). Ancient Israel demanded a king, and they got what they wanted. They pursued this because they were in unbelief; they rejected God's revealed will. The prophet Hosea later said: 'So in my anger I gave you a king, and in my wrath I took him away' (Hosea 13:11).

The most important thing about prayer is the will of God.

Never – ever – try to upstage God's will. I will say it again: if you want to be a complete fool, try to do better than God's will for your life.

Did You Think to Pray?

And do not grieve the Holy Spirit of God, with whom you were sealed for the day of redemption. Get rid of all bitterness, rage and anger, brawling and slander, along with every form of malice. Be kind and compassionate to one another, forgiving each other, just as in Christ God forgave you.

Ephesians 4:30–32

The key to praying in the Spirit is learning to pray without any bitterness in our hearts. It means manifesting the fruits of the Spirit – 'love, joy, peace, patience, kindness, goodness, faithfulness, gentleness and self-control' (Galatians 5:22–23). This equally means learning not to grieve the Holy Spirit, and the chief way we tend to do this is by being bitter.

Not grieving the Spirit and manifesting the fruits of the Spirit come to the same thing. The fruits of the Spirit will flow in us to the degree we do not grieve the Spirit by bitterness, anger and unforgiveness.

I'm sorry, but I cannot promise you that there will ever be praying in the Spirit if you are holding a grudge and refusing to forgive. You cannot say, 'I think I will try praying in the Spirit for a while in order to get my prayers answered', and expect to do this when you have not been living in total forgiveness. Total forgiveness and praying in the Spirit are as important to each other as breathing and living are to each other. You will recall that the passage concerning prayer that moves mountains was immediately followed by Jesus' words, 'And when you stand praying, if you hold anything against anyone, forgive him.' Jesus said, 'Whatever you ask for in prayer, believe that you have received it, and it will be yours' (Mark 11:23–25), and he repeated this principle in 1 John 5:15: 'And if we know that he hears us – whatever we ask – we know that we have what we asked of him.'

Did You Think to Pray?

Then my enemies will turn back
  when I call for help.
By this I will know that God is for me.

Psalm 56:9

There is no greater feeling than to know that 'God is on my side' (Psalm 118:6, AV). 'If God is for us, who can be against us?' (Romans 8:31). To know that God is with us and 'for' us is a great cause for rejoicing.

This does not mean he approves of all we believe and do. Yes, he is for us – right or wrong; but it does not follow he will uphold my unrighteous cause. He is able to be for me – whether I deserve it or not – in order to demonstrate patience that I might be brought to repentance and get sorted out, if that is what needs to happen. The amazing thing is, he still maintains love and support for me when I am unworthy. He sees the end from the beginning. He does not have to defend his love for me to anybody. In the same way that Jesus did not defend his choice of disciples (some of whom raised the eyebrows of self-righteous people), so does he not have to explain himself for maintaining an everlasting love towards us, even when we are in the wrong. This is why we should not be self-righteous if we feel the presence of the Lord and claim this proves we are in the right. God has a way of manifesting his presence to the most unworthy child! That is why he can be real to me. It does not mean I am better than others or that God approves of all he sees in me. He is that way with all his children! He stays with them until they get sorted out. What love! Amazing love! This is why we rejoice – always . . . in the Lord.

Pure Joy

'Blessed are you when people insult you, persecute you and falsely say all kinds of evil against you because of me. Rejoice and be glad, because great is your reward in heaven, for in the same way they persecuted the prophets who were before you.'

Matthew 5:11–12

If you have a real, relentless, genuine enemy – and you are sure that this person is not a figment of your anxiety or imagination – you should see yourself as sitting on a mine of twenty-four carat gold. Except for the fact that all enemies of Christ are ours as well, not everybody has a fierce enemy. Not everybody is that blessed. But if you are so blessed – and Jesus saves the best for last in the Beatitudes – grasp the opportunity with both hands. You should (in your mind) take this person's picture, enlarge and frame it, and thank God every time you look at it. Your enemy, should you handle him or her correctly, will turn out to be the best thing that ever happened to you.

God has raised up your enemy – possibly just for you! King Saul's pursuing of David was the best thing that could have happened to David at the time. It was part – a most vital part – of David's preparation to be king. He had the anointing without the crown (1 Samuel 16:13) and God was ensuring that when the day came when he wore the crown, he would be ready. Remember the quote of Dr Lloyd-Jones: 'The worst thing that can happen to a man is to succeed before he is ready.' God did David a very special favour: he raised up Saul to keep him on his toes, to teach him to be sensitive to the Spirit (1 Samuel 24:5) and to teach him total forgiveness. Saul was David's passport to a greater anointing.

Total Forgiveness

'But I tell you: Love your enemies and pray for those who persecute you.'

Matthew 5:44

Jesus here puts to us the greatest challenge that ever was. It is a greater challenge to the human spirit than when science put man on the moon. It is, simply, the greatest challenge on earth: to love your enemy. Jesus uses the word *agape*, as Paul would use in 1 Corinthians 13. It is not *eros* (physical or sexual love), nor *philia* (brotherly love). *Agape* is *self-less concern*. It is self-giving love. It is not necessarily affection. You may love a person, and not want to spend a holiday with them. You may love a person and not like them; but you can act unselfishly.

This can be almost overwhelming. The challenge Jesus puts to us is to overwhelm your enemy; not by showing everybody how wrong he or she was – not matching their hatred with yours. The challenge Jesus puts is: overwhelm them by loving them. When you do this you have responded to and achieved the greatest challenge on earth.

We are back to this matter of choice. Love is not what you feel. Forgiving is not doing what comes naturally. It is often said, 'You can't help what you feel.' We therefore ask, is the choice to love someone repressing or denying feelings? No. Repression is almost never a good thing to do. Repressing is playing games with your mind and you may not know you are doing it. Love is a conscious choice to forgive – even if you don't feel like it! Don't wait until you feel like it or you probably never will forgive. Do it because it is right, not because you feel like letting them off the hook. We therefore choose to forgive – or not to forgive.

Total Forgiveness

'But I tell you: Love your enemies and pray for those who persecute you.'

Matthew 5:44

There are five stages, or levels, of praying for one's enemy:

Duty. That's the first level, and there is nothing wrong with that. It is obedience, even if you are doing it because you feel you have to.

Debt. This is when you are so conscious of what you have been forgiven that you cannot but pray for your enemy. You don't want God to spill the beans on you, so you pray that they too will be spared.

Desire. It is what you really want. Not that you felt this way at first; it began as duty. But now you have reached the stage where you actually want to pray for those who have hurt you.

Delight. This is taking desire a step further. It is when you love doing it! You get your joy from knowing that God knows. You know that this is pleasing to him. And not far from your mind is the fact that praying in this manner means a greater anointing and reward in heaven (Matthew 5:12).

Durability. This means that what you took on as a lifelong commitment becomes a lifestyle. The thought of turning back or praying in a different way is out of the question. It has become a habit and it no longer seems like something extraordinary.

As Jackie Pullinger said, 'To the spiritual person the supernatural seems natural.' What began as a duty and seemed insurmountable is now almost second nature.

Total Forgiveness

Praise the LORD, O my soul,
and forget not all his benefits.

Psalm 103:2

Davidlists all the benefits: forgiveness for all his sins, the healing of all his diseases, redeeming his life from the pit, crowning him with love and compassion, satisfying his desires with good things, his youth being renewed like the eagle's (Psalm 103:3–5).

One of the irrefutable evidences for the divine inspiration of the psalms is the repeated praises to God and admonition to praise. Only God could lead a human being to pen psalms like that. The most natural tendency in the world is to forget to be thankful. The Apostle Paul described those whom God has given over to a reprobate mind, that they were unthankful (Romans 1:21–28), but the psalms are full to running over with thankfulness and the exhortation to all of us to be thankful. These words are combined with the promise never to forget.

If God prospers you he is putting you on your honour – to be thankful. And to show it. So tell him!

Thanking God

We all stumble in many ways. If anyone is never at fault in what he says, he is a perfect man, able to keep his whole body in check.

James 3:2

We will never be perfect in this life. This is because we always have our fallen nature with us. 'The heart is deceitful above all things and beyond cure. Who can understand it?'(Jeremiah 17:9). What we inherited from our first parents in the Garden of Eden we will have until we are glorified, when we are totally changed (1 Corinthians 15:51). Until then we are conscious of indwelling sin, the propensity to impure thoughts, unguarded comments, imperfections that keep embarrassing us and weaknesses that reveal we have not been glorified yet. Until then we will err.

But that does not mean we do not try to be and do better! It is being a Christian that makes one want to get it right. This is one of the big differences between the Christian and the non-Christian. We have a motivation to be more like Jesus. We want to please God more and more. We want a greater testimony before others – saved and lost. Because we can indeed improve! I think of John Newton's words to his friend William Cowper, when they were discussing Paul's words, 'But by the grace of God I am what I am, and his grace to me was not without effect' (1 Corinthians 15:10). Newton looked across the breakfast table at Cowper and said: 'I'm not what I ought to be. I'm not what I want to be. I'm not what I hope to be. But thank God I'm not what I used to be.'

Your Words Have Power

Now these things occurred as examples to keep us from setting our hearts on evil things as they did.

1 Corinthians 10:6

The infallible word of God describes fallible men and women between its covers. What Scripture says about them we can believe, but what some of them *did* and *said* at times was very often wrong. So even the best of God's servants described in the Bible frequently turn out to be examples of how *not* to be! We don't need to repeat the same mistakes!

I have lived long enough to observe that every person I began to admire a little bit too much disappointed me sooner or later. We may wish that we lived in Bible times – and witnessed first hand some of the great people in biblical history – Abraham, Isaac, Jacob, David, Elijah, for example, and found out what they were really like; but you would have been shocked to see how human they were. They were not perfect. The imperfection was almost always traceable to the tongue.

What we say reveals the heart. 'Out of the overflow of the heart the mouth speaks' (Matthew 12:34). This is why Jesus said by our words we are either 'acquitted' or 'condemned' (Matthew 12:37) when the verdict is given as to our reward at the Judgment Seat of Christ. Our words, which reveal to what extent we truly sought after true wisdom, therefore indicate what was in the heart.

Your Words Have Power

*Give thanks in all circumstances, for this is God's will for you in
Christ Jesus.*

1 Thessalonians 5:18

Thanking God *for* everything and thanking him *in* everything are not
exactly the same thing. Not many people thank him for everything.
We may end up doing that – when enough time rolls along that 'all
things work together for good' (Romans 8:28, AV). Then we may thank
him for things that were once evil and which caused grief. But I do
not counsel that we must thank him *for* everything at any given moment.

When I sin or fail I do not say, 'Thank you, Lord.' I cannot say
that I thank God for the events of 11 September 2001. It may well be
that all who read these lines live long enough to see God's sovereign
hand in it all and find reasons to be thankful. But we are not required
to be thankful for everything. For being robbed. Or raped. Or lied
about. Or being betrayed.

We therefore are not asked to be thankful *for* all these ordeals. But
it is another thing to give thanks *in* such adversities. And this we are
asked to do in 1 Thessalonians. Paul and Silas were in jail but they
were praying and singing hymns to God (Acts 16:25).

What separates the Christian from the non-Christian is not whether
bad things happen to them but whether we can make the choice to
rejoice in all circumstances.

Thanking God

Submit yourselves, then, to God. Resist the devil, and he will flee from you.

James 4:7

The king of Assyria sent his forces into Jerusalem to address Hezekiah the king and the common people who sat on the wall. These soldiers shouted insults to Israel's God and to the king. They hoped to cause a revolt among the ordinary people. 'Now do not let Hezekiah deceive you and mislead you like this. Do not believe him, for no god of any nation or kingdom has been able to deliver his people from my hand or the hand of my fathers. How much less will your god deliver you from my hand!' (2 Chronicles 32:15).

Hezekiah sent word to Sennacherib's men not to speak in Hebrew to the people. Hezekiah was fearful that the people would weaken and give in. It was the greatest national crisis during the reign of King Hezekiah.

But King Hezekiah need not have worried. It was a grand and historic moment. 'But the people remained silent and said nothing in reply, because the king had commanded, "Do not answer him"' (Isaiah 36:21). It was a wonderful moment. It was a beautiful sign of unity in Israel that not one person succumbed to Sennacherib's men. Shortly afterwards God supernaturally defeated Israel's enemies and Sennacherib's own people cut him down (Isaiah 36:36–38).

Satan will always try to persuade the people of God to interact with him and negotiate with him. When you feel pressured to speak, remember this account in Scripture. In such cases, when the exact word is not given to you, the best thing to do is to say nothing.

Your Words Have Power

*To him who is able to keep you from falling and to present you
before his glorious presence without fault and with great joy – to
the only God our Saviour be glory, majesty, power and authority,
through Jesus Christ our Lord, before all ages, now and for evermore! Amen.*

Jude 24

When Jude says we will be presented to God 'with great joy' it is
impossible to infer whether it is our joy or God's! The Authorised
Version translates the Greek word – *agalliasei*, used only five times in
the New Testament – as 'exceeding joy'. It is a word that means *extreme
joy*. This is Jude's word to describe what will be experienced – by us
and by the Lord himself – when we are presented to him. No greater
joy can be conceived. It will be joy for us, partly because it will mark
the end of sin and evil, the end of suffering and questioning. But it
will also be the sheer joy of the Holy Spirit in us without measure –
as Jesus had all along – and which we will be able to accommodate.
I think of D. L. Moody's experience when he was baptised with the
Spirit and asked the Lord to stop as he thought he would literally die
from the joy! But on that day we will have this joy, but with the capacity
to endure it!

But it will bring joy to the Lord as well and, for all I know, it will
be even more joyous for him than for us. He will receive joy by seeing
us so happy, but he will also know a joy that comes from the final
and undoubted vindication that will be his. For nobody – nobody –
has endured suffering and false accusation as God himself has. It will
mean that never again will he endure such. The joy, indeed, will be
extreme.

Pure Joy

Thinking he was in their company, they travelled on for a day.
Then they began looking for him among their relatives and friends.
When they did not find him, they went back to Jerusalem to look
for him. After three days they found him in the temple courts,
sitting among the teachers, listening to them and asking them ques-
tions.

Luke 2:44–46

It wasn't enough for Joseph and Mary to go to Jerusalem when they
were searching for Jesus. Once arriving there they still had to find *him*.
Obviously he wasn't where they thought he would be, for they took
three days to find him. You can step out of a flowing stream but you
can never step back in at the same place. For the flow moves on. They
had to go where they hadn't thought necessary.

A familiar theology is also a very common comfort zone. So too
with a familiar liturgy, clichés or style of worship. We almost certainly
will begin to look for Christ in our comfort zone. But what if he isn't
there? Will we admit to this too?

Seeking the face of the Lord is to settle for nothing but him. We
must seek him until we find him. It may require examining teaching
we had previously dismissed out of hand. It may mean associating
with people we once said we'd have nothing to do with. It may be
singing lines we previously felt had nothing in them for us. Those who
have concentrated only on the things of the Spirit may have to go
seeking God's word in a manner they never thought they'd have to do.
Those who were at home with the word and the finer points of theology
may have to submit to a ministry of prayer carried out by people they
had once sneered at. Traditionalists may have to begin singing, 'Shine,
Jesus, shine'; contemporary-style worshippers may have to seek God
by singing 200-year-old hymns. Once God has succeeded in getting
our attention we will have to repent and then carry through by seeking
our Lord's face and not giving up until we find him. A lot of humbling,
climbing down and sheer embarrassment may be part of the journey
back.

The Sensitivity of the Spirit

But Jonah ran away from the LORD *and headed for Tarshish. He went down to Joppa, where he found a ship bound for that port. After paying the fare, he went aboard and sailed for Tarshish to flee from the* LORD.

Jonah 1:3

Nothing gives me more pleasure than the realisation that God has a plan for my life. He is in the process of leading me from A to Z. I don't know what Z is, therefore I wait for the knowledge of what B is. I am often asked, 'Can we avoid God's will?' I answer, 'Only if we want to avoid it.' Yet Jonah wanted to avoid God's will. But the end of Jonah's story convinces me that Jonah both avoided and did not avoid God's will. Nothing took God by surprise. God knew what Jonah's reaction would be to the initial news that he must go to Nineveh. I suspect that God began preparing Jonah's fish before Jonah disobeyed.

God looks after his family. After all, he sent his one and only Son into the world to bring 'many sons to glory' (Hebrews 2:10). Those sons are adopted sons (Romans 8:15; Galatians 4:6; Ephesians 1:5). Jesus was God's only 'natural' Son. The rest of us have been brought into God's family by adoption. As adopted sons, moreover, we are made 'co-heirs with Christ' (Romans 8:17). This means that I am called to inherit all that Jesus will inherit. This is because *God loves us as much as he loves Jesus*. I know of no more dazzling thought. I base this statement not only on Romans 8:17 but also on John 17:23 where our Lord prayed for us: 'that you sent me and have loved them [that is, us] even as you have loved me [that is, Jesus]'. Therefore God loves us as much as he loves his only Son and looks after us as he did his Son. This means he plans for us as he did for his Son. Paul said that he knelt before the Father, 'from whom his whole family in heaven and earth derives its name' that through him we may receive 'immeasurably more than all we ask or imagine' (Ephesians 3:14, 20). All because we are a part of his family.

Does Jesus Care?

Look, he is coming with the clouds,
  and every eye will see him,
even those who pierced him;
  and all the peoples of the earth
    will mourn because of him.
      So shall it be! Amen.

Revelation 1:7

There *is* coming a day in which God will clear his name. 'God has a lot to answer for,' says the unconverted person. 'If God is perfectly just and loving he would not allow famine in Africa, earthquakes in South America, the low standard of living in Calcutta, violence in Northern Ireland, hurricanes in the Gulf states of America, ruthless men taking innocent people hostage in aircraft and airports, sexual crimes against helpless children.'

But God *does* allow evil. God does let man suffer. And he is just and holy and merciful. 'The LORD is righteous in all his ways and loving towards all he has made' (Psalm 145:17). 'Rubbish,' says the scoffer and the infidel. But God quietly suggests that we lower our voices. 'For my thoughts are not your thoughts, neither are your ways my ways . . . As the heavens are higher than the earth, so are my ways higher than your ways and my thoughts than your thoughts' (Isaiah 55:8–9).

The differences between the Christian and the non-Christian can be summed up briefly. The Christian vindicates God now; the non-Christian will vindicate God later. To do so now is to do it willingly and by faith. To do so later is to do it by constraint and without faith. For faith is being sure of what we hope for and certain of 'what we do not see' (Hebrews 11:1). Secular man says 'seeing is believing'. The Christian says 'believing is not seeing'.

Does Jesus Care?

'Lord,' Martha said to Jesus, 'if you had been here, my brother would not have died. But I know that even now God will give you whatever you ask.'

John 11:21–22

Most of us protect ourselves by affirming our orthodoxy rather than our simple faith that God will act in the here and now. I sometimes wonder if our orthodoxy is but a camouflage for our unbelief. Because we don't really believe that God will work today we take refuge in what he will do tomorrow.

There are those who believe that God once worked powerfully in men's lives. When? In the days of the early Church. They therefore believed in the book of Acts with all their hearts. They believe in the miracles of Jesus. They believe in his resurrection. They believe in his ascension. They believe in his intercessory work at God's right hand. They are orthodox, yes. But that is about all. Their faith in God's power is either limited to the distant past or the Last Day. In between it is mostly soundness of doctrine that counts.

Most of us are afraid to put ourselves on the line as Martha did. We don't want to look like fools. We content ourselves with the orthodox statement, 'I know he will rise again in the resurrection at the last day.' It is like those who state the Apostles' Creed. That seems to be the extent of their faith. What God *did* and *will do*.

What zeal Martha had! Many of us would stand on the sidelines and say, 'I'm not going to be found talking to the Lord like that. After all, if God wants to do something, fine. No need to be so unsubtle about what we hope God will do. Let God do it if that is what he wants to do.'

Not Martha. This dear child of God saw in Jesus the power to do something *on the spot*.

Does Jesus Care?

*Who has believed our message and to whom has the arm of the
LORD been revealed? He grew up before him like a tender shoot,
and like a root out of dry ground. He had no beauty or majesty to
attract us to him, nothing in his appearance that we should desire
him. He was despised and rejected by men, a man of sorrows, and
familiar with suffering. Like one from whom men hide their faces he
was despised, and we esteemed him not.*

Isaiah 53:1–3

From a letter to Rabbi David Rosen, former Chief Rabbi of Ireland:

All I am asking of you, David, is to *consider* certain aspects of my
theology: for example, how Isaiah saw hundreds of years in advance
that Israel's promised Messiah would be called the 'Mighty God,
Everlasting Father' (Isaiah 9:6). Is this not a promise that the coming
Messiah would be *God in the flesh*? Is it not true that Isaiah also saw
long before the event that the people of Israel would by and large
completely reject their Messiah? 'Who has believed our message and
to whom has the arm of the LORD been revealed?' (Isaiah 53:1). Isaiah
foresaw that the very One Israel had prayed for would indeed show
up – but be completely underestimated and, sadly, missed entirely by
most Jews. This is because, far from being charismatic and obvious,
the Messiah would be like a 'root out of dry ground', a lacklustre
figure without apparent attractiveness (Isaiah 53:1–3). On top of that,
he would be perceived by Jews as being severely but rightly judged by
God (verses 4–5) *and* he would die as a substitutionary atoning sacrifice for our sins: 'the LORD laid on him the iniquity of us all' (verse
6). I will stop at that verse for now, only to point out that the Jews
who *did* believe in Jesus as their Messiah two thousand years ago –
and since – have found incalculable comfort and hope from Isaiah 53.

The Christian and the Pharisee

'Do not think that I have come to abolish the Law or the Prophets;
I have not come to abolish them but to fulfil them.'

Matthew 5:17

From a letter to Rabbi David Rosen, former Chief Rabbi of Ireland:

It is my opinion that when Jesus promised personally to fulfil the Law
in Matthew 5:17, meaning not merely the Ten Commandments but –
when you add them up in Exodus, Leviticus, Numbers and
Deuteronomy – not only 613 but over 2,000 pieces of Mosaic legisla-
tion, it was the most stupendous statement he made: 'I have not come
to abolish them [the Law or the prophets] but to fulfil them.' Nobody
had done that, truly fulfilling the Mosaic Law in every jot and tittle.
Nobody. Even James, who was a great defender of the Law in the
earliest Church, finally agreed with Peter that even their Jewish ancestors were not able to bear the yoke of the Law (Acts 15:10–21). But
when Jesus said, 'I will fulfil the Law,' it was a major statement fairly
early on in his ministry. So when he uttered the words on the cross,
'It is finished' (Greek *tetelestai* – John 19:30), he was stating he had
accomplished what he had promised to do – fulfil the Law – because
tetelestai was a word also understood as 'paid in full'.

This brings us back to the nature of faith. You are right, David, in
saying we regard faith in itself as being of 'redeeming value' – with
one proviso: that the object of that faith is in Jesus whose substitutionary death atoned for our sins. We believe that Jesus was our
substitute. He not only took our place by bearing the wrath of God
we deserve (Matthew 27:46; 2 Corinthians 5:21) but was also our
substitute in having performed the righteous deeds of the Law *on our
behalf* (1 Corinthians 1:30). Therefore, faith justifies when I *rely* on
Jesus as a person and as my Redeemer.

The Christian and the Pharisee

'Why were you searching for me?' he asked. 'Didn't you know I had to be in my Father's house?' But they did not understand what he was saying to them.

Luke 2:49–50

Jesus was lovingly confronting his parents with the truth they didn't want to hear. And yet, as Calvin put it, 'The wonder is that Joseph and Mary did not understand this reply.' They knew better than anybody the truth about Jesus.

The unfolding of God's glory is also the unfolding of truth. This may mean truth we hadn't wanted fully to accept – at least not yet.

This can be exceedingly difficult for those in leadership, especially if we have espoused teaching that we may have to abandon. It is harder if we have to accept teaching we had opposed, and harder still if we have gone to print – and have to retract! I have had to do so, but the inner peace and joy far outweigh the fear of criticism which may or may not follow. Sadly, I know some people who wouldn't change *because* they were committed to print. If this unwillingness to change is in the face of clear biblical teaching, I would fear becoming yesterday's man overnight – like King Saul.

Jesus said, 'If anyone chooses to do God's will, he will find out whether my teaching comes from God or whether I speak on my own' (John 7:17). That means if I am obedient I will come to truth and can be preserved from grievous error. But if that truth is right there before my eyes but I can't bear the thought of embracing it, my prayer for an ever-increasing anointing is not sincere.

The Sensitivity of the Spirit

But they did not understand what he was saying to them.

Luke 2:50

Jesus had a way of asking a question that might have tended to make one feel a bit stupid – but it was always done to rebuke unbelief. For example, when Jesus enabled Peter to walk on the water all went well until Peter saw the wind. He cried out to be saved as he began to sink. 'Immediately Jesus reached out his hand and caught him. "You of little faith," he said, *"why did you doubt?"'* (Matthew 14:31). On another occasion, when asked about the parable of the sower, Jesus said to his disciples, 'Don't you understand *this* parable?' as if saying, 'This is an easy one,' for he added, 'How then will you understand any parable?' (Mark 4:13). He did not really do this to make them feel stupid but to force them to look again at what he had just said and conclude for themselves what he felt was obvious.

So too with any manifestation of God's glory. At first our reaction may be bewilderment. But looking again in the light of what we have already learned will reveal that there is a credible explanation for what God chooses to do.

The Sensitivity of the Spirit

For you created my inmost being;
  you knit me together in my mother's womb.
I praise you because I am fearfully and wonderfully made.

Psalm 139:13–14

The way you have been shaped is the way God chose to make you. It is all a part of forming you into the person you now are.

Therefore you must accept that your birth and all that has happened to you since is a part of the way God has determined to make you. But that is not all; you are a new creation in Christ Jesus (2 Corinthians 5:19). The consequence is that you are a new person. All that God did at the natural level – creation – is augmented by what he has been doing at the supernatural level – by the Holy Spirit. The result: you are his 'workmanship': 'God's work of art' (Jerusalem Bible), 'God's handiwork' (New English Bible), and 'what we are' (Phillips Modern English) because of the Holy Spirit (Ephesians 2:10).

You are no accident. 'My parents did not want me,' you may reply to me. I believe you. But God wanted you. You were known from the foundation of the world, before the beginning of time (2 Timothy 1:9). God not only 'determined' the time when you were born and the 'times set for them' – meaning the cultural, social, political and environmental situation of the particular generation in which you were born. Not only that; he determined 'the exact places' where each person born should live (Acts 17:26).

Here is the goal God has envisaged for you: that you will agree with all he has said about you, namely, that God created your 'inmost being'; you were 'knit together' in your mother's womb. God did that. Not you. Not your parents. God.

Totally Forgiving Ourselves

*And we know that in all things God works for the good of those
who love him, who have been called according to his purpose.*

Romans 8:28

I call it Paul's most extreme statement. Paul has made some stupendous claims in his epistles, among them: (1) ungodly people are regarded
as righteous the moment they put their faith in Jesus Christ (Romans
4:5); (2) that the Christian can overcome impossible odds: 'I can do
everything through Christ who gives me strength' (Philippians 4:13);
or (3) those who give generously and cheerfully to the Lord will be
made 'rich in every way' (2 Corinthians 9:11).

But when Paul says that 'we know that all things work together for
good to them that love God, to them who are the called according to
his purpose', he put his pastoral, theological and personal integrity
on the line.

Call to mind your most difficult moment. Your most shameful. The
hardest to understand. When you were at your worst. When the greatest
injustice was thrust upon you. When you were involved in the most
tragic accident − whether your fault or not. I could go on and on.
Please think about this.

Romans 8:28 guarantees to every person who loves God and is
among the called according to his purpose, that anything and everything that was negative, wrong or unfair which has happened to them
will eventually turn out for good. Why does God give us this promise?
Two reasons: (1) because it is true, and (2) because he does not want
you to feel guilty about the past. He wants you to believe that all will
turn out for good. If you really believe that, you will feel less guilty;
and when you know that God himself wants you to believe that, I
would have thought you are home! He says to you right now as you
read these lines, 'As for the past, leave it with me. It is not your problem.
It is my problem. It is my job to make all that has happened to you
work together for good. It is what I do.'

Totally Forgiving Ourselves

Eagerly desire the greater gifts. And now I will show you the most excellent way.

1 Corinthians 12:31

In the Greek, this passage means: 'The excellent *way by which you discover* your gifts is by love.' It sounds almost too simple to be true: you can best discover your gift when you demonstrate *agape* love. Yet it is true. When we love people and long to serve them, when we totally forgive, and keep no record of wrongs, then we spontaneously find ways of expressing that love: and the gifts of the Spirit emerge in us. There are no short cuts to finding the gifts. We must have hearts devoid of bitterness.

Worshipping God

Scripture Index

The Old Testament

Isaiah 58:3	January 24	Habakkuk 1:3	October 8
Isaiah 58:9–10	June 21	Habakkuk 2:3	October 6
Isaiah 64:4	July 2	Habakkuk 2:4	October 5
Jonah 1:3	December 22	Habakkuk 3:17–19	October 9
Jonah 3:3	June 27	Malachi 3:10	June 7
Habakkuk 1:2	October 7		

The New Testament

Matthew 3:7	August 26	Matthew 22:29	April 29
Matthew 3:17	November 20	Matthew 22:39	September 23
Matthew 3:20–22	August 2	Matthew 25:41	May 7
Matthew 5:5	December 5	Matthew 26:55–56	March 24
Matthew 5:7	June 23	Matthew 26:75	October 20
Matthew 5:11–12	November 26, December 12	Matthew 27:3–4	November 4
		Matthew 27:45	May 4
Matthew 5:17	December 26	Matthew 27:46	June 5
Matthew 5:33–37	June 30	Mark 8:36	February 20
Matthew 5:44	August 6, December 13, December 14	Mark 11:25	May 17
		Luke 2:43–44	January 22, September 8
Matthew 6:8	May 14	Luke 2:44	March 17
Matthew 6:9	March 1, March 2, March 3, March 4	Luke 2:44–46	December 21
		Luke 2:46	November 18
		Luke 2:48	September 29
Matthew 6:10	March 5, March 6	Luke 2:49–50	December 27
		Luke 2:50	December 28
Matthew 6:11	March 7	Luke 6:37–38	July 28
Matthew 6:12	March 8	Luke 7:7–10	April 12
Matthew 6:13	March 9	Luke 9:49–50	November 17
Matthew 6:14	August 8	Luke 10:20	November 25
Matthew 6:14–15	March 10	Luke 10:31	February 10
Matthew 7:1	May 26	Luke 10:40–42	September 9
Matthew 7:1–2	September 1	Luke 14:11	October 22
Matthew 7:3	September 2	Luke 15:24	February 28
Matthew 7:5	September 4	Luke 16:10	February 1
Matthew 8:11–12	September 5	Luke 16:15	October 23
Matthew 10:32	February 14	Luke 17:11–14	April 10
Matthew 10:32–33	January 16	Luke 17:15–19	April 11
Matthew 10:36	August 12	Luke 17:20–21	May 22
Matthew 12:34	June 24	Luke 18:1	February 7
Matthew 12:36	March 16, May 31	Luke 18:4–7	December 3
		Luke 19:37	September 15
Matthew 13:13–15	September 12	Luke 23:34	May 25
Matthew 16:4	February 15	John 1:32–33	January 10
Matthew 18:32–34	August 18	John 3:8	January 21
Matthew 19:19	October 19	John 3:14–15	January 11
Matthew 21:12	March 28	John 3:16	January 8, January 12, April 24
Matthew 21:15–16	January 9		

John 4:24	August 15	Romans 8:32	April 3
John 5:44	June 18, July 19,	Romans 8:34	January14
	August 28,	Romans 10:9–10	November 21
	November 19,	Romans 11:33–34	February 26
	December 6	Romans 12:1	August 14
John 7:17	September 30	Romans 12:19	March 25
John 7:38	June 1	Romans 14:9	August 23
John 11:4	November 14	Romans 14:17	August 11
John 11:6	November 23	Romans 14:19	July 1
John 11:14–15	March 29	1 Corinthians 1:18	October 11
John 11:15	July 16	1 Corinthians 1:27	July 18
John 11:21	August 20	1 Corinthians 1:27–29	April 9
John 11:21–22	September 10,	1 Corinthians 2:3	January 19
	December 24	1 Corinthians 2:4–5	January 17
John 11:32	August 9	1 Corinthians 3:9	August 3
John 11:32–33	March 26	1 Corinthians 3:11	August 1
John 11:32–35	February 25	1 Corinthians 3:12	August 30
John 11:37	September 19	1 Corinthians 3:13–15	August 31
John 13:38	October 24	1 Corinthians 3:14–15	June 9
John 14:13	November 16	1 Corinthians 4:3–4	September 24
John 14:14	January 23,	1 Corinthians 5:19	February 18
	August 21	1 Corinthians 6:19	October 21
John 14:26	October 16	1 Corinthians 9:27	June 8
John 17:26	September 17	1 Corinthians 10:6	December 17
Acts 1:8	May 23	1 Corinthians 10:11	March 18
Acts 2:14	October 20	1 Corinthians 10:13	April 4
Acts 2:42	March 30, June 3	1 Corinthians 11:25	March 31
Acts 3:1	April 7	1 Corinthians 11:31	February 24
Acts 4:24	April 20, April 21	1 Corinthians 12:7–10	September 27
Acts 4:31	January 26	1 Corinthians 12:14–16	February 3
Acts 5:41–42	October 25	1 Corinthians 12:28	July 8
Acts 7:9–10	February 16	1 Corinthians 12:31	July 3,
Acts 12:5	August 22		December 31
Acts 16:6	April 17	1 Corinthians 13:1	July 9
Acts 19:15–16	November 1	1 Corinthians 13:5	June 13,
Acts 24:24–25	January 18		September 13,
Romans 1:8	January 6		September 22
Romans 1:9–10	September 26	1 Corinthians 13:10	July 6
Romans 1:14	May 12	1 Corinthians 14:12	July 7
Romans 1:16	January 15	1 Corinthians 15:3	April 5
Romans 1:17	May 2	2 Corinthians 2:10–11	October 2
Romans 1:22–23	February 19	2 Corinthians 3:17	February 5,
Romans 3:22–23	May 2		December 4
Romans 4:13–14	April 25	2 Corinthians 3:18	May 27
Romans 5:1–5	September 6	2 Corinthians 5:10	June 4
Romans 8:16	August 16	2 Corinthians 5:18–19	June 12
Romans 8:27	December 8	2 Corinthians 5:21	May 1
Romans 8:28	June 25,	2 Corinthians 7:8–10	February 29
	September 11,	2 Corinthians 9:6–8	June 15
	December 30	2 Corinthians 11:30	July 26

2 Corinthians 12:7	July 24, July 25	Hebrews 9:27	May 3
2 Corinthians 12:7–9	February 8	Hebrews 10:25	December 1
2 Corinthians 12:8–9	July 29	Hebrews 11:6	November 9
Galatians 2:7	February 12	Hebrews 11:7	July 15
Galatians 5:16	April 26	Hebrews 11:8	April 1
Galatians 5:25	April 18	Hebrews 11:24–26	January 7
Ephesians 2:8–9	May 24	Hebrews 11:39	October 28
Ephesians 4:16	February 2	Hebrews 12:2	April 15
Ephesians 4:30–32	March 11,	Hebrews 12:5–6	February 27
	June 2,	Hebrews 12:6	April 27,
	December 10		July 30,
Ephesians 5:10	January 1		October 12
Philippians 2:8	April 2	Hebrews 12:10–11	March 21
Philippians 3:1	November 24	Hebrews 12:11	October 29
Philippians 3:3	February 9	Hebrews 12:28	August 27
Philippians 4:4	October 17,	Hebrews 13:8	May 13
	November 24	Hebrews 13:15	November 30
Philippians 4:6	January 5,	James 1:2–3	June 16
	May 9,	James 1:2–3	June 17
	September 25	James 2:2	June 6
Philippians 4:11–12	October 10	James 3:2	December 16
1 Thessalonians 1:5	May 20,	James 3:5–6	February 13,
	October 15		September 20
1 Thessalonians 5:18	December 18	James 3:8	October 3
1 Thessalonians 5:19	July 13	James 4:7	December 19
1 Thessalonians 5:19–22	September 14	James 5:16	October 14
1 Timothy 1:12–14	January 4	James 5:17–18	November 29
1 Timothy 1:16	July 27	1 Peter 1:6	November 27
1 Timothy 6:6	November 6	1 Peter 2:15	August 19
1 Timothy 6:6–10	October 26	1 Peter 4:17	February 23
1 Timothy 6:10	November 10	1 Peter 5:7	November 12
2 Timothy 1:8–9	April 28	2 Peter 1:10–11	January 27,
2 Timothy 1:8–10	November 28		March 19
2 Timothy 1:14	July 11	2 Peter 1:20	November 3
2 Timothy 2:3	March 20	1 John 1:6	August 7
2 Timothy 3:16	April 30	1 John 1:8	July 12
2 Timothy 4:1–2	September 7	1 John 4:4	October 31
2 Timothy 4:2	April 6,	1 John 4:18	June 22,
	June 20,		October 1
	November 8	1 John 5:15	December 8
2 Timothy 4:6–8	June 28	Jude 20	April 19,
Hebrews 3:7–10	July 14		December 7
Hebrews 4:15	August 5,	Jude 24	December 20
	November 22	Revelation 1:7	January 13,
Hebrews 6:4–6	May 6, May 16		December 23
Hebrews 6:16–18	May 5	Revelation 3:20	January 25
Hebrews 8:12	June 14	Revelation 12:10–11	November 2